# Advance Praise

'Financialization, defined as growing scale and profitability of the finance sector at the expense of the rest of the economy, is a relatively new term in the lexicon of economics. In this timely, well-researched and thought-provoking book V. Anantha Nageswaran and Gulzar Natarajan not only examine the causes and the consequences of financialization but offer specific policies that can help reduce its negative impacts on the real economy. The authors break new grounds by linking central banks' policies with the increased financialization of national economies, offering India as a case study of how smart financial deregulation could be a force for sustainable economic growth in emerging economies. Anyone who wants to understand the roots of increasing inequality and instability in the global economy must read this book.'

**Hossein Kazemi**, Michael & Cheryl Philipp Distinguished Professor of Finance and Director of CISDM Isenberg School of Management, University of Massachusetts

'Anantha Nageswaran and Gulzar Natarajan's work is a courageous and comprehensive commentary on the reasons, ramifications and possible response to the excessive financialization and financial market liberalization that characterized the global economy over the last quarter century or so. The authors lament that the world has not learnt the right lessons from the recent global financial crisis, the major manifestation of unbridled financialization by re-emphasizing and reinforcing, through painstaking analysis and new perspectives, the thesis that beyond a point financial sector growth can have inverted U-shaped effect on the real economy and the society.

They provide a strong critique of the role of the major central banks led by the Federal Reserve in fostering and furthering financialization leading to misallocation of resources away from the real economy to the financial markets, excessive risk taking and speculation, bourgeoning indebtedness, cycles of booms and bursts with serious economic and social costs and spillovers effects of cross-border flows on emerging countries. Their singular focus on price stability under the inflation-targeting framework to the detriment of the financial stability and the consequences of the unconventional monetary policy with potential for stoking the next financial crisis have been subjected to sharp scrutiny in the book. Authors have unhesitatingly suggested policy choices like using capital-flows management and stricter macro-prudential measures by the central banks, curbs on banks' capacity for asset creation in sync with the need for 'boring banking', ending the craze for debt pile-up, restraints on central banks' put option for the rescue of the financial assets and overarching imperative of building consensus for safe and sustainable financial system.

In a separate section on India the authors provide a somehow different perspective that India suffers from too little rather than too much of finance and hence has to focus on institutions and innovations for financial sector deepening and broadening while remaining on guard against potential for excessive speculation in certain areas and disproportionate financialization.

This bold and brilliant book is a must-read for all those who are concerned with a fragile financial future of economies and societies.'

**Harun R. Khan**, former Deputy Governor, Reserve Bank of India

'An iconoclastic but persuasive account of the excessive financialization that has come to dominate and distort advanced economies over the past three decades. *The Rise of Finance* is a comprehensive, painstakingly researched and documented account of all that has gone wrong as the finance-dominated advanced economies struggle to emerge from the North Atlantic Financial Crisis. An immensely readable, accessible and valuable contribution that will be a must-read for laymen, finance aficionados, market participants, researchers, academics and policymakers alike. Coming from practitioners and teachers of finance, their bold nostrums for a radical overhaul of the global financial and monetary systems deserve a serious hearing.'

**Rakesh Mohan**, Senior Fellow at the Jackson Institute for Global Affairs, Yale University, and Distinguished Fellow at Brookings India

'Anantha and Gulzar have tackled an important issue in this book – the financialization of the world economy and its consequences. Is financialization a case of the tail wagging the economic dog? Why is it a risk to macro-stability and what should be done about it? The book explores options and remedies. Agree or not, it is a must-read for all breeds of economists – academic, financial and policy-maker.'

**Sanjeev Sanyal**, Principal Economic Adviser, Government of India

# The Rise of Finance

Financialization, or the disproportionate importance of financial considerations in economic decisions, has been a defining feature of the economic history of the last 30 years. The wave of deregulation that accompanied the neoliberal agenda in the US, aided by the dominance of the US dollar and the American economy, has resulted in the globalization of finance.

The current instability in the world economy provides a window for a radical overhaul of the global financial and monetary systems. Measures such as simple capital adequacy rules for banks, acceptance of capital flows management, measures to discourage debt accumulation, anti-trust action, and replacement of elements of the neoliberal framework are crucial in realizing and effecting that change.

This book examines the rise of financialization globally while charting its drawbacks and prescribing suggestions for a definitive overhaul of the structure. Bringing together various strands of the latest research and evidence generated in recent years, empirical analysis, and views of reputed experts in the field, it presents a counterpoint to the canonical frameworks of analysing financial market dynamics and financial globalization. It proposes a revision of the current monetary policy paradigm to correct its excessive focus on equity markets and their 'wealth effect', embrace a more symmetric response to the economic cycle, and a mandate to focus on financial stability as much as price stability.

**V. Anantha Nageswaran** is Dean of the IFMR Graduate School of Business at Krea University, India. He has published *Economics of Derivatives* with T. V. Somanathan (2015) and *Derivatives* (2017) with T. V. Somanathan and Harsh Gupta.

**Gulzar Natarajan** is Senior Managing Director at Global Innovation Fund. He is a serving officer of the Indian Administrative Service.

V. Anantha Nageswaran and Gulzar Natarajan have co-authored *Can India Grow?* published by the Carnegie Endowment (India) in 2016.

# The Rise of Finance

*Causes, Consequences and Cures*

V. Anantha Nageswaran
Gulzar Natarajan

CAMBRIDGE
UNIVERSITY PRESS

# CAMBRIDGE
## UNIVERSITY PRESS

University Printing House, Cambridge CB2 8BS, United Kingdom

One Liberty Plaza, 20th Floor, New York, NY 10006, USA

477 Williamstown Road, Port Melbourne, vic 3207, Australia

314 to 321, 3rd Floor, Plot No.3, Splendor Forum, Jasola District Centre, New Delhi 110025, India

79 Anson Road, #06–04/06, Singapore 079906

Cambridge University Press is part of the University of Cambridge.

It furthers the University's mission by disseminating knowledge in the pursuit of education, learning and research at the highest international levels of excellence.

www.cambridge.org
Information on this title: www.cambridge.org/9781108482349

First published 2019

Printed in India by Nutech Print Services, New Delhi 110020

*A catalogue record for this publication is available from the British Library*

ISBN 978-1-108-48234-9 Hardback

# Contents

# Figures

# Tables and Boxes

**Tables**

**Boxes**

# Foreword

The developments leading to the global financial crisis and experiences with policy responses have led to an inconclusive but fundamental rethinking on the practice of public policy. We know that the intellectual framework that prevailed before 2008 was not sustainable. We are yet to agree on what the new normal should be, except that money and finance are critical, though one part, and that excess finance is injurious to health. But right sizing finance cannot happen if the attention is confined to finance. We are in search of new balances not only between finance and real economy, but also between state and market, between national and global, and between old global economic order and evolving new one.

It is often argued that the ongoing financial crisis reflects excessive belief in the efficiency and self-correcting mechanisms of markets. It is, therefore, argued that the state should be empowered so that the balance between the state and the market is restored. Consequently, the policy prescriptions are essentially in the nature of creating a strengthened role for state, broadly defined to include intervention in the functioning of markets by the public policy.

It is possible to argue that the recent financial crisis represents the failure of both the market and the state. The apparatus of the state, in particular the independent central banks and regulators, seem to have failed to discharge the duties assigned and deliver the outcomes that they had assured. There are sufficient grounds to believe that the crisis is a result of the capture of the governments by the markets, especially by the financial institutions and financial markets. In other words, it can be argued that the crisis was caused by not a mere failure of regulators but a capture of the regulators and the governments by the financial markets. This plausible explanation of the crisis warrants an entirely different dimension to the traditional debate of state versus market. The debate may have to focus on the relationship between the state and the market in each country, on one hand, and the relationship between the nation states, national financial markets and international financial markets, on the other. At the same time, the role of large non-financial corporates cannot be ignored in the analysis.

The corporate sector seems to have developed a larger-than-life identity of its own but is not necessarily maintaining continuity of individual identities as corporates. The mergers, amalgamations and takeovers of corporates have become common and thus the corporate identities are fast changing. However, the corporate sector as a whole has developed a global domination and a global presence. Their influence over politics is now no longer necessarily through a national government, but cuts across several countries. The managements of corporates seem to have developed their own spheres of cross-country influence and interests. More importantly, some of their institutional capacities often exceed that of some national governments.

Technological developments are constraining the capacity of the individual nation-state to exercise its power of intervention in the economic activity of individuals or corporates that it was able to do in the twentieth century. Technological developments have a tendency to make cross-border movements economical and hence can undermine the instruments available for the nation-states. At the same time, the consequences of cross-border movements on a nation's population have to be often managed by the state. It is possible that globalization of business, especially finance, has been premature relative to the globalization of public policy or globalized governance.

In the past, finance was viewed as powerful but mainly as an enabling part of the real politics and real output or employment. In recent years, the financial sector has acquired a life of its own, with capacity to influence politics not only at a national level but also in terms of relations between nations, and equally in terms of the influence of the financial sector over the real sector. A possible disconnect between the real sector and the financial sector may also be emerging. For instance, currently while the financial markets seem to have rebounded globally and are thriving, employment and growth appear to be lagging behind, particularly in developed countries. It is not clear whether the booming financial markets are in anticipation of a definitive surge in real output and employment globally.

The common elements in the narration of events that led to the current financial crisis indicate that there has been close cooperation between the financial conglomerates and the ruling elite; that there has been competition for resources among these constituents within each country; and that these forces resulted in contagion in different degrees to different countries. Thus, there have been different strategic elements of cooperation, competition and coordination between state and market, nations and supra-nations, financial and non-financial corporates.

Interestingly, the surging public debt of many countries in recent years may place the sovereign at the mercy of the financial markets that were bailed out by the sovereign in the first place. How will these be resolved? In any case, the path towards the new normal is not only a political process but also one in which business—big business—especially the financial sector, plays a major role.

Optimal level and role of finance is, thus, not merely a question of regulation and supervision. Just as the influence and impact of finance has spread well beyond its initial role of provision of funds to enterprises, determining its optimal role, size, power and influence in the future requires an examination of the motivations and incentives of various players and institutions that finance touches. The authors of the book, V. Anantha Nageswaran and Gulzar Natarajan, have brought out these multiple dimensions and oft-overlooked areas relating to the future of finance. They have embarked on this intellectually demanding and, yet, ambitious task with courage, conviction, open minds and scholarship of considerable depth and breath.

The story of India may not fully fit into this narration as far as the role of finance is concerned, but it is part of the pattern in link between politics and business.

During the independence movement, there were observable links between indigenous business and policies. Post-independence, politicians and big businesses continued to be distinct and a dynamic mutually reinforcing on occasions and restraining each other at other times existed. The position seems to have changed rapidly after the reforms of 1991. Politics and business were merged in India. Many businessmen have joined active political life while many politicians turned to business as an additional occupation. Some people comment that the regime of gentlemen-politicians has been replaced by businessmen-politicians or politician-businessmen. Further, after the onset of the process of economic reform, there have been large elements of deregulation and liberalization, but the role of the government continues to be dominant in a significant way in the area of access to natural resources, privatization of public enterprises or disinvestment and public–private participation in physical infrastructure and possibly social infrastructure such as education. More importantly, public policy in India under the reform period seems to have created a conducive atmosphere for rapid growth by being business-friendly but not necessarily market-friendly. Public sector banking and, in fact, dominance of public sector in finance may be the institutional link between politics and business embedded in government.

In India, banking dominates finance and public sector dominates banking. Finance in India thus becomes an extended arm of politics. It provides extra-budgetary resource to the government. It also provides the largest source of fiscal gains, taxes, next only to taxes on energy. It enables decisions outside direct parliamentary accountability. Hence, the debate on excessive financialization in India has far larger political economy dimensions than in other countries. It has lesser global finance dimensions. The challenge for India is to move towards optimal market-based financialization from repressive political patronage–based financialization.

The authors had taken upon themselves the ambitious task of bringing together empirical evidence pertaining to this complex reality from multiple disciplines, thought processes and sources and have succeeded in weaving them together into a cogent narrative, culminating in a set of interesting and bold recommendations. The value of the book lies in its departure from simplistic prescriptions or predominantly scholarly exposition, but focusing on pragmatism derived from both theory and practice.

Readers will find in this book insights and observations that are not readily available in the plethora of literature being churned out on the subject of bloated global finance in need of re-orientation.

24 September 2018                                                     **Y. V. Reddy**

# Prologue

As the Clinton presidency entered its final year in 2000, America removed the last vestiges of control on the financial services industry. The Commodities Futures Modernization Act was passed, paving the way for an explosion in the creation of financial derivatives. The Glass–Steagall Act that separated commercial banking from investment banking was repealed, enabling the creation of financial conglomerates.

The new millennium began with the collapse of the Internet and technology bubbles in the United States and elsewhere. The NASDAQ composite index crashed from 5,300 points to around 1,300 points. Then, there was 9/11. Surprisingly, the US economy endured only a brief and mild recession. In December of that year, China joined the World Trade Organization (WTO). In the United States, the Federal Reserve lowered the federal funds rate to 1.0 per cent. From 2002, a global economic recovery ensued, notwithstanding the invasion of Iraq in 2003, in search of weapons of mass destruction.

America pursued simultaneous wars in Afghanistan and Iraq. Government spending rose rapidly, and consumer spending even more so. The US dollar weakened but foreign governments, led by China and oil-producing nations, bought American debt copiously. Interest rates stayed low despite swift and big increase in government and private debt. Prices of commodities, including crude oil, boomed. Real estate prices boomed everywhere. Millions, including those with no income, no jobs and no assets, became homeowners, as lending standards were continuously diluted by successive governments. Securitization of mortgages happened at an unprecedented pace. New over-the-counter financial derivative contracts such as credit default swaps (CDSs) were created in the trillions. It all ended in 2007 as mortgage borrowers began to default and the real estate boom ended in America. The malaise soon spread to the rest of the world through financial channels. It climaxed with the collapse of Lehman Brothers, a big name on Wall Street. The world economy teetered on the edge of collapse.

In response, monetary policy turned unconventional. Unprecedented measures were adopted. The Federal Reserve set its policy rate – the federal funds rate – at 0 in December 2008 and held it there for seven years. In addition, the Federal

Reserve targeted long-term interest rates through asset purchases. The Federal Reserve 'printed' money. It was called quantitative easing (QE). The balance sheet of the Federal Reserve went from USD 898.61 billion nearly a month before the collapse of Lehman Brothers on 15 September 2008 to USD 4.516 trillion on 14 January 2015. In many countries in Europe, central bank policy rates turned negative. That is, commercial banks had to pay interest to leave money in their accounts with the central banks.

# Part A | The Causes

# 1 | Introduction

In 2015, ethicist Dirk Philipsen wrote a book on GDP – gross domestic product. The book was titled *The Little Big Number: How GDP Came to Rule the World and What to Do About It.* Katy Lederer,[1] who reviewed the book for the *New Yorker*, quotes this gem from the book:

> ... a pill-dependent smoker who, on the way to his divorce lawyer, crashes his oversized car into a school bus because he is texting about an impending derivatives trade.

Philipsen has used this extreme example to make the point that GDP makes no distinction between ethical and unethical activities. All of the above boost GDP but do little to boost economic welfare or well-being. Yes, it includes the derivatives trade.

A piece of news from *Financial Times* in June 2018 proved that Philipsen was not exaggerating. A financial market trader, running a hedge fund inside the private equity firm Blackstone, used to take positions in credit default swaps (CDSs) (an insurance contract that compensates the owner if the borrower defaults on payments – interest and/or principal repayment – on the bond on which the insurance was bought). Nothing exceptional. Hedge fund managers and traders routinely do this. The difference was that he then used it to lean on the companies that had to make the payment to miss payments or delay them such that they constituted a technical default. His CDSs would then pay him out the compensation. Few days later, the companies would make their delayed payments to bondholders. In one of his last trades, he did the opposite. He sold CDSs to other hedge funds on a company that looked very likely to default on its next payment and collected premiums from those who

---

[1] Katy Lederer, 'The End of G.D.P?' *New Yorker*, 9 September 2015, available at https://www.newyorker.com/business/currency/the-end-of-g-d-p (accessed on 8 June 2018).

bought the CDS. Then, the company was lent enough money such that it did not default on the payment. The insurance was for nothing. Those who bought the CDS lost their premiums! Several months later, the company defaulted and filed for bankruptcy. This is the equivalent of fixing matches in sports. We are also reminded of *Almighty*, a novel by fiction writer Irving Wallace, in which a newspaper owner would begin to create news-stories and make them happen so that his newspaper could be the first one to report the exclusive breaking news!

What was this trader's strength? Apparently, he used to pore over hundreds of pages of bond or loan documents for details that others would miss. 'Once he identifies chinks in the wording of particular clauses he plots a way to construct trades using derivatives on whether a company will default on its debts, which would lure rivals to take the other side.'[2]

Did his extraordinary diligence contribute to economic growth or quality of life of the people? It only left a trail of bitterness and howls of protest at the blatant unfairness of it all even though nothing illegal could be established.

Close on the heels of this big report in *Financial Times* came the news that the Australian financial regulator was charging Citibank and Deutsche Bank with criminal misconduct when they underwrote the share issuance of ANZ Bank. Reportedly, they had held back on certain number of shares from being available for sale and did not disclose that. Both the banks are contesting the charge. But financial regulators are not known to press criminal charges lightly.[3] Separately, from another news,[4] we learn that previously unreported court documents reveal that American prosecutors were aware of high-level executive involvement in SocGen bank in France and directed the rigging of the London Interbank Offered Rate (LIBOR). None of them were personally prosecuted or extradited to America to face trial. So, none went to jail either.

By now, if you think you have an idea of where the book is going, then you are wrong. This book is not a chronicle of personal or institutional misconduct by financial institutions over the years. We have nothing more to add to what

---

[2] 'The Mystery Trader Who Roiled Wall Street', *Financial Times*, 4 June 2018, available at https://www.ft.com/content/5e23e516-5cdc-11e8-ad91-e01af256df68 (accessed on 8 June 2018).

[3] 'Former Citi and Deutsche Bankers Charged in Australian Cartel Case', *Financial Times*, 5 June 2018, available at https://www.ft.com/content/851bfcf6-68a5-11e8-8cf3-0c230fa67aec (accessed on 8 June 2018).

[4] 'SocGen Executives Ordered Libor Rigging, US Prosecutors Believed', *Financial Times*, 8 June 2018, available at https://www.ft.com/content/05dfb112-6a53-11e8-b6eb-4acfcfb08c11 (accessed on 8 June 2018).

Raghuram Rajan, former governor of the Reserve Bank of India (RBI), had said in a speech about five years ago:

> No wonder bankers today, and unfortunately, have a social status somewhere between that of a pimp and a conman.[5]

## 1.1 The story of this book

This book tells the story of how finance came to dominate economies, our lives and the evolution of societies disproportionately heavily from the 1980s. Of course, as will be seen later, it was not the first time it had happened. Finance had been dominant before, and on those occasions too, it had caused grief. Our purpose in this book is not to present a history of finance from its origins. Ours is a more recent tale.

In the wake of the Great Depression of the 1930s that followed the 'Great Gatsby' decade of the 1920s, the Roosevelt administration had taken several steps to improve the lives of the people. Social security was introduced (the Social Security Administration [SSA] was founded on 14 August 1935) as was Deposit Insurance (the Federal Deposit Insurance Corporation [FDIC] was founded on 16 June 1933) for bank deposits. Interstate banking was prohibited and interest rates on deposits and loans were regulated. Post World War II, the Bretton Woods Agreement was concluded, which created a system of stable exchange rates with the US dollar as the global anchor currency. Stock market tickers did not run continuously below the morning breakfast television shows in America.[6]

The world economy, led by the United States of America as the leader of the victorious Allied nations, recovered nicely from the ravages of war. Reconstruction and catch-up growth were state-led and were low-hanging fruits. Households held bank deposits and pension funds bought bonds to hold until maturity as the coupon on them was deemed adequate compensation against inflation. Compensation in the financial sector (see Chapter 3) was no different from the rest of the economy and trading derivatives was not easy. Not too many financial innovations happened in any case. Stock broking commissions were too high and analysts' research reports on stocks were not

---

[5] Raghuram Rajan, 'A Step in the Dark: Unconventional Monetary Policy after the Crisis', First Andrew Crockett Memorial Lecture, 23 June 2013, available at https://www.bis.org/events/agm2013/sp130623.htm (accessed on 8 June 2018).

[6] Wikipedia informs us that the first fully automated stock ticker to appear on television was in 1996 (https://en.wikipedia.org/wiki/News_ticker).

the equivalent of sales promotion literature and retirement planning was not a gamble on stock market returns. Emerging markets (EMs) were a long way off from emerging as a viable and promising asset class. There was West and then the rest. Financial and banking crises were rare. Banking was boring. Then, it changed.

It all began as America fretted about the too successful Germany and Japan and about the spread of communism to faraway shores. It entered the costly Vietnam War and also began running a loose monetary policy with a view to making American exports competitive. The Bretton Woods arrangement soon unravelled in the 1970s. Without the anchor country guaranteeing price stability, there cannot be a fixed exchange rate regime. Arab nations flexed their oil muscle; mullahs took over Iran and they held America hostage. Oil prices became a big factor in economic growth and the decade of the 1970s was a decade of stagflation for the West.

As economic growth opportunities were exhausted, the West had to find other ways to maintain economic growth. Financial liberalization was the next growth driver and academic studies played a catalysing role in placing it at the centre of economic activity. The economy was no longer the dog that wagged the finance tail. In ordinary terms, one can say that the 'rise of finance' or *financialization*[7] is the process by which the tail wagged the dog or finance became the dog!

The facts[8] are staggering:

Credit market debt and market value of equities in America were 212 per cent of GDP in 1981 and 514 per cent of GDP in 2014.

The balance sheet of the Federal Reserve exploded from USD 200 billion to USD 4.5 trillion. Call that a 23× gain.

According to Forbes, Warren Buffett's net worth was USD 2.1 billion back in 1987 and it is now about USD 73 billion. Call that 35×.

---

[7] These two terms will be used interchangeably throughout the book. To us, it means one and the same.

[8] These facts are based on a blog post by David Stockman, the former Director of the Office of Budget Management under President Ronald Reagan: 'The Warren Buffett Economy: How Central-Bank-Enabled Financialisation Divided America', 7 August 2016, available at http://www.zerohedge.com/news/2016-08-07/warren-buffett-economy-how-central-bank-enabled-financialization-divided-america (accessed on 14 May 2017). We have updated the figures using FRED database of the Federal Reserve Bank of St. Louis for as many of the bullet points as possible. We cannot vouchsafe for their accuracy.

During those same years, the value of non-financial US corporate equities rose from USD 2.3 trillion to USD 23.6 trillion. Call it 10.3×.

During those same years, credit to the private non-financial sector rose from USD 5.9 trillion to USD 28.0 trillion. That was 4.7×.

Nominal GDP rose from USD 4.9 trillion to USD 18.6 trillion during the same 29-year period. That was 3.8×.

The value of corporate equities rose from 46 per cent to 125 per cent of GDP during that 29-year interval.

Wage and salary disbursements paid to employees (from gross domestic income data) rose from USD 2.26 trillion to USD 8.2 trillion over the period. That is 3.6×.

Then comes the median nominal household income. That measurement increased from USD 26,000 to USD 565,000 over the period. Call it 2.2×.

Then comes the real median household income (2015 dollars). That measurement increased from USD 52,000 to USD 565,000 over the period. Call it 1.2×.

The median nominal income of US families increased from USD 31,000 to USD 71,000 over the period. Call it 2.3×.

The real median income (2015 dollars) of US families increased from USD 618,000 to USD 707,000 over the period. Call it 1.14×.

The sum of aggregate labour hours supplied to the non-farm economy by real people rose from 185 billion hours to 240 billion hours during those same 29 years. Call it 1.27×.

The average weekly wage of full-time workers in constant 1982 dollars was USD 330 per week in 1987 and is currently USD 340. Call that 1.03×.

This book tells the story of how this happened and more. What or who caused this? What are its consequences? What is the cure? Yes, we consider the rise of finance to such staggering levels as a disease that the world is suffering from. We suggest some therapies. Others have suggested them too. We do not claim originality. But we think that the more they are discussed and their circulation greater in public domain and discussions, the better are the chances of their acceptance. Of course, this sounds somewhat naïve. Reforms and regime shifts are neither voluntary nor are they products of intellectual persuasion. Crises and revolts are the likely parents. The crisis of 2008 was an opportunity. But financiers and their godfathers dug their heels in. Temporarily, they have succeeded. The more things changed, as a consequence of the 2008 crisis, the more they have remained the same. In 2018, the Federal Reserve relaxed the capital requirements for eight systemically important financial institutions (Chapter 6). Therefore, it might take another bigger crisis to force end the dominance of finance that has been the feature of nearly the last four decades.

We are aware that the stakes are more than about finance. It is also a clash between the interests of capital and labour. It is not a mere coincidence that the rise of finance has gone hand in hand with the decline of labour unions and labour share of income not just in the US but in several other developed nations as well. The dominance of the West over the rest has also been bound up with the rise and success of capitalism of which finance is a crucial component. So, we realize that taming and reversing the rise of finance is not just a simple matter of making banking boring again. It may come to redefine the course of capitalism in the twenty-first century and reshape the global power balance between the West and the rest. After all, with aging populations, the West has relied considerably on debt to deliver economic growth. Finance has ferried global savings to the shores of the America so that it could consume and grow. While Germany is different, the rest of Europe needs global capital to help them honour their pension, social security and health care promises to their public. If the genie of finance is put back in the bottle, the collapse of the western model might follow in short order. They know that and consequently they did not allow the crisis of 2008 to upend the financial edifice they had carefully constructed over the previous three decades.

At the same time, change has to come because the rise of finance has meant the rise of debt mountains around the world – debt in the hands of governments, businesses and households. As debt climbed, interest rates have plumbed. Strange as it may sound, that has happened since the 1980s. Without that, such vast and rapid debt accumulation would not have transpired, nor would it have been possible to service them. But interest rates cannot go much lower. All interest rate bullets had been fired to stave off the consequences of the last crisis and there has been resistance to reloading the policy guns. Consequently, the world finds itself saddled with much more debt in 2018 than it did in 2008. In the process, it has woken up to another problem that has grown silently if unsurprisingly: glaring, persistent and pervasive income and wealth inequality.

It should not be surprising because when capitalists got the better of labour in the 1980s, labour share of income began to fall. As capitalists managed to retain their dominance, it kept falling. Debt goes and on favourable terms where there is collateral. That is, assets facilitate debt growth and debt facilitates asset growth. It is a convenient marriage. In contrast, the working class relies on debt, available at not-so-favourable terms, for survival and for smoothing out consumption from one period to the next. As a result, the household net worth distribution is skewed and is disproportionately in the hands of the top deciles of the population. The rest are managing with less savings in banks that earn them nothing. It does not look like a sustainable state of affairs to us.

In 2011, Wolfgang Streeck wrote:[9]

> More than ever, economic power seems today to have become political power while citizens appear to be almost entirely stripped of their democratic defences and their capacity to impress on the political economy interests and demands incommensurable with those of capital owners. In fact, looking back at the democratic-capitalist crisis sequence since the 1970s, one cannot but be afraid of the possibility of a new, however temporary, settlement of social conflict in advanced capitalism, this time entirely in favour of the propertied classes now firmly entrenched in their politically unconquerable institutional stronghold, the international financial industry.

Changing this is far more urgent and important than preserving the existing pecking order between nations of the West and aspiring powers of the East. It is a humane thing to do. That requires stopping the rise of finance and plotting its decline. This book is a small effort in that direction.

## 1.2 The questions we seek to answer

This book answers three questions: What caused the rise of finance? What are its consequences? What can cure it? The first part examines the causes and it is also a chronicle of the rise of finance. But the chronicle is only brief for we are more interested in examining and presenting the consequences of its rise and in proposing cures that would cap and reverse its rise. The second and third parts of the book deal with them. The reader may notice that 'cures' is a play on the word 'curse'.

The story of the twentieth century was a tale of two halves – a bloody first half and a peaceful second half. The second half of the second half witnessed

---

[9] Wolfgang Streeck, 'The Crisis in Context: Democratic Capitalism and Its Contradictions', MPIfG Discussion Paper 11/15, Max Planck Institute for the Study of Societies, October 2011.

the rise of finance. Such a phenomenon which quickly became global has to have multiple causes and actors who helped it along. We will take the risk of being accused of oversimplification but we will say that the Federal Reserve and Alan Greenspan, its chairman from 1987 to 2006, emerge as the biggest creators and champions of financialization. The institution, under his leadership, seeded it and nurtured it and safeguarded it. He handed the baton over to Ben Bernanke in 2006 who ran with it faithfully. The Federal Reserve and its leadership are the prime forces that propelled financialization and its globalization. America's leadership in the non-Communist world and unipolar position after 1990 ensured that the rest of the world had to accommodate and accept the rise of finance, willingly or otherwise.

In the quarter century between 1990 and 2015, that is, in a period of 300 months, the Federal Reserve had either been lowering the federal funds rate or kept it on hold for a total of 240 months. Yes, 80 per cent of the time. When it raised the federal funds rate by 25 basis points in December 2015, it was doing so for the first time in 114 months. Monetary policy decisions of the Federal Reserve were central to the extraordinary wealth accretion to financial traders, fund managers and executives and to the rewards that investors and other participants collected from speculative activity in financial and other asset markets. That is why for David Stockman financialization is the process by which the Federal Reserve monetary policy over the last quarter century to three decades rewarded financial speculators at the expense of mainstream America. This may be sensational but also true, even if only partially.

The Federal Reserve enabled the rise of finance not just through its conduct of monetary policy but also through the intellectual contributions made by its leadership on issues such as deregulation, budget deficits and social security. Their larger-than-life roles influenced opinion formation in the media, society and the US Congress. The importance of the US economy to the rest of the world influenced opinions and financial sector evolution globally too. We are convinced that reversing financialization or de-financializing America and the rest of the world would require a change of heart or a different philosophical outlook towards finance at the Federal Reserve. That is where it has to begin. But it is not going to be easy. In the aftermath of the crisis of 2008, Alan Greenspan expressed some remorse for his role in the deregulation of the US financial industry, in his memoirs. He admitted that his faith in the self-regulating capacity of the financial markets had been misplaced. But by the end of his testimony, he had largely retracted his confession.

## 1.3 Why did we omit the crisis of 2008?

Some readers might be surprised that the book does not have a chapter dedicated to the crisis of 2008. After all, it was the Wile E. Coyote moment for finance and it was global. Then, why are we silent on the crisis of 2008? We are silent not because the crisis is now 10 years old, that it is time for the next one and that it made more sense to us to discuss why the conditions for it are in place rather than doing a post-mortem on the last one. After all, many have already done that. Although these explanations have more than a kernel of truth, they only partially explain our silence. A more important reason is that we see the crisis of 2008 as a symptom, an apparent manifestation of underlying causes that were themselves the consequences of the rise of finance. Chapters in Part II of the book deal with consequences of the rise of finance.

The extraordinary rise in executive compensation in finance, which then spread to non-financial sectors, is one of them. A related phenomenon is the misallocation of human resources in the economy. Much talent flowed to finance where it created far too much private gains and too little social gains. Just remember the fund manager in Blackstone who knew how to read the arcane details of bond covenants and set up profitable trades for himself and his firm. Then, there is inequality of income and wealth.[10] The most important consequence of the rise of finance was the changes it wrought to the monetary policy framework in the world.

In the 1980s, central banks went from targeting the quantity of money and credit to setting interest rates to target inflation. That was a momentous change – one that mistook price stability for financial stability and sacrificing the latter in the process. This important change in the monetary policy framework then spawned a series of subsidiary consequences: sustained growth in debt, which, in turn, meant that monetary policy had to support asset prices for assets represented collateral to debt. It meant that monetary policy had to become predictable and transparent to financial market participants and speculators. If they were surprised and if asset prices fell, debt burdens would be hard to service

---

[10] We must record here that Wolfgang Streeck thinks that inequality is not so much the consequence of financialization as it is a cause of it! In his widely cited essay 'How Will Capitalism End?', in the *New Left Review* in 2014 (May/June), he wrote, 'As Keynes would have known, concentration of income at the top must detract from effective demand and make capital owners look for speculative profit opportunities outside the "real economy". This may in fact have been one of the causes of the "financialisation" of capitalism that began in the 1980s.'

and defaults would mount. Pain all around. In short, the capture of monetary policy was an important consequence of the rise of finance. Unfortunately for the world, that led to a pivotal role for monetary policy in setting off a slew of undesirable economic and social consequences post 2008.

The rise of finance had multilayered consequences and the crisis of 2008 was an outcome of these underlying forces that the rise of finance had unleashed.

The third and final part of the book has three chapters. There are some incipient danger signs in some pockets of finance and equally, there are areas where finance has barely registered its presence. As with most things, India presents a picture of contradictions and complexity. Hence, we present that chapter separately. But the lessons that the world has learnt about finance will eventually apply to India too. It neither has to reinvent the wheel nor repeat the mistakes that other nations have made. The advantage of a late-starter is that it can leapfrog over the mistakes that others made in their journey.

We offer several suggestions and proposals on managing, taming and reversing the rise of finance. The ones with the greatest potential for change are to do with monetary policy and banking regulation. As we said before, the Federal Reserve and its leadership over the last 30 years have played a very big role in helping finance rise to its present state of undesirably excessive domination over the economy and, increasingly, over society too. Finance has returned the favour by capturing monetary policy. Monetary policy has to be freed of the considerations of finance. Mind you, these considerations are not and will never be official. If it were so, it would be easier to resist it and change it. It is subterranean. It is insidious.

Reversing the financialization of the global economy requires fixing the prevailing monetary policy framework in America and Europe. Yes, Europe too. Europe was relatively late to the party. It favoured fixed exchange rates and the discipline that went with it. For a long time, capital controls were in vogue in the continent. But aging populations, faltering growth, a broken banking system and a huge debt burden have forced their hand. The European Central Bank (ECB), under Mario Draghi, has enthusiastically embraced America's policy framework. They have to keep their fiscally broken sovereigns with heavy interest rate subsidies. In doing so, they have fallen into the ditch and are still digging. Their policies have created more problems than solving them. Real estate bubbles have popped up everywhere in the continent and zombie companies have been kept alive.

Fixing the monetary policy framework requires fixing not just their economic models and but also their mental models. That explains a separate section on asymmetries and non-linearity in economics and finance in Chapter 6. In the end, solutions to seemingly intractable problems lie in the recognition of the limitations of the human mind and intelligence and the need for humility.[11] Otherwise, policymakers will lurch from one unprecedented experiment to another with nary a thought for consequences that they do not or cannot foresee. The road to hell has always been paved with good intentions.

Fiscal policy rules, automatic triggers on spending cuts and fixed exchange rate regimes are as much about prudence and discipline as they are about the recognition of the dangers of unconstrained policy-making. Those rules are a recognition that governments, as much as humans, have to and need to restrain or chain themselves with hard stops to avoid slipping into unsustainable and undesirable policy habits. Much the same applies to monetary policy. Monetary policymakers are human, not immune to human failings and hence not exempt from such hard stops. Monetary policy experiments with unforeseen and unforeseeable consequences need to be hard-stopped.

## 1.4 Organization of the book

Chapter 2 looks at the origins of financialization in the twentieth century and its subsequent evolution. It also looks at how deregulation set the stage for financialization and how the pivotal role of the US dollar and the American economy contributed to the globalization of financialization.

Chapter 3 explores how the dominance of financial markets contributed to the divergence of financial sector wages and widening inequality. This may also be the most politically salient feature of financialization and therefore the most compelling reason for reversing it. Even the elites at Davos, the biggest beneficiaries of financialization, recognize the threat posed by this trend.

Chapter 4 examines the role that central banks and monetary policy play in entrenching and strengthening financialization. Importantly, we stress that the evolution of the monetary policy framework according primacy to asset prices, financial market considerations and the interests of the financial sector (for example, see Section 4.4 on monetary policy transparency and predictability) is a consequence of financialization and its globalization. We discuss the multiple channels through which this manifests – through low interest rates, debt accumulation, the importance accorded to financial markets and asset

---

[11] 'The Man Who Tried to Redeem the World with Logic' must be compulsory reading for intellectuals before they begin work as policymakers. Amanda Gefter, *Nautilus*, 5 February 2015, available at http://m.nautil.us/issue/21/information/the-man-who-tried-to-redeem-the-world-with-logic (accessed on 9 June 2018).

prices in general in economic models, through orienting communication to suit the horizons and return preferences of the financial sector and through regulation of the financial sector, including rules on bank capital and so on. We round off the chapter with examining the costs of not using monetary policy to 'lean against the wind'. That monetary policymakers chose not to preemptively deal with asset price bubbles but felt more comfortable cleaning up after the bubble burst (clean vs. lean) is an important consequence of the rise of finance. Needless to add, this important policy choice comes with economic costs attached.

Nothing illustrates the two-way cause and effect between monetary policy and financialization better than the unconventional monetary policy (UMP) pursued in response to the global crisis of 2008. Chapter 5 takes a comprehensive look at the consequences of the biggest financial experiment of our times – both intended and unintended – and its contribution to financialization. In particular, it carries detailed discussions on the failure of UMP to boost capital formation and the causes of such a failure, on its contribution to resource misallocation, on its encouragement of excessive debt accumulation, on the obstruction of capitalism by policy stability and policy transparency, on the inducement it offers to excessive risk-taking and the consequent risk to financial and economic stability including the risk of prolonged economic stagnation and, finally, on its role in driving the widening inequality.

This brings us to the third and final part of the book which puts forward a set of cures. Accordingly, in Chapter 6 we endorse the recommendations for simple capital adequacy rules for banks – higher tangible equity to tangible assets. Emerging economies should not be embarrassed about invoking capital controls and they should strive to keep their currencies slightly undervalued as long as unbridled capital flows and their sudden surges and stops remain a threat. The centrepiece of this chapter is Section 6.5, where we call for the abandonment of the obsession with asset prices at the Federal Reserve Board (FRB). We argue that while it may not solve all the problems that currently bedevil the global economy, it would go a long way in making the world safe from finance. It then outlines a set of proposals including adoption of full reserve banking, dealing with spillovers including actions at both national and multilateral levels, eliminating the tax exemption on interest expenses, focusing on anti-trust measures to combat the growing business concentration and rise of oligopolies, and changing prevailing narratives.

Chapter 7 takes a detour from the global context of financialization and explores financialization in India. In contrast to the developed economies, India's challenge is not so much in reversing financialization as it is in deepening its financial markets and promoting greater financial inclusion. Further, while the RBI has rightfully been very cautious with capital account liberalization, there may perhaps be a case for further liberalization given the relatively limited aggregate external financial exposure of the Indian economy. The chapter also explores financial repression and the central bank's attendant monetary policy transmission challenge and the changing nature of financial intermediation given the increasing salience of capital markets. Finally, in the context of the growing and globally integrating financial markets, it explores certain financialization challenges – resource misallocation and the speculative excesses of the derivatives markets, the central bank's balance sheet expansion and external vulnerabilities as manifested during the taper tantrum and regulatory capacity constraints.

Chapter 8 concludes with a summary of the proposals for revision of the prevailing monetary policy paradigm as well as a call for democratic accountability and leadership by the US.

### 1.5  What is the message of the book?

1.  Finance matters but it should not be the only matter.
2.  Asset prices should reflect economic fundamentals but should not dominate or dictate fundamentals.
3.  Finance must be regulated for three reasons. It has mostly private benefits and public costs. Second, financial sector and financial market behaviours are inherently pro-cyclical. Third, competition in the financial sector is inimical to economic system stability.
4.  Money creation by banks has been mostly socially harmful. Full reserve (as opposed to fractional reserve) banking is an idea worth trying. Along with that, the idea of 'too big to fail' (TBTF) banks must be buried. It creates moral hazard as does deposit insurance.
5.  Financial markets have not priced risk well at all. Either they have been forgotten or monetary policies over the years have made them forget.
6.  Investors (aka financial market participants) do not learn their lessons from previous crises well. They simply repeat their errors in different areas. That is why most regulations that follow crises address the last one well but fail miserably in preventing the next one. Indeed, they fail to anticipate them, because they cannot. The only effective insurance against unbridled investor greed and risk-taking is a cost of capital that adequately reflects risk.

7. Therefore, there is no escape from financial stability considerations being at the front and centre of monetary policy. But central banks ignored financial stability before 2008 and are still at it, 11 years after the last crisis in 2008.

8. Financial market behaviour, relationship between economic variables and between economic variables and asset prices and responses of asset prices to economic policy decisions are both non-linear and asymmetric. Academics and policymakers are well aware of this but their decisions often do not reflect this reality.

9. Given integrated capital markets and the unipolar importance of the US dollar to the international payment system, commodities and capital markets, spillovers from policies pursued in developed countries to developing countries is inevitable. Developing countries lack instruments and coercive power to dissuade advanced nations from pursuing domestic policies that have negative spillover effects for them. Since the world has no alternative to the US dollar presently, the only option left to avoid spillovers is to reverse integration of capital markets and free capital flows. In the absence of restrictions on capital flows, both the impossible trinity and the financial market trilemma have been reduced to the impossible duality and financial market dilemma, respectively. Therefore, capital controls cannot be the policy of last resort to be deployed in the event of financial instability. It is central to ensuring financial stability. Developing countries must be cautious in liberalizing external commercial borrowings for their domestic borrowers and in inviting foreigners to invest in domestic debt.

10. Secular stagnation is absent in returns to capital – returns generated in stock and real estate markets and corporate profit margins have been rising at disproportionately high rates despite mediocre and moderate economic growth and wage growth. Returns to capital are bulked up by monetary policies that have helped capitalists lever up their gains with enormous but cheap debt. This is deepening and worsening economic and social schisms. Politically, it has contributed to the rise of economic populism and nationalism. It is futile to blame populists for the problems that preceded them.

If the Federal Reserve were to signal, categorically and unambiguously, the withdrawal of the Federal Reserve Put on stock markets, much of the problems associated with financial capitalism – poor returns to labour, excessive absolute and relative executive compensations, short-term investment horizons, preference to financial over real investments, investor indifference to market risk, build-up of public and private debt and systemic risk – would begin to sort themselves out.

## 1.6  What do readers get out of this book?

For policy experts and perceptive financial market participants, much of the contents of our book must be familiar. Some concerned academics and ex-policymakers have suggested the recommendations made in this book before.

This book is different for the following reasons:

1. It assembles data, evidence and findings from many allied social sciences and does not restrict itself to finance and economics.
2. In doing so, it challenges orthodox thinking in finance and economics.
3. While specific recommendations have been made in specific areas, very few books offer a comprehensive and integrated perspective on multiple dimensions – finance, economics and society – as this book does.
4. For those readers who do not think about these issues constantly, the book not only offers an excellent introduction but also affords to get them up to speed quickly with the current thinking, debates and viewpoints of several scholars from different yet related disciplines.
5. The rise of finance has been too steep and has crossed the peak of usefulness for many societies. Hence, the points made in this book, even if they have been made before and elsewhere, are useful reinforcements. It takes concerted and sustained effort to move the world to a different paradigm. Therefore, we feel that this book is an important, if incremental, contribution towards a more financially stable and less inequitable world.
6. We would like to believe that the language we use in the book makes the subject accessible to readers and not arcane.

# 2 | The Rise of Finance: Origins

This chapter begins by establishing a common understanding of financialization in Section 2.1. In Section 2.2, it underscores the important point that is often missed in the discourse on reining in finance. Its rise was part of the neoliberal agenda that began to be assembled in the 1980s. Section 2.3 traces the rise and growth of financialization in the twentieth century to the onset of economic stagflation in the 1970s in much of the developed world. That propelled many forces that have dominated and shaped the world economy in unforeseen ways. Globalization of trade and financialization are two important forces that the economic troubles of the 1970s spawned. In Section 2.4, we show that deregulation propelled and strengthened financialization and made it inexorable even though finance is far less amenable to the free and untrammelled play of market forces compared to other economic activities. In Section 2.5, we establish that financialization went global, thanks to the hegemony of the US dollar and the dependence of the rest of the world on American economic growth.

## 2.1 What is financialization?

The most comprehensive analysis or a more formal treatment of financialization comes from Thomas Palley. For him, financialization is 'a process whereby financial markets, financial institutions, and financial elites gain greater influence over economic policy and economic outcomes'.[1] He identifies three principal impacts – elevation of the significance of financial sector relative to the real sector, transfer of income from the real sector to the financial sector and increase in income inequality and contribution to wage stagnation. He also points to three different conduits – changes in the structure and operation

---

[1] Thomas I. Palley, 'Financialisation – What It Is and Why It Matters', The Levy Economics Institute of Bard College Working Paper no. 525, December 2007.

of financial markets, behaviours of non-financial corporations and economic policy.[2]

Donald Tomaskovic-Devey and Ken-Hou Lin of the University of Massachusetts in Amherst (the alma mater of one of us)[3] go one step further than Palley. They define financialization as consisting of two interdependent processes: the increasing importance of financial services firms to the American society in economic, political and social terms and the increased involvement of non-financial firms in financial activity. So, they view financialization as a process that placed financial services firms at the centre of American society and not just at the centre of the American economy. We lean towards this formulation. Financialization not only influenced the economy but also had social consequences through its impact on wages and compensation. For instance, the rise of finance shaped students' preferences for skills and higher educational qualifications.

Ewa Karwowski, Mimoza Shabani and Engelbert Stockhammer investigated[4] empirically the dimensions and determinants of financialization in seventeen Organisation for Economic Co-operation and Development (OECD) countries between 1997 and 2007. They estimate correlations between five indicators of financialization – household debt, gross financial income of non-financial corporations, debt of non-financial corporations, value added in the financial sector and debt in the financial sector – and seven hypotheses of financialization. These hypotheses may be causal factors for financialization or simply associated with financialization. The hypotheses are that real investment slowdown precedes financialization, financial deregulation leads to financialization, financialization is associated with market-based as opposed to bank-based systems, financialization occurs in debt-driven as opposed to

---

[2] In this context, Greta Krippner argues that unlike other long-term structural shifts in the economy, the signatures of financialization cannot be found in the changes in employment or the mix of goods and services produced. Instead, she suggests looking at where profits are generated and the changes in the respective shares of different sectors. See Greta R. Krippner, 'Financialisation of the American Economy', *Socio-Economic Review* 3 (2005): 173–208.

[3] Donald Tomaskovic-Devey and Ken-Hou Lin, 'Income Dynamics, Economic Rents, and the Financialisation of the U.S. Economy', *American Sociological Review* 76, no. 4 (1 August 2011): 538–539.

[4] Ewa Karwowski, Mimoza Shabani and Engelbert Stockhammer, 'Financialisation: Dimensions and Determinants. A Cross-country Study', Post Keynesian Economics Study Group Working Paper no. 1619, December 2016.

export-driven aggregate demand in the economy, financialization is associated with strong foreign investment inflows and that asset price inflation is a feature of financialization.

What they find is that rising debt and rising asset prices are associated with financialization because there is strong correlation between these two and at least one indicator of financialization across all the three sectors – households, non-financial corporations and the financial sector. Interestingly, financialization of the non-financial sector is strongly associated with market-based (vs. bank-based) financial systems. In other words, the more a country relies on capital markets for financial intermediation, the more financial activities play an important role in the businesses of non-financial corporations (Figure 2.1). One would have expected financial deregulation to be correlated with the increasing financialization of the non-financial sector. They did not find evidence of it in their sample. They rule out real investment slowdown and foreign investment flows as causal or associated factors for financialization. Debt and asset price dynamics are the subjects of extensive analysis in Chapters 4 and 5.

**Figure 2.1  Spearman rank-order correlation coefficients for financialization hypotheses and economic sectors (1997–2007)**

| | *Household debt* | *NFC gross financial income* | *NFC debt* | *Financial sector value added* | *Financial sector debt* |
|---|---|---|---|---|---|
| Investment slowdown | −0.358 | 0.282 | 0.081 | −0.762 | −0.521 |
| Financial deregulation | 0.423** | 0.266 | 0.042 | 0.43** | 0.669*** |
| Market-based/ bank-based systems | −0.032 | 0.473** | 0.536* | −0.476 | −0.385 |
| Debt-driven/ export-driven demand regimes | 0.598** | −0.097 | 0.379* | 0.531** | 0.194 |
| Foreign financial inflows | 0.174 | 0.227 | 0.2 | 0.27 | 0.833*** |
| House price inflation | 0.371* | 0.176 | 0.455* | 0.27 | 0.436* |

*Source*: Ewa Karwowski, Mimoza Shabani and Engelbert Stockhammer, 'Financialisation: Dimensions and Determinants. A Cross-country Study', Post Keynesian Economics Study Group Working Paper no. 1619, December 2016.

Delivering the Per Jacobsson Memorial Lecture in 2012,[5] Dr Y. V. Reddy, the former governor of the RBI, who earned plaudits for keeping India out of the harm's way during the GFC in 2008, made a distinction between optimal financialization and excessive financialization. In his view, optimal financialization referred to a situation where the financial sector is allowed to intermediate credit and savings at the right price without the interference of the state that results in financial repression. He then defined excessive financialization as not just the rise in importance of the financial sector, financial markets or the financial institutions in the economy. They are important. But what constitutes excessive financialization, according to him, is the (disproportionate) influence of financial considerations and the influence and role of finance in commodities markets, in corporate balance sheets and in household budgets. Throughout this book, when we refer to 'financialization', we mean the 'excessive financialization' that Dr Reddy had in mind.

## 2.2 Financialization and the neoliberal agenda

Financialization grew on the ideological soil of neoliberalism. James Montier of GMO, an asset management firm, wrote a thoughtful long essay[6] on the recent rise of popular politicians (populists) in western economies and its causes. He attributes it to the public anger against the neoliberal economic agenda pursued by the United States and other advanced nations. What is the neoliberal economic agenda?

According to him, it has four pillars:

1. Shareholder value maximization
2. Inflation targeting and the concept of non-accelerating inflation rate of unemployment (NAIRU)
3. Globalization and free trade
4. Flexible labour markets

It is important to note that Montier and Pilkington use 'financialization' and 'neoliberalism' interchangeably in their paper (Figure 2.2). However,

---

[5] Y. V. Reddy, 'Society, Economic Policies and the Financial Sector', The Per Jacobsson Foundation Lecture 2012, Basel, Switzerland, 24 June 2012, available at http://www.perjacobsson.org/lectures/062412.pdf (accessed on 17 March 2017).

[6] James Montier and Philip Pilkington, 'The Deep Causes of Secular Stagnation and the Rise of Populism', *GMO*, March 2017, available at https://www.gmo.com/docs/default-source/research-and-commentary/strategies/asset-allocation/the-deep-causes-of-secular-stagnation-and-the-rise-of-populism.pdf (accessed on 17 March 2017).

as Tomaskovic-Devey and Lin did, we see financialization as an important component of the neoliberal agenda. 'Financialization was rooted in a series of political decisions to deregulate existing finance activities, which took place during an era of emerging neoliberal corporate and state governance ideologies'.[7] Indeed, if neoliberalism was a policy and intellectual movement away from state regulation, financialization was its most important product.[8] We explore the theme of 'movement away from state regulation' as the progenitor of financialization later in this chapter.

**Figure 2.2 The model of 'financialization'**

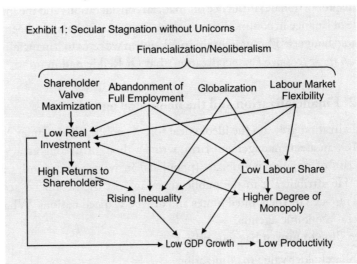

*Source*: James Montier and Philip Pilkington, 'The Deep Causes of Secular Stagnation and the Rise of Populism', *GMO*, March 2017, available at https://www.gmo.com/docs/default-source/research-and-commentary/strategies/asset-allocation/the-deep-causes-of-secular-stagnation-and-the-rise-of-populism.pdf (accessed on 17 March 2017).

Central bankers are the architects of the second pillar in Figure 2.2. Their focus on inflation as a measure of economic stability before the crisis of 2008

---

[7] Ken-Hou Lin, 'The Rise of Finance and Firm Employment Dynamics, 1982–2005', *SSRN*, 24 June 2013, available at https://ssrn.com/abstract=2284507 or http://dx.doi.org/10.2139/ssrn.2284507 (accessed on 18 March 2017).

[8] Donald Tomaskovic-Devey and Ken-Hou Lin, 'Income Dynamics, Economic Rents, and the Financialization of the U.S. Economy', *American Sociological Review* 76, no. 4 (2011): 538–559.

led them to ignore the signs of imbalances and instability building up through credit markets and various other channels. These imbalances were threats to the sustainability of full employment but not to price stability. Hence, the Federal Reserve ignored them. In remarks made in a public discussion at the University of Michigan in March 2017,[9] Janet Yellen, the former chairperson of the Federal Reserve, said that the Federal Reserve was doing pretty well in meeting the twin goals of low and stable inflation and full employment. Ms Yellen's remarks were a reminder that the economic models of the Federal Reserve have barely mutated in response to the crisis, which could have spelt the end of the dominance of the western alliance. Indeed, nearly a year later in March 2018, with asset prices boiling over all across the globe, it appears that the chickens may be coming home to roost again, a decade after the last crisis.

In the next chapter, we discuss in detail the economic model at the Federal Reserve that privileged price stability (not of assets but of goods and services) and not financial stability. The 'Great Moderation' was about achieving price stability and stable economic growth. That led to the Federal Reserve and other regulators taking their eyes off financial stability. That is an important consequence – undesirable for the economy – of financialization of the economy. Putting financial stability at the apex of monetary policy and banking regulatory framework would have led the Federal Reserve to the conclusion that financialization was indeed harming the economy and the society, precipitating, in turn, action to roll it back. Hence, an intellectually elegant excuse was needed to avoid walking down that path. The belief (or the hope) was that the financial markets were self-correcting and hence financial stability did not require regulatory oversight and action provided that excuse. That had been proven wrong in the past. It went wrong again in 2008 in a big way and it will happen again. An important reason is that activity in financial markets is motivated and governed by a different set of considerations (see Box 2.1).

## 2.3 The modern origins of financialization

The world economy experienced very sluggish growth for 18 centuries in the Common Era. Then, the fruits of industrial revolution began to appear. Growth picked up in the nineteenth century. The 35 years before World War I were really a golden era for world economy. There was mobility of capital and labour.

---

[9] 'Fed's Janet Yellen Says Era of Stimulative Monetary Policy Is Ending', *Wall Street Journal*, 11 April 2017, available at https://www.wsj.com/articles/federal-reserve-chairwoman-janet-yellen-sees-monetary-policy-shifting-1491865770 (accessed on 15 April 2017).

There was price stability and strong growth. Technological breakthroughs from the industrial revolution chipped in too to aid growth. For the most part, the next 30 years were bad for the world economy with two world wars, the collapse of the Gold Standard and the Great Depression. Reconstruction from the ravages of World War II helped the world economy experience strong growth from 1945 to 1965.

When the reconstruction era had run its course by the 1970s, it became more difficult to sustain growth in developed countries. Once those low hanging fruits were plucked, war and strife returned and the world experienced economic stagflation in the 1970s.

By the early 1970s, a different dynamic had gripped the world economy. Consumer prices rose almost 50 per cent between 1975 and 1980 in the United States. Inflation rate peaked at 14.3 per cent in June 1980. Donald Tomaskovic-Devey and Ken-Hou Lin write:[10]

> In 1973, surges in oil prices increased the cost of manufacturing and transportation while transferring income to oil producing firms and countries. The rise in union and consumer power put real limits on corporate autonomy in the labour process and the market. Manufacturing competition from Japan and northern Europe ended the post-war era of U.S. global manufacturing hegemony.

This put pressure on governments to rekindle growth through other means. Economist and former Greek finance minister, Yanis Varoufakis, wrote in his essay, 'The Vicious Disequilibrium': [11]

> The Bretton Woods system oversaw capitalism's Golden Era (1950–1970) in America. What tripped it up on 15 August 1971, causing the economic system itself to lose its footing? It was the US government's inability to restrain abuse of its exorbitant privilege – its ability, as custodian of the world's reserve currency – to print global public money at will to finance (without substantial new taxes) a stupendous military-industrial complex, the Vietnam war, the space program, Lyndon Johnson's (otherwise splendid) Great Society policies, et cetera.

---

[10] Tomaskovic-Devey and Lin, 'Income Dynamics, Economic Rents, and the Financialization of the U.S. Economy'.

[11] Yanis Varoufakis, 'Vicious Disequilibrium', *Los Angeles Review of Books*, 3 April 2014, available at http://lareviewofbooks.org/essay/vicious-disequilibrium (accessed on 3 May 2017).

US policy makers made an audacious strategic decision: faced with the rising twin deficits that were building up in the late 1960s (the budget deficit of the US government and the trade deficit of the American economy), Washington decided to turn a blind eye to them. Rather than imposing stringent austerity, whose effect would be to shrink both the twin US deficits and America's capacity to project hegemonic power around the world, they allowed the deficits to rise and economic growth to resume....

The expansion of US deficits generated the increases in aggregate demand that kept factories in the surplus countries going. On the other hand, almost 70 percent of the profits made globally by Eurasian capitalists were transferred to the United States, in the form of capital flows to Wall Street.

This was not just an isolated view. Many social and political scientists share this view of the rise of finance and the neoliberal agenda as being motivated by the economic stagnation and high inflation of the 1970s. Both of them were attributed to militant labour unions and the consequent high wage growth. James Montier and Pilkington, whose work we had cited in Section 2.2, note that 1948–1969 was the Golden Age of Keynesian full employment policy, that 1970–1982 was the crisis period of rising inflation due to OPEC oil price hikes and poor labour relations and that 1983–2015 was the period of inflation targeting.

The last was part of the emergent neoliberal agenda. The post–World War II world featured the commitment and responsibility of the state to citizens. That is how an elaborate system of social security, unemployment and pension benefits and state-funded health care came up. This was a fallout of the Depression of the 1930s which was seen (somewhat wrongly, in our view) as a consequence of the outcome of the Gold Standard era that tied the hands of the state from acting to prevent its damaging consequences. In the 1980s, this was pushed back through an intellectually clever argument that the representative Homo sapiens was a rational economic agent and that she was very well capable of looking after herself. This argument served a dual purpose. One was to discourage and dismantle state regulation and the second was to roll back or, at least, arrest the spread of the welfare state.

Although mathematics and econometrics were very much part of the academic economic literature, mathematical models were more prominently pressed into service in the cause of the neoliberal economic agenda from the late 1960s or 1970s, gathering further momentum in the 1980s. The use of mathematics lent a (false) touch of precision to the policy prescriptions of economists in favour of 'laissez faire' and against state intervention in the economy. That is, an impression was created that economic policies can be 'programmed' to deliver deterministic results like in the case of physical sciences, even though counterfactual scenarios cannot be constructed or controlled experiments cannot be done in economics, in social sciences and in real life![12]

This shift towards a pro-business (pro-capital) policy agenda would be meaningful only if the cost of capital could be brought down. The cost of borrowing, even for the US government, had doubled in the 1970s. The yield on the 10-year US government bond was around 5 per cent in the late 1960s. By October 1979, it was over 10 per cent. Businesses naturally faced even higher interest costs. So, inflation had to be brought down because the yield on loans was first, and foremost, a compensation for the loss of purchasing power.

Recall from Section 2.2 that inflation targeting by central banks was the second of the four pillars of the neoliberal regime, according to Montier and Pilkington. Reducing inflation meant restraining wage growth since labour costs were the biggest item of cost for most businesses – service or manufacturing. Thus, monetary policy, targeting inflation, in effect, began to target wage growth, completing the transformation of the interventionist, compassionate and pro-labour state to a non-interventionist, pro-business and empowering state that allowed individuals to determine their own destinies. That was a nice way of stating that elected political leaders were now condemning individuals to their own fate even as they decided to side with capital in pursuit of economic growth and political advancement.

Figure 2.3 shows how the shares of employee compensation and corporate profits in GDP moved in the opposite direction. Before 1980, the former was rising and the latter was falling and post–1980, the trend reversed, except for a

---

[12] In his essay 'The New Monetarism', Nicholas Kaldor had this to say about the followers of Milton Friedman: 'The new school, the Friedmanites (I do not use this term in any pejorative sense, the more respectful expression "Friedmanians" sounds worse) can record very considerable success, both in terms of the numbers of distinguished converts and of some rather glittering evidence in terms of "scientific proofs", obtained through empirical investigations summarised in time-series regression equations. Indeed, the characteristic feature of the new school is "positivism" and "scientism"; some would say "pseudo-scientism", using science as a selling appeal. *They certainly use time-series regressions as if they provided the same kind of "proofs" as controlled experiments in the natural sciences*' (emphasis ours). V. Ramanan, 'Nicholas Kaldor on Milton Friedman's Influence', *The Case for Concerted Action*, 13 July 2013, available at https://www.concertedaction. com/2013/07/13/nicholas-kaldor-on-milton-friedmans-influence/ (accessed on 4 March 2018).

few years in the second half of the 1990s when stock options and stock grants in technology companies briefly drove up employee compensation.

**Figure 2.3 Labour share of GDP peaked and profits share of GDP bottomed in the 1970s**

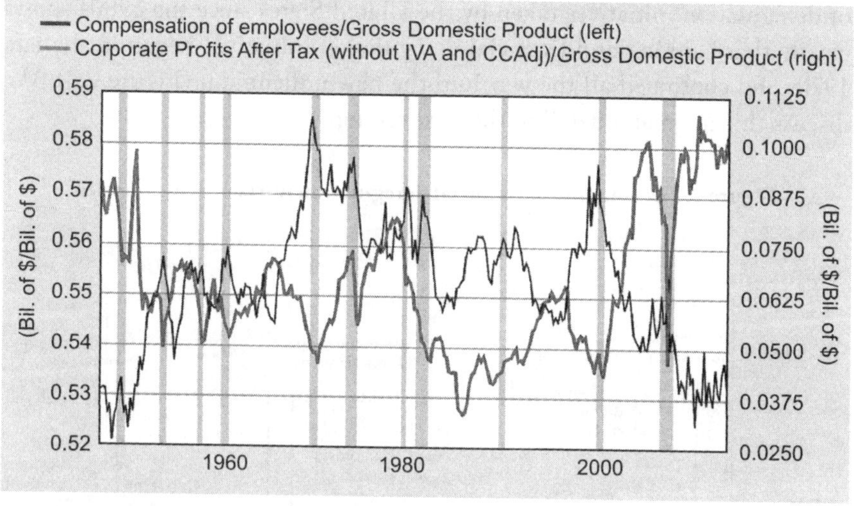

*Sources*: Bureau of Economic Analysis and the FRED Database of the Federal Reserve Bank of St. Louis.

It was not entirely coincidental that the collapse of the post–World War II consensus on government regulation, welfare state, government-led economic reconstruction and recovery also saw the collapse of the exchange rate arrangement agreed upon in Bretton Woods, anchored by the United States. Rising inflation, the exigencies of the Vietnam War and the fear of eroding competitiveness as Japan and Germany rapidly rebuilt their economies as competitive export machines led Nixon to end the dollar's anchor role. In its wake, other central banks abandoned their fixed exchange rates to the US dollar. This happened earlier in the 1970s.

Towards the end of the decade of the 1970s, after Paul Volcker, the newly appointed chairperson of the US Federal Reserve, abandoned targeting of money supply and began to target interest rates, the intellectual consensus in the developed ('free') world paid less attention to money supply. All that central banks had to do was to credit the accounts of commercial banks with more money. Creating base money became as easy as that. In a sense, the base money became the margin money on top of which the mountain of debt was created – many times as big. This should have led to higher inflation but it did not because monetary policy was now on the prowl for any nascent sign of acceleration in wage growth, to nip it in the bud.[13] The stage was set for the rise of finance or too much finance.

Shackles imposed on banks too began to loosen. The following timeline of deregulation initiatives taken by the United States since the 1980s shows clearly that banking and financial deregulation initiatives began in the late 1970s and continued all the way into the new millennium (Figure 2.4). We discuss this in greater detail in the next section.

**Figure 2.4  A timeline of financial deregulation initiatives in America**

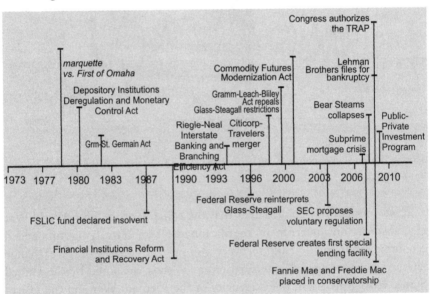

*Source*: Matthew Sherman, 'A Short History of Financial Deregulation in the United States', Centre for Economic and Policy Research (CEPR), July 2009.

In their discussion of the unintended consequences of economic policy advice that ignores the political economy, Daron Acemoglu and James Robinson provide a succinct summary of the chronology of financial deregulation

---

[13] Indeed, we argue in Chapter 4 that inflation has become less of a monetary phenomenon, if it ever was one. We explore the dynamics of inflation in the chapter.

('Money and Politics in the United States') and how it bolstered the political power and influence of finance, facilitating further deregulation.[14]

Consequently, bank credit growth picked up. The figure below (Figure 2.5) shows the 'structural break' in the evolution of bank credit and bank assets in the world from the 1970s and, more pronouncedly, from the 1980s. Something changed in the 1980s. Alan Taylor, an economist from the University of California, Davis, concedes that one of the goals of current and future research would be to pin down exactly why the period from the 1940s to the 1970s was so unusually quiescent, with no financial crisis at all.

**Figure 2.5 The inflection point in the global leverage cycle**

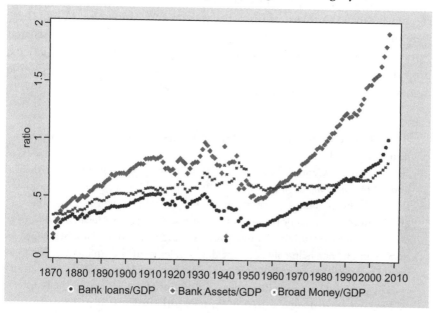

*Source*: Alan Taylor, 'The Great Leveraging', National Bureau of Economic Research, Working Paper no. 18290, issued in August 2012, revised in October 2012.

He refers to the century between 1870 and 1970 as the 'Age of money'. In this age,

---

[14] Daron Acemoglu and James A. Robinson, 'Economics versus Politics: Pitfalls of Policy Advice', *Journal of Economic Perspectives* 27, no.2 (2013): 173–92, doi: 10.1257/jep.27.2.173.

the ratio of loans to money was more or less stable. Loans to GDP hovered in a range around 0.4 to 0.5, with broad money to GDP sitting a little higher at an average of about 0.6 to 0.7. From the 1970s, the picture changed dramatically, and we entered what might be called the 'Age of Credit'. Although broad money relative to GDP remained almost flat at around 0.7 (rising a little only in the 2000s), the asset side of banks' balance sheets exploded. Loans to GDP doubled from 0.5 to 1.0 and assets to GDP tripled from about 0.7 to roughly 2.0.

What changed in the 1980s? Alan Taylor pointed to two possible factors: first, banks' risk tolerance changed over time as enterprises were rebuilt after the economic depression followed by the devastation of World War II and second, financial liberalization played its part. He did not examine these hypotheses rigorously since the thrust of his paper was on something else. While these were proximate reasons, the important underlying causes were, as discussed earlier in this section, the American policy choices to accept and grow deficits, drop the nominal anchor for money supply and to target interest rates while money supply expanded unhindered by any nominal anchor.

---

**Box 2.1  The British playbook for America's financialization – three hundred years later**

'The Origins of Central Banking' written in 1998 by Lawrence Broz for the journal *International Organisation* is a brilliant paper.[1] Every generation thinks that the problems it faces are unique and unprecedented challenges. Either they are not aware of economic history or they are short on memory (deaths come in the way!). But the truth is that most often issues repeat themselves. Studying history might not help solve present-day problems all the time but at least would reassure that no condition – no matter how unpleasant – stays forever.

The paper by Lawrence Broz traces the origins of the creation of the Bank of England and, along the way, it chronicles the balance of power tussles between the citizenry, the elites, the rent-seeking classes and workers. These have been playing out in our times, especially since the 1980s.

The monarchy committed to cede to the Parliament the power to provide it credit and to the newly created Bank of England with an express proviso in the charter that the government could not utilize a current loan if it had failed to honour its past obligations. That proved to be a crucial difference for Britain. That took away a big risk from providing war financing for the government. In turn, the government granted favours to the sub-groups that 'organised to support central banking'. One was the monopoly on bank note issuance (notes could be issued against the loans extended to the government) and the other was the special relationship with the state. For example, the government deposited its funds with them and the bank paid no interest on them.

The monopoly on notes issuance and the special relationship with the government meant that other banks used its notes as reserves. Thus, this special bank evolved to become a central bank. A rival bank – the Land Bank – was set up by others who were excluded from this arrangement. It failed and the promoters of the Bank of England ensured that its special privileges were protected and the bank received tax exemption too. In the first century of its existence, the bank's monetary policy discretion was circumscribed by a gold standard rule – it had pledged to redeem its notes in gold at a fixed price. So, excessive note issuance meant that its value dropped and the public could buy the notes with their gold and trade the notes for gold with the bank. Thus, the note–specie convertibility restrained inflation in the first century of the existence of the Bank of England. In that century, the general inflation rate in the country was statistically indistinguishable from zero.

However, in the initial years of the Napoleonic war, between 1797 and 1821, the government persuaded the bank to suspend gold standard, resulting in inflation and depreciation of the sterling. That brought tenant-farmers, manufacturers and industrial labour together since farmers earned higher prices for commodities but paid rents fixed in nominal terms. Prices of tradeable goods and wages rose as well. However, landowners wanted the gold standard restored. 'Government bondholders joined landlords in supporting the return to the gold standard.'

The return to the gold standard was a commitment by the government to ensure that the government would not resort to inflation tax and depreciate the currency too. That is why landowners who received rents from tenant-farmers fixed in nominal terms and government bondholders preferred it.

Came one data point – the Great Depression – and it was abandoned. It was reinstated partially after World War II in a modified form (the Bretton Woods fixed exchange rate system). However, that did not stop the working class from still being compensated well for the following reasons: social welfare net was comprehensively created and economic growth was a low-hanging fruit. There was plenty to go around, for all, for capital and for labour. It lasted two decades.

Once the Bretton Woods was abandoned on 15th August 1971 – again a war was the principal reason and worries over erosion of competitiveness to Germany and Japan was another – the inflation floodgates opened. It had multiple causal factors but excesses of labour unions and wage growth were important.

So, in the 1980s, the American government copied the playbook of the British monarchy in setting up the Bank of England. No, it did not set up the Federal Reserve only then. That was set up long ago. They made the same pact with the financial sector as Britain did with a group of creditors who set up the Bank of England. The parallels are uncanny and yet unsurprising. History revisits. Always.

The financial sector was arranged to finance the massive fiscal deficits of the Reagan government. America was in the final stage of its 'Cold War' with the Soviet Union. In return, finance was given concessions like the British government did. Restrictions on finance and barriers to interstate banking were removed; derivatives contracts were made legally enforceable, Glass-Steagall Act was dismantled by stealth, and so on. What was missing was the specie–note exchange to preserve its value.

Hence, inflation targeting in the 1980s – but with a lovely twist. The gold standard had served the capitalists well by protecting the real value of their rents. But its discipline too could rebound, as 'The Great Depression' proved. In the circumstances, inflation targeting appeared a brilliant winner.

Historical experiences should have made it amply clear that money supply was not the causal factor for inflation. The decade-long experience with quantitative easing is only the latest example. Only money supply created to finance fiscal expansion (war financing) was inflationary. Wages were the real driver of inflation. Charts of wage growth and inflation in the UK and in the USA provide powerful confirmation of the causal power of wages for inflation. That central banks, post-1980s, adopted inflation targeting after dumping money supply growth targeting, despite swearing by Milton Friedman, was an acknowledgement that inflation was caused not by monetary factors but by real factors. Hence, 'inflation targeting' in practice meant leashing wage growth.

At the same time, capitalists wanted no restraint on money and credit creation. Central banks obliged with no other target for money supply growth or credit growth. So, leverage-aided and induced asset price growth. Win-win!

The result? Working class contained and restrained; profit growth and wealth creation unrestrained and unconstrained! But, as recent events show, this may have been a Pyrrhic triumph.

What next? Now that we know that banks create money and not the central bank (courtesy of Bank of England), can we bring back the gold standard that would restrain money creation? But will it matter if banks are creating money? What is the point in restraining the central bank and not commercial banks? Further, neither the working class nor the capital class will want the discipline of the gold standard. The capital class is too spoilt and has travelled too far down the road of asset bubbles to walk back. There is risk of too much dislocation. The working class will be worse off. For them, the gold standard is a stiffer anti-labour policy straitjacket than inflation targeting. It reinforces the anti-inflation commitment of the central bank. That, in practical terms, is anti-wage growth. Only stricter.

So, what can central banks do to restore some balance between labour and capital, to address inequality and to avoid the destabilizing effects of leverage and asset price bubbles?

Higher inflation target of 4 per cent in the western world and 6 per cent for the developing world and a much higher capital adequacy ratio for banks. In the context of this book and its theme, we do not dwell upon the need for a higher inflation target in the western world. However, we make the case for higher capital ratio for banks in Chapter 6.

[1] Lawrence Broz, 'The Origins of Central Banking: Solutions to the Free-rider Problem', *International Organisation* 52, no. 2 (Spring 1998). Massachusetts Institute of Technology.

While bank assets and bank credit are important markers of financialization, there are other indicators too.

One such indicator is the trend in finance's share of corporate profits in the US.[15] Mathew Klein at *FT Alphaville* points out that after staying roughly the same size relative to the rest of the economy for nearly 40 years, profits in the financial sector shifted to a higher plane starting in the 1980s.[16] The share almost quadrupled in the early noughties before settling down around double the earlier share (Figure 2.6).

Interestingly, he went on to compare the US business productivity growth adjusted for utilization and changes in composition (or productivity due to just technological and managerial progress) and found systematically higher productivity growth when finance sector was smaller, and vice versa. In fact, in comparison to the period 1948–1974, productivity growth halved, and the share of financial sector in corporate profits doubled in the period 1975–2014.[17]

---

[15] Greta R. Krippner, 'Financialisation of the American Economy', *Socio-economic Review* 3 (May 2005): 173–208.

[16] Matthew C. Klein, 'Crush the Financial Sector, End the Great Stagnation', *FT Alphaville*, 16 February 2015, available at https://ftalphaville.ft.com/2015/02/16/2119138/crush-the-financial-sector-end-the-great-stagnation/ (accessed on 11 August 2017).

[17] We discuss the formal academic investigations by Cecchetti and Kharroubi that corroborate this in Section 2.4.

**Figure 2.6 The rising share of finance**

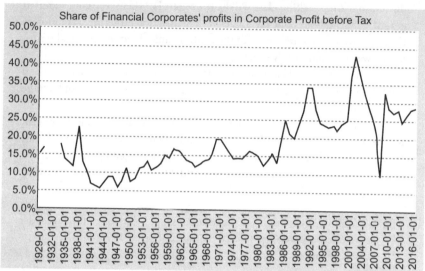

*Source*: US Bureau of Economic Analysis and FRED. Share of financial corporations' profits before tax derived from data on corporate profits before tax and non-financial corporations' profits before tax (without inventory valuation adjustment and corporate consumption adjustment). Figures for 1931–1933 are removed because of extreme swings in the data those three years. The numbers were 103 per cent, -52 per cent and 44 per cent, respectively, for those three years.

Gretta Krippner's work firmly establishes the empirical basis for financialization.[18] She begins her analysis with data on the employment, share of GDP and share of profits of the financial (Finance, Insurance and Real Estate) sector. She then considers the share of financial income in the overall profits of the non-financial sector. She accommodates potential objections such as the fact that a higher share of financial sources of income for non-financial businesses could simply be an artefact of offshoring of manufacturing. She looks at profits earned overseas and their breakdown into financial and non-financial components. Financialization of the US economy since the 1980s is evident and is established.

Table 2.1 provides a useful snapshot of the issues, the actors, the challenges that originated in the pre-financialization world, the responses to them and the institutional and income shifts that they caused in the post-financialization world.

---

[18] Greta R. Krippner, 'Financialisation of the American Economy', *Socio-Economic Review* 3 (May 2005): 173–208.

**Table 2.1  Summary of institutional account of financializaion**

| 1970s: Pro-financialization | | | 1980s to 2000s: Financialization | |
|---|---|---|---|---|
| *Precipitating factors: oil crisis, low-growth, high-inflation economy, global economic competition* | | | | |
| *Actors* | *Challenges* | *Reaction* | *Institutional* | *Income Shifts* |
| State | Stagflation and political pressure from corporate actors | Adopt deregulation policies | Neoliberal consensus: financialization of state. regulatory capture. dismantling of Class-Steagall regulations. | Favorable treatment of financial sectors income through regulation and bailouts. |
| Nonfinancial | Reacting national market limit, facing global competition | Demand economic deregulation. lower taxes, and a smaller state. | Rise of shareholder value conception of firm : focus on short-term financial goals rather than long-term capital investment. | Rise of finance CEOs. CEO pay tied to stock market performance. income transfer to finance sector and top management. |
| Financial | High inflation threatens bank profits from traditional banking activity; reaching local market limits. | Demand deregulation of interest rates. mergers, cross-state banking: function limits. | Developing unregulated financial instruments and cross-sector activity, and increased industry concentration; rise of gigantic bank holding companies; increased systemic risk tied to concentration and scale. | Overall increased sector income. unregulated fee-based business model: growth in bank profits and compensation for investment bankers. |

*(Contd.)*

| 1970s: Pro-financialization | | | 1980s to 2000s: Financialization | |
|---|---|---|---|---|

*Precipitating factors: oil crisis, low-growth, high-inflation economy, global economic competition*

| Actors | Challenges | Reaction | Institutional | Income Shifts |
|---|---|---|---|---|
| Consumers | High inflation, low growth undermines savings. | Demand deregulation of interest rates. | Easier consumer credit, rise of predatory lending, rise of investment mentality. | High interest rate on consumer debt, low interest on savings, banking fees. |
| Institutional Investors | High inflation, low growth undermines traditional investment strategy | Number and size of institutional investors increases. | Increased investment in speculative financial instruments, increased expectations for stable or high returns. | Inflates financial bubbles |
| Foreign Capital | Japan, later China and others, seek to invest capital surplus. | Investment in U.S. financial instruments increases. | | Finances federal deficits keeping interest rate low |
| Neoclassical Economists | Dominance of Keynesian policy model. | Legitimates neoliberal policy. Advocates self-regulating market, efficient markets hypothesis. agency theory. | | |

*Source*: Donald Tomaskovic-Devey and Ken-Hou Lin, 'Income Dynamics, Economic Rents, and the Financialisation of the U.S. Economy', *American Sociological Review* 76, no. 4 (2011): 538–559.

Along with the change in the monetary policy framework and the rise of bank assets, financial liberalization and the development of bond markets meant that both governments and companies could tap capital markets directly for their borrowing requirements. To grow the bond markets, capital had to be allowed to move across borders freely. That is where intellectuals stepped in. The free-market doctrine was extended to finance. Theory suggested that, under certain conditions, free markets should know better. Academics and ideologues concluded that markets knew best, regardless of circumstances. Propelled by a combination of conviction and convenience, they provided the intellectual and ideological cover for authorities to overlook the finer distinctions between the financial and the real economy. Competition rather than regulation might be a desirable state of affairs to achieve optimal economic outcomes in the real sector, they argued.

The financial sector is different, however. The wave of financial market deregulation that America launched in the 1980s and encouraged in the rest of the world (or, more precisely, thrust on) ignored the differences (see Box 2.2).

---

**Box 2.2 Why is finance different?**

There are three crucial distinctions between the marketplace for goods and non-financial services and markets for financial assets. The laws of demand and supply usually worked well for normal goods, as long as markets were reasonably competitive. All things being equal, lower prices led to higher demand and higher prices boosted production/supply. In financial markets, it worked the other way. Lower prices created panic and more supply followed. Higher prices boosted animal spirits and greed, resulting in higher risk-taking and demand went up for assets whose prices were rising.

When it comes to normal goods and services, human beings could be relatively more rational. Of course, it is a different matter with luxury goods and prestige goods. Further, consumer-marketing efforts are directed at making individuals make irrational purchase decisions. That is a different matter. But when it comes to financial assets, rational expectations fail miserably. Humans are motivated by greed and fear. Humans are possessive about assets. Further, financial assets are a store of wealth, desire for which is usually limitless. Therefore, emotions are central to the purchase and sale of financial goods. It is not so with respect to consumption goods and services. Thus, investor behaviour is pro-cyclical and that makes cyclicality and instability inherent features of finance.[1] Bubbles and busts follow.

The second distinction is with respect to contagion, correlation and connectedness. Contagion arises from information asymmetry that, when problems surface, can trigger perceptions of asset–liability mismatches, which in turn leads to, for example, bank runs. The financial engineering of the past two decades has dramatically increased the correlation of assets and interconnectedness among institutions. This has also expanded the 'dark corners' to cover large swathes of the financial market.

The third distinction is that competition between financial firms encourages risk-taking. For example, as banks compete for business, they charge lower interest rates in order to entice more borrowings. They also relax lending standards. In the process, the economy as a whole becomes more indebted. Debts make economies unstable and vulnerable to downturns. Further, debt makes economic downturns deeper and longer. Thus, competition between banks increases systemic risk. Seldom does competition between firms in other sectors increases systemic risk as competition in the financial sector does.

The sub-prime crisis stands out as the best illustration of the confluence of all the three. The alphabet soup of securitized mortgage loans dispersed risk anonymously far and wide across both instruments and institutions, leaving the entire financial system vulnerable to any trouble in the housing sector. Market participants, spooked by information asymmetry and misperceptions, responded with fire sales and credit squeezes which paralysed the entire financial sector. Liquidity problems led to decline in asset values, which triggered fire sales and solvency problems. A localized problem became global.

In the circumstances, a unique dynamic affects the financial market. Outside of finance, when a firm collapses, other firms usually benefit. The industry or the economy is not destabilized. In finance, when a financial institution collapses, panic can ensue. All the three factors come into play, reinforcing one another. Other sectors and firms in those sectors carry idiosyncratic risk that is diversifiable. In contrast, financial sector represents non-diversifiable economic risk making panic inevitable. Hence, unregulated financial markets were theoretically infeasible and practically unwise.

Academics ignored these crucial differences. They advocated financial market liberalization as they advocated the liberalization of markets for normal goods. They advocated free movement of capital across borders as they did for free movement of goods between countries. As capital markets became globally integrated, sovereign and corporate borrowers could tap into international savings. They forgot that, in crises, money ceases to be fungible. National origins of money begin to matter. That is why emerging economies encounter sudden rush of capital inflows and sudden stops as well. However, it is a different matter that developing country governments forget the fickleness of capital flows and go all out to court hot money once a crisis passes.

[1] Claudio Borio and William White have a very good discussion of the many aspects and dimensions of cyclicality in Finance. See Borio and White, 'Whither Monetary and Financial Stability? The Implications of Evolving Policy Regimes', Bank for International Settlements (BIS), Working Paper no. 147, February 2004.

## 2.4 Financialization and deregulation

Amplifying the effects of these trends was the wave of financial market deregulation that was initiated in the 1980s. Financial market deregulation was initially only a small part of the larger Reagan era deregulation movement, but soon came to dominate it.

The Gramm–Leach–Bliley Act, 1999 repealed the Glass–Steagall Act which prohibited commercial banks from offering investment banking and insurance-related services. The Commodity Futures Modernization Act, 2000 exempted derivatives from regulation. Both the regulators and regulated came to implicitly embrace a view of voluntary regulation by the financial industry.[19] Ken-Hou Lin and Donald Tomaskovic-Devey write, 'Although key shifts in the regulatory field that led to financialization happened in the early 1980s, the 1999 Financial Services Modernization Act increased concentration of the finance industry and the centrality of the largest financial institutions to the economy.'[20]

Only part of this deregulation was rolling back oversight. A major part involved financial engineering and the emergence of new forms of opaque and lightly regulated financial instruments. Derivative securities like CDS quickly came to occupy a significant chunk of the market and were very lightly

---

[19] Matthew Sherman, 'A Short History of Financial Deregulation in the US', CEPR, July 2009.
[20] Tomaskovic-Devey and Lin, 'Income Dynamics, Economic Rents, and the Financialisation of the U.S. Economy'.

regulated (see Box 2.3).[21] Securitization allowed loans to be sliced and diced, packaged and sold off, thereby triggering both moral hazard among banks (in their lending decision diligence) and creating completely opaque securities.

Rather unusually, the Federal Reserve had a big role to play in rolling back oversight and in deregulating different products and segments of financial market activity. This was largely due to the larger-than-life image that Greenspan, the chairman of the Federal Reserve from 1987 until 2006, enjoyed. His response to the American stock market crash of 1987 – flooding the economy with liquidity – won praise for it restored confidence in the market. It might have played some role in precipitating the Savings and Loan (S&L) crisis. But people ignored it.

His apparent successes gained salience. Again, after keeping interest rates low for too long until 1993, he raised them aggressively in 1994. That is said to have prevented the emergence of inflationary pressures and engineered a soft landing in the economy. Then, in the aftermath of the Asian crisis in 1997–98, he cut interest rates aggressively and that is said to have prevented the US economy from being affected by the recession. Strong growth in the United States and a strong US dollar in that period helped Asian economies recover in 1999. All these successes, attributed widely to his stewardship of American monetary policy and his acute understanding of trends in the economy, earned him the sobriquet 'maestro'. He had acquired a cult status.

In March 1999, he gave a speech[22] that proved, in hindsight, to be the pivotal movement in the deregulation of the derivative industry. That speech helped cement the case for self-regulation by banks of derivatives through their risk management models rather than through 'the traditional approach based on regulatory risk management schemes'. Interestingly, some of his cautionary notes and potential risks he identified only to dismiss them were to eventually prove prescient.

---

[21] The testimony by Brooksley Born, the then chairperson of Commodities Futures Trading Commission, concerning the 'over-the-counter' derivatives market before the US House of Representatives Committee on Banking and Financial Services on 24 July 1998 is an essential read for its clarity and prescience on the dangers of de-regulation of derivatives trading (available at http://www.cftc.gov/opa/speeches/opaborn-33.htm, accessed on 23 February 2018).

[22] 'Financial Derivatives', remarks by Chairman Alan Greenspan before the Futures Industry Association, Boca Raton, Florida, 19 March 1999, available at https://www.federalreserve.gov/boarddocs/speeches/1999/19990319.htm (accessed on 23 February 2018).

He noted that the possibility of increased systemic risk appeared to be an issue that required fuller understanding. He added that the resilience of the derivatives markets had not been tested by a significant downturn in the economy. He was right on both counts. Derivative markets were not only not resilient to the economic downturn but their brittleness also exacerbated it. Evidently, the Federal Reserve had failed to understand the extent of systemic risk that these products posed. Although he talked about stress testing of correlation assumptions and counterparty credit risks, they were to prove inadequate in anticipating and being prepared for the crisis of 2008 as neither he nor the Federal Reserve or market participants had any idea of the extent of overall risk that had been accumulated.

Since there was no central repository for over-the-counter derivatives and since they were not regulated, no one had any idea of the sizes of the leveraged derivative bets that had been built up by all participants. In the circumstances, only credit-rating agencies had some idea of the systemic risk exposures since market participants came to them shopping for better ratings for their securitized products. But they chose not to pay attention to the systemic risk that the rising volume of such products was posing. In the aftermath of the crisis of 2008, one area that required deregulation and the induction of fresh blood was the credit-rating industry. But, to date, that has not happened.

---

**Box 2.3 Deregulation and over-the-counter (OTC) derivatives**

Prior to 2000, derivatives traded outside regulated exchanges suffered from legal infirmities that made them difficult to enforce because they ran the risk of being treated as gambling contracts. In the US, restrictions on OTC derivatives were removed by the Commodity Futures Modernisation Act of 2000 leaving them completely unregulated. The Glass–Steagall Act (Banking Act 1933) of the US was gradually relaxed and finally repealed in 1999 and this made it possible for investment banking to be combined with commercial banking. These changes facilitated the growth of the CDS industry whereby banks and financial institutions offered credit insurance, albeit named credit default 'swap'. Unlike a true swap, a CDS does not involve the swapping of streams of cash flows. It is nothing but an insurance contract—an agreement to pay a sum in the event of a particular uncertain event occurring in return for a fixed premium paid in advance. However, a key difference is that normal insurance contracts require an insurable interest, that is, the person taking out the insurance must have an interest in the preservation of the asset. For instance, a person cannot take out insurance on an asset owned by a stranger or on a stranger's life. The use of the term credit default swap instead of credit default insurance was to avoid the industry being regulated by insurance regulators. CDSs were not traded in recognised exchanges where the exchange becomes the 'buyer to every seller' and the 'seller to every buyer'. They were traded bilaterally between counterparties. Therefore, they were subject only to the regulations of the International Swaps and Derivatives Association (ISDA) and this is an industry body. It is not a regulator.

The severe weaknesses of self-regulation in this area were illustrated in 2012 by the debt restructuring that Greece announced, which was tantamount to a sovereign default. The ISDA initially ruled that they would not treat this as a default event and Credit Default Swaps would not be paid (on the grounds that the original proposal supposedly only invoked voluntary participation on the part of debt-holders) nullifying the very purpose of buying credit default protection. Subsequently, when the Hellenic Republic invoked collective action clauses to force all debt-holders to participate in the debt restricting, ISDA ruled that a credit event had occurred triggering payments under the Credit Default Swaps that had been bought (either by bond holders to protect from losses or by speculators to profit from a Greek default or debt restructuring). The episode illustrated that credit default swaps carried an element of 'discretion' to be exercised by the self-regulatory body, possibly in its own interest, and could not necessarily be relied upon when they were most needed.

*Source*: V. Anantha Nageswaran and T. V. Somanathan, *The Economics of Derivatives* (New Delhi: Cambridge University Press, 2015).

In 2008, after the collapse of Lehman Brothers, Greenspan testified to the Congress (the House Committee on Oversight and Government Reform) on the crisis. He admitted that he had put too much faith in the self-correcting power of free markets. Yet, towards the end of his testimony, he said, in contrast to his prescience in 1999, 'whatever regulatory changes are made, they will pale in comparison to the change already evident in today's markets. Those markets for an indefinite future will be far more restrained than would any currently contemplated new regulatory regime'.[23]

As we survey stock markets around the world, the real estate market in several countries including in the United States, the high-yield bond market and the market for exotic products such as short volatility, what we see is pervasive irrational exuberance and not rational restraint. Greenspan has been wrong

---

[23] 'Greenspan Concedes Error on Regulation', *New York Times*, 24 October 2008, available at http://www.nytimes.com/2008/10/24/business/economy/24panel.html (accessed on 23 February 2018).

again. The principal reason (if not the only reason) for this state of affairs is the monetary policy framework of the United States before and after the crisis of 2008. Lest we forget, the policy framework is itself a consequence of its capture – intellectually or otherwise – by financial interests. The consequences of financialization are the subject matter of Chapters 3 and 4.

Greenspan completed his reversion to 'form' in 2011 in a sense when he wrote in *Financial Times* that regulatory reforms could lead to excess buffers at the expense of the nation's standard of living.[24] Put differently, curbing finance would lead to lower economic growth and lower standard of living. An International Monetary Fund working paper,[25] widely cited for its seminal conclusions, proved that it was false. It stated rather simply and bluntly that one can always have too much finance. No ifs and buts. It does not matter whether the country enjoys macroeconomic stability or has a volatile economy and whether the country experiences banking crises or not. Only the thresholds at which finance starts to hurt economic growth vary in different circumstances. But it does hurt and always. The inverted U-shaped relationship between finance and economic growth survived different specifications, estimators and data. At some point, the effect of finance on growth vanishes. It happens for all countries. Therefore, they concluded that higher capital requirements that international regulators were prescribing for banks might actually be what the doctor ordered for the global economy and for individual countries. Several countries would be better off with smaller financial sectors.

Cecchetti and Kharroubi of the Bank for International Settlements (BIS) did a series of investigations too.[26] They found that the relationship of several finance-related variables to the real economy has an inverted U-shape. In this, they corroborate the work by IMF researchers. Whether it is total credit, bank credit or employment in the financial services sector, all were positively correlated to GDP per capita and then the correlation reaches a peak before the relationship turns negative. They tested the correlations using econometric techniques and they controlled for other factors. Their findings remained

---

[24] Cited by Jean-Louis Arcand, Enrico Berkes and Ugo Panizza, 'Too Much Finance?', IMF Working Paper no. WP/12/161, June 2012, available at https://www.imf.org/ external/ pubs/ft/wp/2012/wp12161.pdf (accessed on 9 January 2018). See Klein, 'Crush the Financial Sector, End the Great Stagnation'.

[25] Arcand, Berkes and Panizza, 'Too Much Finance?'

[26] S. Cecchetti and E. Kharroubi, 'Reassessing the Impact of Finance on Growth', BIS Working Paper no. 381, Monetary and Economics Department, Bank for International Settlements, July 2012.

robust. They also noticed that there was a clear inverse relationship between employment in financial intermediation and economy-wide productivity growth. They set out to investigate this inverse relationship in a second paper.[27]

They concluded that as the financial sector attracts skilled workers with higher pay, it affects the ability of other businesses, particularly new enterprises to attract talent, adversely.

Thus, with enterprises lacking skilled workers, their ability and willingness to take risks and innovate diminishes. After all, more than the collateral, the intellectual property (IP) embedded in their skilled workers is crucial for the survival and growth of new businesses. As they lose this important factor crucial for their success, financing too becomes more difficult to obtain. That also means that industries that can more easily post collateral are the ones that obtain funding. That is why credit booms usually coincide with construction booms. The property and real estate sector, with its tangible assets, is able to post collateral more easily.[28]

The paper's conclusions are rather unambiguous:

> The growth of a country's financial system is a drag on productivity growth. That is, higher growth in the financial sector reduces real growth. In other words, financial booms are not, in general, growth-enhancing, probably because the financial sector competes with the rest of the economy for resources. Second, using sectoral data, we examine the distributional nature of this effect and find that credit booms harm what we normally think of as the engines for growth: those that are more R&D-intensive. This evidence, together with recent experience during the financial crisis, leads us to conclude that there is a pressing need to reassess the relationship of finance and real growth in modern economic systems.

---

[27] S. Cecchetti and E. Kharroubi, 'Why Does Financial Sector Growth Crowd Out Real Economic Growth?' Paper presented at the Institute for New Economic Thinking-Federal Reserve Bank of San Francisco conference 'Finance and the Welfare of Nations', September 2013.

[28] Alan Taylor and his co-authors point to BIS capital adequacy requirement changes as one of the contributory factors to the boom in real estate lending. Since such lending is collateralized, it attracted lower risk weights than uncollateralized lending to businesses. See Òscar Jordá, Moritz Schularick and Alan M. Taylor, 'The Great Mortgaging: Housing Finance, Crises, and Business Cycles', Working Paper no. 2014–23, September 2014, available at http://www.frbsf.org/economic-research/publications/working-papers/wp2014-23.pdf (accessed on 23 February 2018).

Thomas Philippon and Ariell Reshef found that[29] 'most of the rise in living standards after 1870 was obtained with less income spent on finance and less financial output than what is observed after 1980; and the relationship between financial output and income has changed after 1980'. Similar to Cecchetti and Kharroubi, they concluded that it was difficult to make a clear-cut case that, at the margin reached in high-income economies, further expansion of the financial sector increases the rate of economic growth. These authors concede that, until countries reach the maximum point on a curve, finance does provide a positive impetus to growth. In countries whose per capita incomes are below that level, the traditional position is likely to be still valid. However, regulators in those countries have to learn from the experience of the developed countries that finance is not always benign. They should let the financial sector expand but not allow it to reach destabilizing levels.

This has huge implications for developing economies starting from a small size of the financial sector and wanting to expand it to benefit economic growth. It is the correct thing to do but up to a point and with a gradually rising level of checks and balances on the sector as it expands. At some point, the growth of the financial sector has to stop. It does not matter how sophisticated the regulatory regime or how evolved the institutional strength in the country is. But that is easier said than done.

In a recent IMF working paper, Jihad Dagher explored the political economy of financial policy in 10 of the most infamous financial crises since the eighteenth century and found 'consistent evidence of pro-cyclical regulatory policies by governments'.[30] He writes:

> Financial booms, and risk-taking during these episodes, were often amplified by political regulatory stimuli, credit subsidies, and an increasing light-touch approach to financial supervision ... post-crisis regulations do not always survive the following boom ... in most cases regulation has been pro-cyclical, effectively weakening during the boom and strengthening during the bust. Regulators do not operate in a vacuum, and ... in most cases, political interventions have helped fuel the boom in similar ways across time and countries.

---

[29] T. Philippon and Ariell Reshef, 'An International Look at the Growth of Modern Finance', *Journal of Economic Perspectives* 27, no. 2, (Spring 2013): 73–96.

[30] Jihad Dagher, 'Regulatory Cycles – Revisiting the Political Economy of Financial Crises', IMF Working Paper no. 18/8, 15 January 2018, available at http://www.imf.org/en/Publications/WP/Issues/2018/01/15/Regulatory-Cycles-Revisiting-the-Political-Economy-of-Financial-Crises-45562 (accessed on 11 March 2018).

Unsurprisingly, deregulation had a prominent role in the crisis of 2008 too. Atif Mian and Amir Sufi too have shown that regulatory standards in the mortgage markets were lowered consistently since the 1990s.[31] The affordable housing mandate given to federal mortgage re-financiers Fannie Mae and Freddie Mac in 1992 encouraged them to dilute quality standards in an attempt to drive down borrowing costs. This was complemented by a slew of measures that deregulated both instruments and institutions in the name of expanding access to housing credit.

America did not just stop with embracing financial deregulation with enthusiasm. It evangelized it around the world. The role of the US dollar as the global monetary standard played no small part in those persuasion efforts.

## 2.5    How financialization went global

Banks are nothing if not manufacturers of debt (leverage). Therefore, it is unsurprising that the rise in debt levels in the global economy has gone hand in hand with the rise of the importance of finance for economic activity. The financial sector and its participants prospered as finance, financial markets and asset prices drove economic growth rather than reflecting economic growth. The crisis of 2008 was a reminder that this process has run its course and it was time to go back to the basics of promoting economic growth through savings, investment, employment and consumption. In the debt-driven growth model, consumption, instead of being a consequence of economic growth, became its cause.

Nowhere is this more starkly evident than in the case of the United States whose consumption proclivity, while supporting economic activity around the world, has also made the global economy unbalanced and unipolar. This was the case before 2008 and it is repeating itself in the current cycle too. American personal savings rate has declined again to very low levels. It was 2.4 per cent in December 2017, having reached a peak of 11.0 per cent exactly five years earlier. The previous (historical) low was 1.9 per cent in July 2005.

The emergence of the American consumer as the buyer of first and last resort has helped to cement the role of the US dollar as the global transaction and reserve currency. Despite abandoning Bretton Woods and the fixed rate US dollar standard, America was able to ensure that the orbit of money around

---

[31] Atif Mian and Amir Sufi, *House of Debt* (Chicago: The University of Chicago Press, 2014), available at http://press.uchicago.edu/ucp/books/book/chicago/H/bo20832545.html (accessed on 27 March 2018).

the world was centred on the US dollar. It involved some deft diplomacy and geopolitical bargaining with other countries, particularly oil-producing nations. Besides crude oil, the US ensured that international trading of other commodities too was settled in US dollars. Delving into details of how the US ensured such a supreme stature for the US dollar is beyond the scope of this book. That other economic powers were not only a fraction of the size of the US economy but also beholden to it for their rise from the ashes of World War II helped.

However, the rest of the world's dependence on her consumption habits has resulted in a de facto world of fixed exchange rates and synchronized monetary policies around the world. Thus, the global economic cycle and the global policy cycle are but extensions of the American economic cycle and policy cycle.

Integration of economic and policy cycles is reflected in the integration of financial market cycles. Global stock and bond markets provide investors with very few, if any, avenues for diversification when they need it the most – during market downturns. When America is healthy, other economies and markets may still be unhealthy for domestic reasons but when the US is not, other economies and markets have no choice. They are infected.

The pre-eminent position of the dollar as an internationally accepted medium of exchange and store of value helped lower the borrowing cost for a country that, otherwise, would have paid more to borrow, considering the perpetual deficits that it had signed up to in pursuit of economic growth sans competitiveness. Hence, the US enjoyed the advantages of having the world's anchor currency without the concomitant responsibilities. From that day onwards, spillover effects were unavoidable for the rest of the world.

It is important to remember that the country's decision to run trade deficits would not have amounted to much had global capital markets remained segmented. How could the US finance trade deficits without making it possible for capital to flow across borders and reach its shores? Hence, the US had to be willing to let non-residents buy American assets and they, in turn, must allow American financial institutions intermediate these flows. Financial liberalization went global. Other countries were leaned on to allow capital to flow out of their countries so that they could finance American deficits.

Unimpeded, unrestricted and open capital flows are one leg of what Dani Rodrik calls 'hyperglobalization':

The transition to hyper-globalization is associated with two events in particular: the Organization for Economic Cooperation and Development's decision in 1989 to remove all restrictions on cross-border financial flows, and the establishment in 1995, after almost a decade of negotiations, of the World Trade Organization, with wide-ranging implications for domestic health and safety rules, subsidies and industrial policies.[32]

Further, these countries had to allow Wall Street firms – banks and insurance and asset management companies – to operate in their countries so that the process of facilitation of capital outflows to America was made easier. America imported goods and exported services, especially financial services. It enjoys a big trade surplus in services except that it is dwarfed by an even bigger deficit in merchandise trade (Figure 2.7).

**Figure 2.7 America's surplus in services**

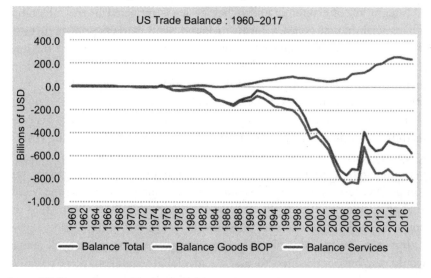

*Source*: US Census Bureau, Economic Indicator Division.

Once America became the destination for world exports, it was a short step to making the world dependent on American economic cycle and, by extension, American monetary policy. If a country found itself relying on exports to the United States for its economic growth, it was logical that its economic cycle and policy cycles were aligned with America's. In other words, America

---

[32] See 'Put Globalization to Work for Democracies', *New York Times*, 17 September 2016, available at https://www.nytimes.com/2016/09/18/opinion/sunday/put-globalization-to-work-for-democracies.html (accessed on 18 March 2017).

not only exported financial services but also the intellectual framework that was shaping regulatory policies governing the financial sector. First, major economies fell in line. Then, smaller economies that were part of the supply chain had no choice.

Referring to the Mundell–Fleming lecture made by Hélène Rey of the London School of Economics last year, Martin Sandbu of *Financial Times* wrote:[33]

> The transmission of financial fluctuations through the world economy goes a long way to destroying the supposed monetary independence that can be retained by keeping one's own currency and letting it float.
>
> The traditional view in international economics was one of a 'trilemma': you must choose two out of three among international capital flows, fixed exchange rates and independent monetary policy.
>
> Rey's work shows that it is really a dilemma, not a trilemma: you can have either internationally mobile capital or independent monetary policy – a floating exchange rate does not rescue your monetary freedom as much as the conventional wisdom has it.

What Hélène Rey says is that the exchange rate regime – fixed or floating – that countries have adopted does not matter. That falls out of the equation. Regardless of the exchange rate regime, countries can enjoy independent monetary policy only if they are prepared to restrict capital flows – in and out. Exchange rate regime choice could have been available to countries had they not made their economic growth hostage to consumer spending in the US. For better or worse, the US had become the market of first and last resort for the rest of the world.

The reduction of the policy trilemma into a policy dilemma has two interconnected reasons. First, countries operate as though they are in a de facto fixed exchange rate with the US dollar. Second, the rest of the world is still dependent on the US economy as the ultimate source of demand. Hence, the tendency to curb exchange rate fluctuations vs. US dollar, making the world economy more synchronous than it needs to be. The period between 2002 and 2007 provides overwhelming evidence on the pernicious effects of this unofficial global fixed exchange rate regime.

When the US dollar strengthens due to restrictive monetary policies in the US, other countries tighten policies to avoid excessive currency weakness.

---

[33] Martin Sandbu, 'Lessons Learnt from the Crisis', *Financial Times*, 5 June 2015, available at http://www.ft.com/intl/cms/s/3/d84b1792-0aaa-11e5-a8e8-00144feabdc0.html (accessed on 18 March 2017).

This accentuates the global effect of US tightening. When the US has a loose monetary policy, the US dollar weakens and other currencies appreciate. Other countries respond by following loose policies of their own. Thus, they magnify the impact of US easing. This is what happened between 2002 and 2007. As the US adopted looser policies in this period, most countries followed suit. Therefore, what happened was that the US housing bubble became a global housing bubble. When that bubble burst, it created a global crisis.

As discussed earlier, the costs of excessive growth of the financial sector and the costs of financialization of the economy would have remained confined to the American economy and few others but for the global role of the US dollar. That afforded the US the opportunity to shape the policies of countries around the world intellectually. Figure 2.8 captures this dynamic.

**Figure 2.8  Changing face of US monetary policy and rise of finance**

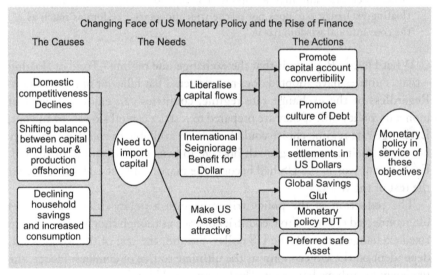

A disturbing feature of financialization is that it not only perpetuates the problem of 'too much finance' but also gives rise to too many undesirable consequences, both in the financial markets (asset price bubbles) and in the real economy, such as low productivity, falling economic growth and accumulation of debt. In other words, the medium-term-to-long-term costs of such a policy exceed short-term benefits.

This concludes this chapter and the section on the causes of financialization and its global reach. We now turn to its consequences.

# Part B | The Consequences

# 3 | Wages, Compensation and Inequality

We examine the consequences of financialization across various dimensions. One is the impact on wages and compensation in America and in the non-financial economy. Second is the human resource misallocation due to financialization. Third is the impact on broader inequality. This chapter analyses these three impacts or consequences and examines the evidence.

Fourth, and perhaps the most important, consequence of financialization is its impact on monetary policy or the capture of monetary policy by finance. In turn, it has global ramifications. Therefore, we dedicate Chapters 4 and 5 to an analysis of the monetary policy framework and monetary policy actions in America and their global consequences. Chapter 4 examines the monetary policy framework that America has adopted. Chapter 5 is an examination of the consequences of UMPs deployed in the wake of the crisis of 2008.

In recent years, attention has turned to the role of finance in the creation and perpetuation of social and class divisions. Inequality is the paramount economic challenge of the twenty-first century. There is increasing realization that financialization has a lot to do with it. That is what we turn to next.

## 3.1 Wages and compensation trends in Finance

Large increases in wages and compensation at the executive levels and widening differential with the remaining employees while not unique to financial markets is most pronounced there. Since the 1990s executive compensation has ballooned (Figure 3.1).

The work of Harvard Law School professor Lucian Bebchuk, an authority on executive compensation trends, has shown how it has distorted incentives all round. His book with Jesse Fried, *Pay without Performance*, is a devastating indictment of modern managerial capitalism.[1] They document that from 1993

---

[1] Lucian Bebchuk and Jesse Fried, *Pay Without Performance* (Cambridge, MA: Harvard University Press, 2006).

to 2002, the aggregate compensation of the top five executives in all US public companies amounted to 7.5 per cent of all corporate earnings!

**Figure 3.1 Executive compensation ratio**

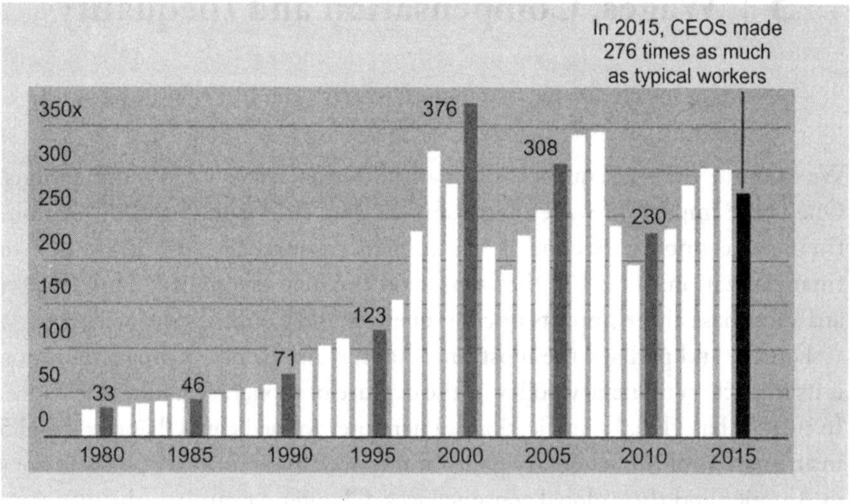

*Source:* Roger Lowenstein, 'CEO Pay Is Out of Control. Here's How to Rein It In', 19 April 2017, available at http://fortune.com/2017/04/19/executive-compensation-ceo-pay/ (accessed on 31 May 2017).

In another work, they attribute the incentive distortionary executive compensation practices to the triumph of managerial power over those of diffuse shareholders and conflicted boards, and the resultant separation of ownership and control.[2] Describing such excessive compensation as a rent extraction arising from failure of corporate governance, they point in particular to two features – compensation that rewards executives even for short-term and reversible results which led to accumulation of latent risks, and its linkage only to returns to equity which resulted in highly leveraged bets.

In a latter work with others, Bebchuk investigated the relationship between the fraction of aggregate compensation of the top five executives accruing to the

---

[2] Lucian Bebchuk and Jesse Fried, 'Executive Compensation as an Agency Problem,' *Journal of Economic Perspectives* 17, no. 3 (2003): 71–92, available at http://www. law.harvard.edu/programs/corp_gov/papers/2003.Bebchuk-Fried.Executive. Compensation.pdf.

chief executive officer (CEO), or CEO pay slice (CPS), and firm performance.[3] They find that the fraction is 'negatively associated with firm value as measured by industry-adjusted Tobin's Q'. They also find that

> in particular, cross-sectional differences in CPS are associated with lower Tobin's Q, lower accounting profitability, less favourable market reaction to acquisition announcements made by the firm, more opportunistic timing of CEO option grants, more luck-based CEO pay, less CEO turnover controlling for performance and tenure, and lower stock market returns accompanying the filing of proxy statements for periods with increases in CPS.

Nowhere have these trends been more pronounced and more corrosive than in finance. To begin with, deregulation in finance drove wages and compensation higher in the financial services industry, well above industry benchmarks. It is possible that financial deregulation and rising compensation were mutually reinforcing tendencies. A deregulated industry is in a position to develop and market complex financial products that are profitable for the originator. That requires talent and skills and both need to be compensated and incentivized with profits to continue developing such products. Conversely, traders and executives, earning high incomes, having to justify their compensation, constantly push for deregulating the regulated parts of the industry such that newer and newer financial products could be developed. Indeed, deregulation helped divert talent from other parts of the economy towards finance. Geologists, physicists and mathematicians, lured by high compensation levels, ended up developing algorithms and financial products embedding complex formula which very few could understand and even fewer knew their sensitivity to and consequences for financial markets.

Thomas Philippon and Ariell Reshef have done extensive research to construct wage trends in the US financial sector on the 1909–2006 period.[4] They show the strong correlation between financial market wages and deregulation, and highlight the steep climb in wages accompanied by deregulation since the 1980s (Figure 3.2).

---

[3] Lucian Bebchuk, Martijn Cremers and Urs Peyer, 'The CEO Pay Slice', *Journal of Financial Economics* 102, no. 1 (2011): 199–221, available at https://www.sciencedirect.com/science/article/pii/S0304405X11001188 (accessed on 9 January 2018).

[4] Thomas Philippon and Ariell Reshef, 'Wages and Human Capital in the US Financial Industry 1909–2006', NBER Working Paper no. 14644, January 2009, available at http://www.nber.org/papers/w14644.pdf (accessed on 9 January 2018).

**Figure 3.2  Deregulation and accelerating wages in finance**

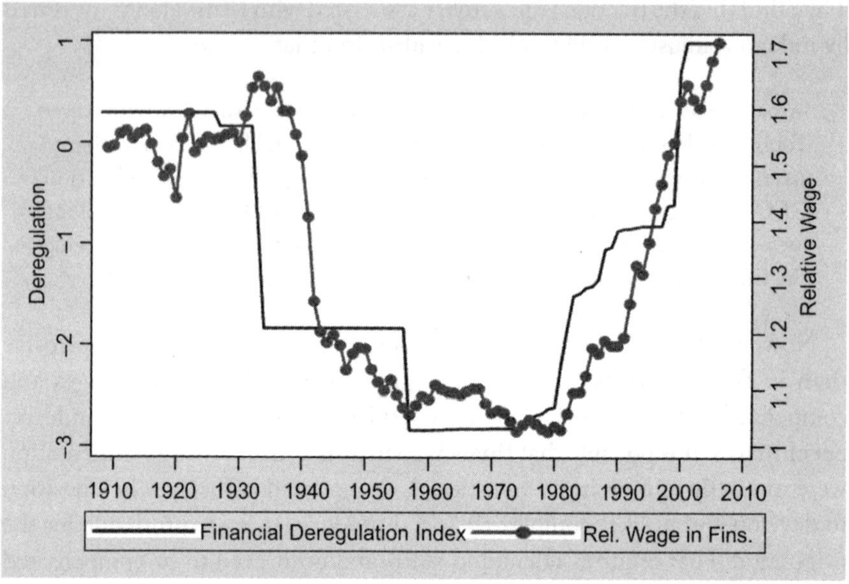

*Source*: Thomas Philippon and Ariell Reshef, 'Wages and Human Capital in the US Financial Industry 1909–2006', NBER Working Paper no. 14644, January 2009, available at http://www.nber.org/papers/w14644.pdf (accessed on 9 January 2018).

Mirroring this, finance's share of total value added and total compensation of financial sector intermediaries as a share of GDP which had been rising slowly since the forties rose vertiginously since 1980.[5] In fact, this was also associated with a similar steep rise in income share of the top 1 per cent, a theme we explore in greater detail later.

Again, the work of Thomas Philippon and Ariell Reshef assumes relevance. They compare a benchmark series for the relative wage in finance, controlling for education and employment risk as well as time-varying returns to education. While the benchmark and actual wages in financial sector have more or less tracked each other, they began to diverge since the 1980s and the financial sector wages have since continued to move upwards (Figure 3.3).

---

[5] Benjamin Landy, 'Graph: How the Financial Sector Consumed America's Economic Growth', The Century Foundation, 25 February 2013, available at https://tcf.org/content/commentary/graph-how-the-financial-sector-consumed-americas-economic-growth/ (accessed on 9 January 2018).

**Figure 3.3 The inflection point for wages in finance in America**

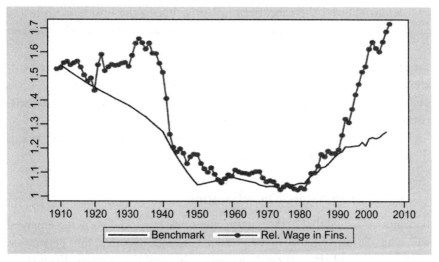

*Source*: Philippon and Reshef, 'Wages and Human Capital in the US Financial Industry 1909–2006'.

These trends have also had the effect of contributing to human resource misallocation between finance and other sectors. Hamid Boustanifar, Everett Grant and Ariell Reshef studied the allocation and compensation of human capital in finance in developed countries in 1970–2005 and found that finance wages explain a large share of the increase in overall skill premium.[6] They found that 'skilled wages in finance account for 36% of increases in overall skill premia, although finance only accounts for 5.4% of skilled private sector employment, on average'. They also find that 'financial deregulation, financial globalization, and bank concentration' drive wages in finance and these wage premia 'attract skilled international immigration to finance'.

Again, Bebchuk and others have shown how these trends and, in particular, the design of pay arrangements in financial firms contributed to excessive risk-taking that imperilled not only their own institutions but also brought

---

[6] Hamid Boustanifar, Everett Grant and Ariell Reshef, 'Wages and Human Capital in Finance: International Evidence 1970–2005', Federal Reserve Bank of Dallas Working Paper no. 266, February 2016, available at https://www.dallasfed.org/~/media/documents/institute/wpapers/2016/0266.pdf (accessed on 9 January 2018).

the entire system to the brink during the GFC of 2008.[7] The standard pay design allowed the executives full exposure to the upside of risks and insulation from the downside, a recipe for excessive risk-taking. The focus on short-term results and returns to equity, as mentioned above, only amplified the problems. Compounding the problems, the compensation arrangements allowed executives to cash out as they liked, with the result that the pre-crisis cashing out of large amounts of CEO compensation by the large financial firms exceeded their losses during the GFC.[8]

The inevitable result of this trend was human resource misallocation towards finance, the subject of Section 3.2.

## 3.2 Human resource misallocation

It cannot be denied that in the past quarter century, a social norm has emerged which has elevated finance as the preferred aspirational career for a generation of youth over and above those like engineering and the sciences. Even those with basic degrees in the latter have preferred the attractions of the former.

Why did finance attract so much talent? A corollary question that poses itself is: why was finance able to pay so much that talent flowed to it? Well, finance made so much of profits that it was able to pay. Actually, the attraction of talent, high wages and profits became mutually reinforcing trends later. But what was the source of profits?

Finance, in modern times (post-1980s because that is when financial liberalization, deregulation and liberalization of capital flows started in right earnest), has not been doing anything unique in comparison to the past. It facilitated much secondary trading of financial securities. But the compensation for it has come down considerably and the fees for active asset management have, for the most part, proven to be wasted and wasteful compensation.

So, what was its source? Andrew Haldane, in his contribution to the volume *The Future of Finance* published by the London School of Economics in 2010 ('Contribution of the Financial Sector: Miracle or Mirage?'), has pointed out that finance generated extraordinary profits because it wrote deep out of the

---

[7] Lucian Bebchuk, 'Executive Pay and the Financial Crisis', World Bank Blogs – All about Finance, 31 January 2012, available at http://blogs.worldbank.org/allaboutfinance/ executive-pay-and-the-financial-crisis (accessed on 9 January 2018).

[8] Sanjai Bhagat and Brian J. Bolton, 'Bank Executive Compensation and Capital Requirements Reform', 9 March 2011, available at https://papers.ssrn.com/sol3/papers. cfm?abstract_id=1781318 (accessed on 9 January 2018).

money options (think CDSs and sub-prime securitization).[9] Deep out of the money options earn premium for the writer but once in a while these options get in the money and the writer has to pay up to the options owner. That is what happened in 2008.

The second source of profits was that much of the profits were risk-unadjusted. One source of risk is that many assets were valued as per models and hence shown at fair value. The second source of risk is high leverage ratios in investment banks' balance sheets. The third arose out of creating products that, willy-nilly, drew the buyers into the web of financial leverage. In fact, that is where the engineering talent was needed.

High profits were required to maintain stock valuation in deference to the pressures exerted by institutional investors. Second, compensation of higher executives was linked to stock price performance. Hence, showing consistently rising profits was an obligation. That required generation of complex financial products which, though based on complex mathematics, were essentially built on unsuspecting clients assuming financial leverage. Developing these products required engineering talent.

Now, the question for policymakers is whether any of this is welfare enhancing. Evidently, they are not. Their welfare-destruction was evident in the crisis of 2008.

Have the policy responses changed the demand for engineering talent and the attraction of finance to such talent? Not much, if at all. That is evident in the continued attractiveness of the sector to students and the high bonuses that continue to be paid in the sector. In March 2018, it was reported that average bonuses on Wall Street had climbed to their highest level since 2006.[10]

So, this is a socially negative phenomenon even though it is positive at the personal level, somewhat like the paradox of thrift that Keynes had discussed, in a different context.

At a very basic level, financial markets compete for not just physical capital but also scarce high-quality human capital by offering exorbitant wages which

---

[9] Andrew Haldane, Simon Brennan and Vasileios Madouros, 'What Is the Contribution of the Financial Sector: Miracle or Mirage?' *Future of Finance: LSE Report* (2010), available at https://harr123et.files.wordpress.com/2010/07/futureoffinance5.pdf (accessed on 1 April 2018).

[10] Jennifer Surane, 'Wall Street Bankers' Average Bonus Jumps to Highest since 2006', *Bloomberg*, 26 March 2018, available at https://www.bloomberg.com/news/articles/2018-03-26/wall-street-bankers-average-bonus-jumps-to-highest-since-2006 (accessed on 1 April 2018).

other industries cannot match. As Cecchetti and Kharroubi brilliantly describe, 'finance literally bids rocket scientists away from the satellite industry'.[11]

In fact, Nandini Gupta and Isaac Hacamo find evidence of precisely this trend:[12]

> We compare U.S. engineering graduates from 12 top schools in the same graduating class and major, and show that engineers from higher ranked schools, and those with graduation honours, are more likely to switch from other sectors to finance. We find that financial sector growth attracts highly talented engineers into financial sector occupations that do not fully use their skills, which leads these engineers to engage in less innovative entrepreneurship in the long-run, compared to their classmates who remain in engineering.

As they suggest, this is a compelling explanation for the wage premium for skilled finance workers and points to the role of Wall Street in driving the competition for talent with Main Street.

As profit and its pursuit bid up wages in finance more than anywhere else, it gave rise to a much bigger problem – economic and social inequality. It is no coincidence that the rise of inequality has accompanied the rise of finance.

### 3.3 Financialization and inequality

Inequality has become a burning topic in several developed nations. There are two main channels of financialization leading to greater inequality. One is the wage channel where, as discussed in Section 3.1, higher and increasing wages in finance widen income disparities. Jon Bakija, Adam Cole and Bradley T. Heim found that in the US between 1979 and 2005 finance professionals were responsible for nearly a fourth of the increase in the share of national income going to the top 1 per cent of the income distribution.[13]

---

[11] Stephen G. Cecchetti and Enisse Kharroubi, 'Reassessing the Impact of Finance on Growth', BIS Working Paper no. 381, July 2012, available at https://www.bis.org/publ/work381.pdf (accessed on 1 April 2018).

[12] Nandini Gupta and Isaac Hacamo, 'Superstar (and Entrepreneurial) Engineers in Finance Jobs', Kellogg School of Business Research Working Paper no. 18-18, 13 March 2018, available at https://papers.ssrn.com/sol3/papers.cfm?abstract_id=3136751 (accessed on 1 April 2018).

[13] Jon Bakija, Adam Cole and Bradley T. Heim, 'Jobs and Income Growth of Top Earners and the Causes of Changing Income Inequality': Evidence from US Tax Return Data (April 2012), available at https://web.williams.edu/Economics/wp/BakijaColeHeimJobsIncomeGrowthTopEarners.pdf (accessed on 1 April 2018).

The other is the wealth channel, famously captured by Thomas Piketty in the famous $r > g$ inequality. This means that the rate of return of capital is generally higher than the rate of economic growth, the proxy for average income growth. In particular, those financial products which offer higher returns are also those which are likely accessible to the wealthier households.[14]

Globalization too has played its part. It has left many relatively under-educated blue-collar workers worse off compared to their parents and grandparents and compared to their peers. Their mental and physical health have suffered consequently and life expectancy has declined. An article in the *Wall Street Journal*[15] has cited from the recent update made by Professors Angus Deaton and Anne Case to their paper first published in 2015:

> Mortality has been rising since the turn of this century for an even broader swath of white adults, starting at age 25, the researchers found, driven by troubles in a hard-hit working class. Death rates for white non-Hispanics with a high-school education or less now exceed those of blacks overall, the pair said—and they're 30% higher for whites age 50 to 54 than for blacks overall of that age…. The analysis paints a portrait of a gradual 'collapse of the white, high-school-educated working class after its heyday in the early 1970s', whose health, mental well-being, and attachment to the labour force have become successively worse for people born after 1945, they said.

Ken-Hou Lin and Donald Tomaskovic-Devey examined[16] the contribution of financialization to income inequality by focusing on the financialization of non-finance industries. The three dimensions of inequality that they examined were reduction of labour share of income, increase in top executives' share of compensation and increasing earnings dispersion among workers. They found that non-financial companies, particularly in the manufacturing sector, began to derive the bulk of their income from financial activities. Their empirical analysis provided evidence for the thesis that 'the increasing reliance on

---

[14] Thomas Philippon, 'Finance, Productivity, and Distribution', *Brookings Brief,* October 2016, available at https://www.brookings.edu/wp-content/uploads/2018/01/philippon-october-2016.pdf (accessed on 1 April 2018).

[15] See Betsy McKay, 'Death Rates Rise for Wide Swath of White Adults, Study Finds', *Wall Street Journal*, 23 March 2017, available at https://www.wsj.com/articles/death-rates-rise-for-wide-swath-of-white-adults-1490240740 (accessed on 1 April 2018).

[16] Ken-Hou Lin and Donald Tomaskovic-Devey, 'Financialization and U.S. Income Inequality, 1970–2008', *American Journal of Sociology* 118, no. 5 (March 2013): 1284–1329, available at http://www.jstor.org/stable/10.1086/669499 (accessed on 1 April 2018).

income through financial channels restructured the social relations and the income dynamics in the non-finance sector. Substituting production and sales investment with financial investment decoupled the generation of surplus from production, strengthening owners' and elite workers' negotiating power against other workers. The result was a structural and cultural exclusion of the general workforce from revenue-generating and compensation-setting processes'.

Dani Rodrik argues, in a different context, that European countries did not experience the kind of stagnation and contraction in labour incomes that America did because of their social security systems.[17] That is an important explanation because elites in all countries were susceptible to the intellectual and commercial charms of globalization.

*Unequal Gains* is an examination of American growth and inequality since 1700. Professors Peter Lindert and Jeffrey Williamson, authors of the book, argue that three episodes establish the link between financialization and inequality in both directions. Causal evidence is hard to produce, especially for the first episode in the early nineteenth century when inequality in the United States surged. The authors provide only tentative evidence.

However, the evidence is somewhat more compelling for the period between 1910 and 1970 when inequality in the United States declined substantially. Definancialization and financial regulation played a big role. Conversely, the re-financialization of the US economy on a massive scale since 1970 has played a direct role in the subsequent rise of inequality. That income inequality since the 1970s rose markedly in the United States had nothing to do with the rise in racial, spatial or gender inequality narrows the potential culprits considerably.

The authors make three policy recommendations to reduce inequality without sacrificing economic growth. The first is investment in public education. Second is taxing inheritance and the third is regulating finance. They admit that the cause of income equality would not be directly helped by financial regulation but it would do so indirectly because the income floor under those near the bottom would be raised by the prevention of unemployment caused by financial busts. That is persuasive. We had argued earlier that finance was different from other sectors of the economy and hence the notion that 'market knows best' does not apply to finance even to the extent that it does to other sectors. That provides a strong basis for regulating finance and we take it up again later in the book.

---

[17] See 'Too Late to Compensate Free Trade's Losers', available at https://www.project-syndicate.org/commentary/free-trade-losers-compensation-too-late-by-dani-rodrik-2017-04 (accessed on 1 April 2018).

The impact of financialization on inequality has not been confined to the US alone. Financial globalization has been the primary channel for the spread of financialization. Davide Furceri and Prakash Loungani of the IMF examined the distributional impact of capital account liberalization in 149 countries from 1970 to 2010, and found that on average it 'increased inequality and reduced the labour share of income in the short and medium term'.[18] They write:

> In particular, we find that, on average, capital account liberalization reforms have typically increased the Gini coefficient by about 0.8 percent in the very short term (1 year after the occurrence of the liberalization reform) and by about 0.7–21/2 percent in the medium term (5 years after).

They argue that 'capital flow liberalization is generally more beneficial and less risky if countries have reached certain levels or thresholds of financial and institutional development'. We discuss this in greater detail in the context of finance in India in Chapter 7.

This chapter examined two of the major consequences of financialization. One was that it influenced, nay, distorted employment and wage patterns in the society. The other consequence is that it widened inequality. The next two chapters examine the effect that the rise of finance has had on the evolution of monetary policy in the US and, by extension, in the rest of the developed world. Over time, given the rising importance of finance to the economy, policymakers adjusted their frameworks, thus accommodating and even contributing to the growth of the financial sector and of financial markets. In this framework, even the UMP that had been adopted since 2008 can be viewed as a consequence of financialization. Thus, all the consequences that UMP generated – the subject matter of Chapter 5 – are, indirectly, the consequences of financialization.

---

[18] Davide Furceri and Prakash Loungani, 'Capital Account Liberalisation and Inequality', IMF Working Paper no. WP/15/24, November 2015, available at https://www.imf. org/external/pubs/ft/wp/2015/wp15243.pdf (accessed on 1 April 2018).

# 4 | The Monetary Policy Framework

This chapter is a continuation of Chapter 3 in the sense that we are still wrestling with the consequences of financialization. In a sense, the previous chapter was about social consequences whereas Chapters 4 and 5 are about consequences of financialization on the economy, on capital markets and on systemic risk, acting through monetary policy.

We had noted earlier that Alan Greenspan favoured and championed deregulation of finance. But once deregulation became a *fait accompli*, the importance of finance to the economy grew and the financial sector became a formidable political and economic force. Therefore, policymakers came to the conclusion that what was good for finance was good for the economy. Consequently, monetary policy was tailored to ensure that it encouraged and did not impede financial sector activity and financial markets.

This needed an intellectual framework. The experience of the 1970s came to the rescue. In the wake of the twin oil price shocks, labour militancy and turmoil in the Persian Gulf, economic growth stagnated but the inflation rate rose sharply in many parts of the advanced world. We had recorded earlier that it gave rise to the neoliberal agenda that put the interests of capital and capitalists at the top and centre of economic policy. Monetary policy had to focus on price stability. Inflation had to be leashed. Since labour costs are the largest portion of cost of production, restraining wages became the prerequisite for preventing inflation from running up. Hence, at the first sign of acceleration in wages, central banks applied the monetary brakes and raised interest rates. The balance between labour and capital had tilted in favour of the latter.

Since central banks were responsible for the creation of money,[1] it appeared logical to give them the responsibility to preserve the value of money. Is it really the case that money supply was the determinant of inflation? It might have been the case when Friedman and Anna Schwartz examined the data and

---

[1] Well, actually, it is commercial banks that create money. Please see Section 6.3.

proclaimed that inflation was always and everywhere a monetary phenomenon. But did it hold true in the modern era when the introduction of credit cards and electronic payments had upended the traditional role of money? Was inflation caused more by real economic factors, with monetary developments playing an auxiliary role? Further, in a well-functioning market, inflation should be taken care of by the natural feedback loop that exists between forces acting on demand and supply. Do central banks really influence inflation expectations? These questions are the subject of inquiry in Section 4.1.

The US economy, in contrast to the high rates of inflation and economic stagnation seen in the second half of the 1960s and in the 1970s, witnessed low and stable inflation and stable growth from the 1980s. It was called 'The Great Moderation' and hailed as a monetary policy success even as debt accumulation was slowly making global economies and financial systems unstable, beneath the surface. The cracks became wider and the earth opened up in 2008. We had the first major GFC in the post-war era. That forms the subject of Section 4.2.

The rise of debt had to be balanced with the rise in collateral values. Hence, asset prices became the de facto purpose of monetary policy, if not de jure. Models of the economy that the Federal Reserve relied on assigned a disproportionate role to the stock market in sustaining private consumption and economic growth. Consequently, monetary policy became captive to the interests of financial markets and financial market participants. That is the topic of Section 4.3.

Section 4.4 offers a brief discussion of the dangers of 'transparency' and 'predictability' that monetary policymakers offer to financial markets. They serve no economic purpose and may even be dangerous to the economy while they reward investors for taking excessive risk. Unpredictability may be a policy virtue and a public good.

Academics, central banks and multilateral institutions like the IMF have seized upon the idea of macroprudential regulations to deal with credit excesses and their impact on asset prices, implying that monetary policy should not be burdened with too many goals. Put differently, the task of maintaining financial stability should fall on macroprudential regulatory framework while the task of maintaining economic stability – stable prices and low unemployment – should be the goal of monetary policy. But the experience of Sweden and Spain in recent years with macroprudential supervision is not encouraging. There is no running away from the use of monetary policy to maintain financial stability. Sections 4.5 to 4.8 are about macroprudential regulation, their empirical record and the cost of not using monetary policy to 'lean against the wind'.

## 4.1 Inflation – 'the dog that did not bark'[2]

We had briefly discussed in Chapter 2 that the policy orientation towards controlling inflation that began in the 1980s has to be seen in the context of the shift from pro-labour, pro-worker orientation post–WW II to a pro-capital stance. It coincided with or brought about the advent of Mrs Thatcher and Mr Reagan in the UK and in the US, respectively.

As we had noted in Chapter 2, the decision of the Federal Reserve (and other central banks followed them) to abandon money supply growth targets as policy instruments but to choose the overnight interest rate as the policy interest rate meant that the central bank would stand ready to meet whatever money demand there was, at that interest rate. Simultaneously, the change in the balance of power between labour and capital meant that the disregard for money supply and the associated (or consequent) surge in debt in all sectors of the economy did not result in a sustained and rapid rise in the cost of living. This was as true of the US as it was for much of the advanced world. Truly, inflation was the dog that did not bark, notwithstanding the tremendous surge in advanced country debt ratios and asset price inflation. Was it because the monetary policy framework had changed and had targeted inflation or was it because the balance of power between labour and capital had shifted in favour of capital and that other factors had chipped in too?

A paper presented at a conference in the Brookings Institution in the US in September 2015 blew a big hole in the prevailing dogma that inflation targeting central banks anchor inflation expectations among the public. Four academics did a survey on the formation of inflation expectations in New Zealand. They chose New Zealand because it was the first country, in the modern era, to target inflation. So, it has had a longer history of inflation targeting than any other central bank. What they found was interesting and humbling for central banks.

The paper presented evidence from surveys of inflation expectations and understanding of inflation conducted among firms in New Zealand. The participants had a good understanding of what inflation was about and did not have any suspicion of official data on inflation. Yet, they formed their inflation expectations based on their personal shopping experience and based on the price of gasoline. Not only that, the majority of managers also reported that the primary use of their inflation expectations was for their personal

---

[2] IMF, 'The Dog That Didn't Bark: Has Inflation Been Muzzled or Was It Just Sleeping?' in *World Economic Outlook* (2013), ch. 3.

shopping decisions rather than in business decisions. Only a small portion seemed aware of the Reserve Bank of New Zealand, its inflation target, and so on. The evidence was a damning indictment of the role of central banks in anchoring inflation expectations. Rather, it confirmed their non-role. These results carried over to the United States too! Interestingly, years after the Federal Reserve began to communicate its strategies and its decisions to the public and had incorporated many educative materials on its website about monetary policy, about the economy, about the currency, and so on, a staggering 70 per cent of those surveyed remained uncertain or unclear about what the Federal Reserve did!

In its annual report 2015–2016, the BIS beautifully summed up the factors that influenced the inflation process in advanced economies. First, it said that inflation was a highly imperfect gauge of how sustainable the economic expansion was. Simply put, achieving low inflation does nothing to keep the economy and the financial system stable. In fact, it may have the opposite effect. Second, BIS added that low inflation was to be expected 'in a highly *globalised* world in which *competitive forces* and *technology* have eroded the pricing power of both producers and labour and have made the *wage-price spirals* of the past much less likely'. In this one sentence, BIS had summed up the forces that influence inflation.

That inflation was an outcome of monetary factors and hence monetary policy was the best policy approach to keep it low and stable was the intellectual contribution of Milton Friedman. All that central banks had to do was to keep money supply growth at a pre-determined rate. Inflation would stay under control and the rest of the economy would take care of itself. The only thing that governments had to do, through their central banks, was to set the money supply growth rate. This policy rule has survived Friedman and is, more or less, still in vogue today. However, at the age of 91, in an interview ('Lunch with FT'), Friedman confessed:

> The use of quantity of money as a target has not been a success. ... I'm not sure I would as of today push it as hard as I once did. (FT, 7 June 2003).[3]

That is astounding. His recanting of his pet theory that set the policy framework in many nations should have led to its rigorous re-examination in the hallowed portals of the Federal Reserve and other central banks. It did not. Perhaps,

---

[3] William Keegan, 'So Now Friedman Says He Was Wrong,' *The Guardian*, 22 June 2018, https://www.theguardian.com/business/2003/jun/22/comment.economicpolicy (accessed 4 March 2018).

had they taken him as seriously when he changed his mind as they did when he first propounded his thesis, we may not have experienced the economic crisis of 2008.

Figures 4.1 and 4.2 show the close association between wages and inflation. Figure 4.1 shows trends in worker compensation growth and inflation in the UK. Figure 4.2 captures the close correlation between hourly earnings of workers and the consumer price index in the US. We admit that we have not formally proven causality. Over time, both trends might have reinforced the other but there is a strong case that wages drive costs and costs drive prices since prices are usually a combination of costs and markups. As the growth rate of wages declined, producers and sellers could maintain their markups or even increase them, leading to higher profits without having to increase the final price to the consumer much. As a result, the rate of inflation trends lower and profits higher. That is a reasonably accurate characterization of the post-1980s world of inflation and corporate profits.

**Figure 4.1  Wages and inflation in the United Kingdom**

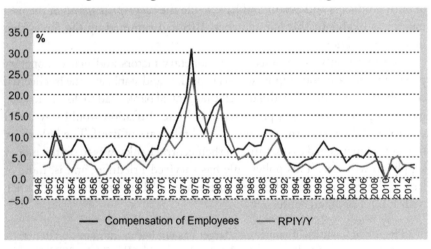

UK: Growth in Compensation Costs and Retail Price Index Inflation

*Source*: Office of National Statistics.

A growing body of literature highlights the increasingly global nature of inflation. Globalization had created a more or less global market for goods and some services as well as for certain factors of production. Integrated markets meant that supply–demand matching took place effectively at a global level.

This was accompanied by the downward pricing pressure exerted by import competition from lower cost producers.[4]

**Figure 4.2 Workers' hourly earnings and CPI inflation in America**

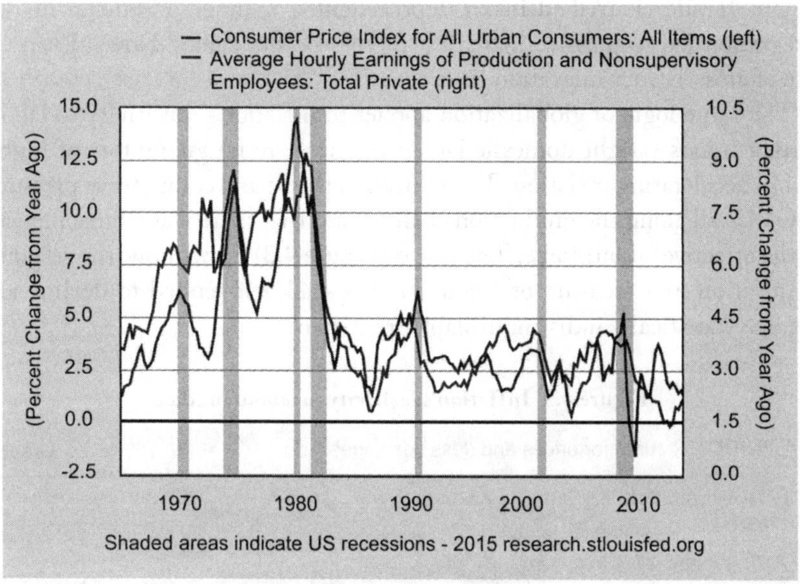

Sources: Bureau of Economic Analysis and the FRED Database of the Federal Reserve Bank of St. Louis.

Claudio Borio et al. have documented how the growth of global value chains (GVCs), which integrate the geographically fragmented global production processes, has created competitive pressures contributing to the 'globalization of inflation'.[5] They find that 'the growth of international input–output linkages explains the increasing sensitivity of domestic inflation to global factors'. They also find that the 'growth of GVCs is associated with both a reduction of the impact of domestic slack on domestic inflation and an increase in that of its global counterpart'. They also show that the trade in intermediate products in the production chain has grown much more than that in final goods.

---

[4] Charles Engel, 'Globalisation of Inflation: A Modelling Perspective', BIS Working Paper no. 70, available at https://www.bis.org/publ/bppdf/bispap70k.pdf (accessed on 4 March 2018).

[5] Raphael Auer, Claudio Borio and Andrew Filardo, 'The Globalisation of Inflation: The Growing Importance of Global Value Chains', BIS Working Paper no. 602, January 2017.

Globalization and the changes ushered in by information and communications technologies were transformational in more ways than one. The most salient manifestation was that it forged new global supply chains that brought in hundreds of millions of people hitherto excluded from the global production system. Trade flourished in an unprecedented manner. Financial market integration led to massive increases in cross-border capital flows. Even the rate of cross-border migration rose.

The same logic of globalization applies to inflation's sensitivity to labour market trends – tight domestic labour markets are no guarantors of higher and/or accelerating inflation. The relocation threat and competitive pressures of GVCs all along the production chain meant that there was a huge increase in the effective labour force. The graph (Figure 4.3) shows how 'the response of inflation to a measure of labour market slack has tended to decline and become statistically indistinguishable from zero'.[6]

**Figure 4.3 Inflation sensitivity to labour market**

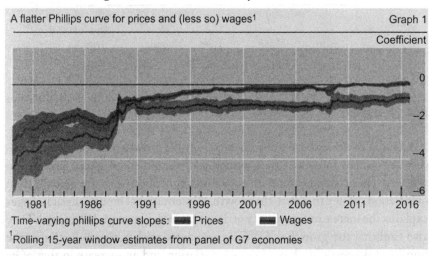

A flatter Phillips curve for prices and (less so) wages[1]    Graph 1

Time-varying phillips curve slopes: ▬ Prices    ▬ Wages
[1] Rolling 15-year window estimates from panel of G7 economies

*Source:* Claudio Borio, 'Through the Looking Glass', OMFIF City Lecture, 22 September 2017.

Another less discussed contribution of globalization was to keep a lid on global inflationary pressures. In its World Economic Outlook published in April 2013, the IMF pointed to a flat and globalized Phillips curve and

---

[6] Claudio Borio, 'Through the Looking Glass', OMFIF City Lecture, 22 September 2017.

anchored inflation expectations (Figure 4.4) to describe inflation as the 'dog that didn't bark'.[7]

**Figure 4.4  A flat Phillips curve**

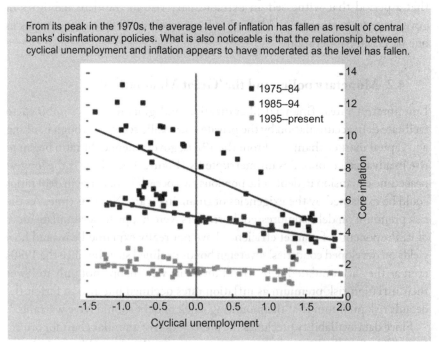

From its peak in the 1970s, the average level of inflation has fallen as result of central banks' disinflationary policies. What is also noticeable is that the relationship between cyclical unemployment and inflation appears to have moderated as the level has fallen.

*Source*: IMF, 'The Dog That Didn't Bark: Has Inflation Been Muzzled or Was It Just Sleeping?' in *World Economic Outlook* (2013), ch. 3.

The net result of all these has been an era of unprecedented stability in the prices of goods and services as well as slow wage growth. That gave rise to two phenomena. Central bankers kept interest rates low because inflation was low. This led to debt accumulation and destabilization of the economy when monetary policy eventually had to be tightened. The second and more insidious consequence is that a mistaken attribution of low inflation to monetary policy led to hubris among monetary policymakers. They concluded that they had found the switch that they could easily turn on and off to moderate business cycles. They thought that they had engineered a 'Great Moderation' in economies.

---

[7] IMF, 'The Dog That Didn't Bark'.

This gave them a false sense of security and comfort and allowed them to experiment extensively with policy measures. It made prophets out of the likes of Alan Greenspan. It allowed governments to pursue debt-fuelled expansionary policies for decades with no apparent discomfort. It was ironical that a period that witnessed an extraordinary rise in the debt liabilities of governments, businesses and households was welcomed by commentators as one of 'Great Moderation'.

## 4.2 Monetary policy and the 'Great Moderation'

Low interest rates, financial liberalization and globalization combined to facilitate debt accumulation by the private and public sectors through banking and capital market channels. From the 1970s, government debt ratio began to rise in advanced economies uninterruptedly (Figure 4.5).[8] This is the longest peacetime expansion in debt. The previous two occasions of surge in debt ratios could be explained by the exigencies of financing wars. Not this time. As the risk premium on debt compressed, borrowers were happy to accumulate more of it. Proponents of market efficiency have not really explained why and how yields on developed countries' sovereign bonds declined steadily since the 1980s even as they accumulated debt. Bond investors were happy not only to lower their inflation risk premium as inflation rates declined but also to forfeit the default risk premium that the mounting stock of debt should have warranted.

Since data availability precludes the presentation of a similar chart for private sector debt for all advanced economies, we present the chart (Figure 4.6) only for the UK and the US, which have a reasonably long history.

Even as debt piled up, the world economy experienced strong growth in the quarter century ending in 2007. In fact, bulk of the global economic growth since the advent of the Common Era happened in this period. That global debt also piled up in this period is no coincidence. In good times, more credit is demanded and supplied. Risk perceptions drop, and people in businesses and governments and even the employed drop their guard. Policymakers patted themselves on the back for having ushered in the 'Great Moderation' – a long period of sustained and stable economic growth on average accompanied by low inflation (see Box 4.1).

---

[8] We do not show the chart for non-financial private sector debt simply because data do not go as far back for all countries. Data availability does not improve much even if we restrict ourselves to advanced economies. Most time series start only around the mid-to-late 1990s.

### Figure 4.5 Largest peacetime expansion in global debt

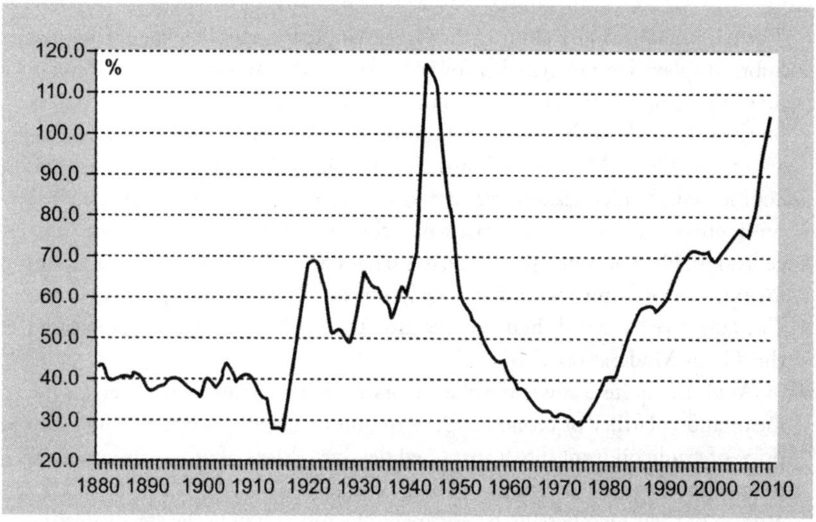

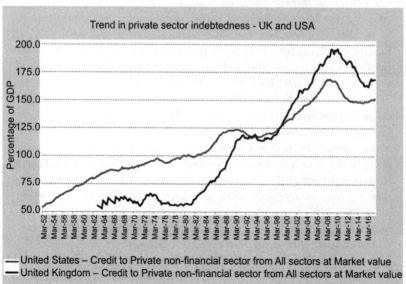

Public debt/GDP ratio in select advanced economies (2011 US dollar GDP-weighted average).

*Source*: IMF WEO database (October 2012).

### Figure 4.6 Non-financial private sector debt

Trend in private sector indebtedness - UK and USA

— United States – Credit to Private non-financial sector from All sectors at Market value
— United Kingdom – Credit to Private non-financial sector from All sectors at Market value

*Source*: Total credit to the non-financial sectors – December 2017 edition. Bank for International Settlements.

## Box 4.1  The Great Moderation and central bankers' hubris

The triumphalism surrounding the Great Moderation was the biggest sign of hubris displayed by policymakers on either side of the Atlantic. Federal Reserve officials, economists that served in the Administration and a Prime Minister on the other side of the Atlantic (Gordon Brown) were all guilty of boasting about the 'Great Moderation' in the economic cycle that policymakers had engineered. Academics too were not immune, with Robert Lucas in his 2003 presidential address to the American Economic Association claiming, 'The central problem of depression-prevention has been solved'! There was no room for extraneous factors or strokes of luck. It was all about skilful policymaking. The narrative has hardly budged even after the 2008 financial crisis punctured the 'Great Moderation' thesis.

Actually, quite a few external factors played their part in lowering the mean and volatility of economic growth and inflation since the 1980s. The price of crude oil went into a sustained decline. Prices of other commodities too declined. Above all, the loss of bargaining power of labour unions and the erosion of their membership base were big factors. Despite the steady decline in labour force growth, which should have pushed up wages, what happened was that globalization expanded the pool of labour, allowing for a massive labour cost arbitrage.

There was only a marginal role for central banks, their monetary policy and inflation targeting in this outcome – the secular decline in the inflation rate – in the last three decades. A serendipitous combination of circumstances ushered in the 'Great Moderation'. It was not the result of central bank policies.

In 2005, shortly before his confirmation as the chairman of the Federal Reserve Board, in words that have, unfortunately, not come to haunt him, Ben Bernanke said that the economic effects of falling asset prices 'depended less on the severity of the crash itself than on the response of economic policymakers, particularly central bankers'.[1] He has continued in that vein since then. The collapse of the housing bubble, the GFC and the rethink by his predecessor Greenspan have not succeeded in making him re-examine his beliefs.

In a speech[2] he made at the American Economic Association in January 2010, he strenuously defended the conduct of monetary policy by the Federal Reserve in the new millennium leading up to the crisis in 2007. His own charts showed that monetary policy was too loose between 2002 and 2004 and perhaps too tight in 2007. A candid admission of the error of judgment (it is no sin) in monetary policy could have sent the right signal to bankers on Wall Street.

Paul Kasriel, then at the Northern Trust Bank, wrote[3] in July 2009 that he would vote against re-nominating Bernanke for the chairmanship of the Federal Reserve Board for the simple reason that not once did he dissent at the Federal Reserve Open Market Committee meetings between 2002 and 2005 when he was a Fed governor. To him, it was a disqualifying sin of omission because the seeds of America's problems were sown in those years.

Before Bernanke's confirmation came the retirement of Greenspan, one of the three members of the 'Committee to save the world' and a Fed chairman who presided over long periods of economic expansion. The annual conference at Jackson Hole in August in 2005 was dedicated to honouring Greenspan. Raghuram Rajan, the former governor of the RBI, presented a paper that argued that financial developments had made the world riskier. Greenspan was a fan of financial innovations and he had used his persuasive skills and his bully pulpit during his tenure as the Fed chairman to prevent them from coming under regulators' preview. It was almost scandalous that a young Indian economist dared to challenge the Greenspan doctrine that 'financial developments arising out of private interest and technological change, interacting in a stable macroeconomic environment, would advance general economic welfare'.[4]

Fed Governor Donald Kohn – who for years had played the role of providing intellectual ballast to the central bank's decisions and served as its vice chairman – said that for central bankers to enact policies aimed at stemming risk-taking would 'be at odds with the tradition of policy excellence of the person whose era they were examining at the conference'.[6] The rest, as we all know now, is history.

The story is not much different across the Atlantic. In 2010, when the Greece crisis struck, the 'Troika' of institutions – the European Commission, the European Central Bank and the International Monetary Fund – bailed out the Greek government with financial assistance. The money was used by Greece to pay off private creditors – financial institutions in Europe. Ambrose Evans-Pritchard of 'The Telegraph' claims that he had seen internal documents of the IMF that suggest that the Greek bailout in 2010 was meant to 'rescue the EMU banking system and monetary union at a time when it had no defences against the contagion'.[6]

However, Karl Whelan, professor of Economics at the University College Dublin, reckons that hubris was at the heart of the 2010 bailout that piled on more debt on the Greek government – hubris that the single currency project was such an outstanding success that no default could be allowed to dilute it.[7]

Hubris is not so much an illness as it is a state of mind. It can be handled by self-reflection. The important thing is to remind oneself that one could turn arrogant and to find ways to deflate (one's ego) in a regular way.[8]

Lord David Owen (a doctor trained in psychiatry), the former foreign secretary in the British government under Mrs Thatcher, had set up the Daedalus Trust to study the onset of hubris among political leaders in the US and Britain in clinical terms. Policymakers everywhere would do well to engage with the Daedalus Trust.

Alas, central bankers were not exempt from hubris.

[1] Nell Henderson, 'Bernanke: There Is No Housing Bubble To Go Bust', *Washington Post*, 27 October 2005, available at http://www.washingtonpost.com/wp-dyn/content/article/2005/10/26/AR2005102602255.html (accessed on 23 October 2017).

[2] 'Monetary Policy and the Housing Bubble,' speech at the Annual Meeting of the American Economic Association, Atlanta, Georgia, 3 January 2010, available at http://www.federalreserve.gov/newsevents/speech/bernanke20100103a.htm (accessed on 23 October 2017).

[3] Paul Kasriel, 'I Come Neither To Praise Nor To Bury Bernanke,' *Northern Trust Global Economic Research*, 30 July 2009, available at http://web-xp2a-pws.ntrs.com/content//media/attachment/data/econ_research/0907/document/ec073009.pdf (accessed on 23 October 2017).

[4] Donald Kohn, 'Has Financial Development Made the World Riskier?' 2005, available at https://www.kansascityfed.org/publicat/sympos/2005/pdf/Kohn2005.pdf (accessed on 23 October 2017).

[5] 'Ignoring the Oracles: You Are With the Free Markets, or Against Them,' *Wall Street Journal*, 1 January 2009, available at http://blogs.wsj.com/economics/2009/01/01/ignoring-the-oracles/ (accessed on 23 October 2017).

[6] Ambrose Evans-Pritchard, 'Greek Debt Crisis Is the Iraq War of Finance,' *The Telegraph*, 19 June 2015, available at http://www.telegraph.co.uk/finance/economics/11687229/Greek-debt-crisis-is-the-Iraq-War-of-finance.html (accessed on 23 October 2017).

[7] See Karl Whelan, 'Greece, The Euro and Gunboat Diplomacy,' 20 June 2015, available at https://medium.com/bull-market/greece-the-euro-and-gunboat-diplomacy-3193983d8336 (accessed on 23 October 2017).

[8] Gillian Tett, 'Hubris and the City', *Financial Times*, 3 October 2014, available at http://www.ft.com/intl/cms/s/0/5d430638-49bf-11e4-80fb-00144feab7de.html (accessed on 23 October 2017).

There is a strong case to be made that the economic growth since the 1980s has been more a product of rising worldwide debt than a consequence of globalization, technological developments and policy competence. As discussed in Section 4.1, inflation remained subdued because globalization crushed the bargaining power of labour and labour income fell. But hubris all around led to an intolerable rise in risk-taking in financial markets.

Borio and White (2004)[9] was one of the earliest examinations of the link

[9] Claudio Borio and William White, 'Whither Monetary and Financial Stability? The Implications of Evolving Policy Regimes', BIS Working Papers no. 147, February 2004. This paper was presented at the Federal Reserve Bank of Kansas City's Symposium on 'Monetary Policy and Uncertainty: Adapting to a Changing Economy' at Jackson Hole,

between the 'Great Moderation', asset price booms and the consequent risks to financial stability. They were the first to raise the prospect that the anti-inflation success and credibility of the central banks could engender financial instability. They were ignored. Something had to give. It did. In 2007. We had the global financial crisis.

Since then, monetary policy has not succeeded in reviving economic growth. The years since the financial crisis of 2008 have witnessed unprecedentedly loose monetary policy and cheap credit. Stock market indices are at record highs. So are profit margins. Bond issuance volumes have exceeded pre-crisis highs. Yet this did not fire up economic growth in the US and Europe. If anything, as Paul Kasriel notes, '23 quarters after the 2009:Q2 business-cycle trough, real GDP growth has been the weakest of any 23-quarter post-cycle trough starting with that of 1961:Q2' (see Figure 4.7 below).

**Figure 4.7 Weakest recovery in five decades in the US**

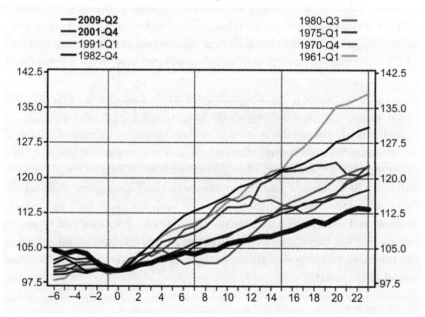

*Source*: Paul Kasriel, 'Those Were the Days, My Friend,' *The Econtrarian*, available at http://www.the-econtrarian.blogspot.sg/2015/06/those-were-days-my-friend.html (accessed on 9 January 2018).

Wyoming, on 28–30 August 2003, available at https://www.bis.org/publ/work147.pdf (accessed on 30 July 2018).

Why has monetary-policy-induced plentiful cheap finance failed to deliver? Well, for starters, there is too much of it. Both efficiency and efficacy are casualties when there is abundance of a resource.

More importantly, there is a rich body of evidence that far from promoting growth, credit expansions end up sowing the seeds of the next recession. Amir Sufi, Atif Mian and Emil Verner have shown that US states with larger household debt increases from 1989 to 1992 experienced larger increases in unemployment and more severe declines in real GDP growth in the same period.[10] They also found that rising household debt-to-GDP ratios were correlated with slower GDP growth and higher unemployment in 30 countries over the past 40 years.

Research by IMF economists led by Nico Valckx examined a large sample of countries and came to exactly the same conclusions.[11] They found that while an increase in household debt is likely to boost economic growth and employment in the short term, its effects are reversed with increased odds of a financial crisis and subsequent recessions in three to five years as indebted households cut back on spending to repay their loans. They show that a 5 percentage-point increase in household debt to GDP over a three-year period is associated with a 1.25 percentage-point decline in inflation-adjusted growth three years ahead. Further, a percentage-point increase in debt raises the odds of a future banking crisis by 1 percentage point, a significant increase given the business as usual (without any debt increase) probability of a crisis is 3.5 per cent.

Sufi and Co describe a 'credit-driven household demand channel' contributing to business cycles through which credit expansion due to lenders either increasing the quantity of credit or lowering the interest rate for reasons unrelated to borrowers' income or productivity. This argument about the financial sector itself contributing to the business cycle goes against the conventional wisdom that attributes such cycles to shocks on real economic factors. Further, they show that instead of increasing investment and, therefore, the productive capacity of firms, such credit expansions end up boosting household demand.

---

[10] Amir Sufi and Atif Mian, 'The Real Engine of the Business Cycle,' *Project Syndicate*, 5 March 2018, available at https://www.project-syndicate.org/commentary/credit-supply-household-debt-drives-business-cycles-by-amir-sufi-and-atif-mian-2018-03.

[11] Nico Valckx et al., 'Household Debt and Financial Stability, Global Financial Stability Report – Is Growth at Risk?' IMF, October 2017, available at https://www.imf.org/en/Publications/GFSR/Issues/2017/09/27/global-financial-stability-report-october-2017 (accessed on 30 July 2018).

Finally, policy has to recognize that asymmetry is a feature of economics. Policy may be effective in one direction, but not in another. For example, monetary policy may be able to slow down economic activity because, among other things, there is no ceiling to interest rates. But it may not be able to revive economic activity as we have seen since 2008. That is not only because on the way down, interest rates are bounded by zero but also because it affects sentiment and psychology negatively. Section 5.2 offers more explanation.

## 4.3 Monetary policy and asset prices

Inflation-targeting central banks, since the 1980s, either failed in or did not mind inflating asset prices as a consequence. Training their guns on consumer price inflation and wages meant being indifferent to sustained and even egregious asset price inflation. It is well accepted now that the crisis of 2008 was triggered, in part, by the failure to take into account the inflation in home prices in the United States, into the Federal Reserve monetary policy framework.

An interesting paradox that emerged from the indifference of monetary policymakers to asset inflation is that monetary policy became the only thing that mattered to asset inflation.

The most disturbing example of the substantial disconnect of the financial market activity from economic activities comes from the differential in US equity market price trends during the days when the Federal Reserve's monetary policy committee (MPC), the Federal Open Market Committee (FOMC), meets and the regular days. James Montier and Philip Pilkington of asset manager GMO studied the changes in S&P 500 on FOMC meeting days and regular days and found that FOMC day bounce account for 25 per cent of the total real returns since 1984, very different from the 0.0086 per cent random statistical probability.[12] They also found that the bounce was more pronounced in the 2008–12 period, which coincided with the peak of quantitative easing (QE). In fact, the average FOMC day returns during this period were a staggering 29 times higher than the returns for non-FOMC days (see Figure 4.8).

---

[12] James Montier and Philip Pilkington, 'The Stock Market as Monetary Policy Junkie – Quantifying the Fed's Impact on the S&P 500', GMO Whitepaper, March 2016, available at https://www.gmo.com/docs/default-source/research-and-commentary/strategies/asset-allocation/the-stock-market-as-monetary-policy-junkie-quantifying-the-fed's-impact-on-the-s-p-500.pdf?sfvrsn=3 (accessed on 17 March 2017).

**Figure 4.8 Stock returns on FOMC days**

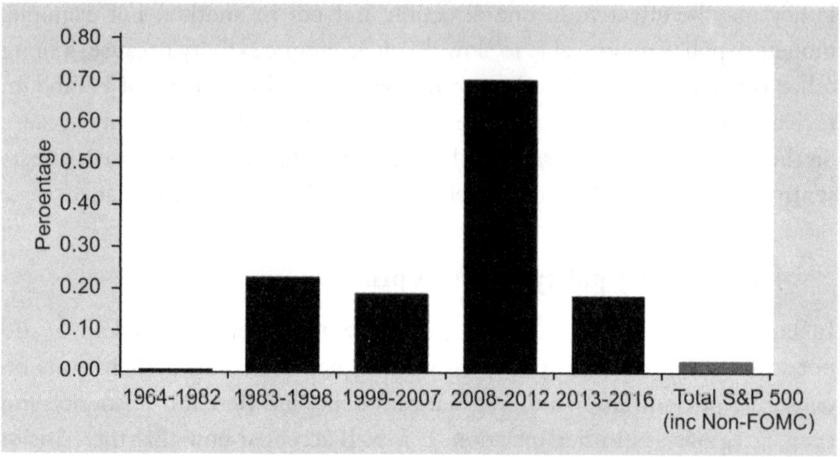

*Source*: James Montier and Philip Pilkington, 'The Stock Market as Monetary Policy Junkie: Quantifying the Fed's Impact on the S&P 500,' *GMO*, March 2016.

Furthermore, dispelling the possibility that the bounce is a natural increase due to rate cuts, they find statistically insignificant difference between the returns on rate cut and rate increase days. In other words, they find that the 'stock market reaction wasn't driven by easing so much as it was by the fact that the FOMC was meeting at all!' Neither economic fundamentals nor corporate fundamentals mattered as much as the fact that the Federal Reserve was meeting on monetary policy!

Research by Anna Cieslak, Adair Morse and Annette Vissing-Jorgensen finds insidious reasons behind this trend.[13] They document that since 1994 the equity premium in the US and worldwide is earned entirely in the even weeks starting from the last FOMC meeting – 0, 2, 4 and 6 weeks. Disturbingly, they attribute the even-week pattern causally to the Fed. In particular, they find 'systematic informal communication of Fed officials with the media and the financial sector' as the 'information transmission channel'. In addition, weak stock market performance in the intermeeting period was a powerful predictor of subsequent FOMC policy easing.

---

[13] Anna Cieslak, Adair Morse and Annette Vissing-Jorgensen, 'Stock Returns over the FOMC Cycle', NBER Working Paper, June 2016, available at https://papers.ssrn.com/sol3/papers.cfm?abstract_id=2687614 (accessed on 15 April 2017).

The authors suggest several possible explanations for the Federal Reserve to maintain communication with financial market participants and the media. One of them is a form of competitive leaking resulting from disagreement among FOMC members.

A somewhat benign explanation is that stock market returns play a disproportionately large role in the economic models that the Federal Reserve relies on, to make decisions. The authors note, 'The stock market explains a significant part of variation in Fed's Green book forecasts of real GDP and unemployment.' Hence, the Federal Reserve is anxious to ensure stock market health and that such anxiety translates into a willingness to cut interest rates and reluctance to raise rates.

More recent work by Cieslak and Vissing-Jorgensen presents evidence and analysis to show that the importance that the Federal Reserve attaches to the stock market for its perceived impact on economic activity is unwarranted.[14] They find that the reaction of GDP growth to excess stock market returns is small and is symmetric for stock market gains and losses. As regards unemployment, they find that its reaction to excess stock market shifts is asymmetric – unemployment rises more when stock market records losses than it falls when the stock market posts gains. But the Federal Reserve expectations for unemployment change much more than actual unemployment changes themselves! Further, belying the Fed's concern over the impact of stock market decline on consumption, the authors find that the sensitivity of actual private consumption to negative stock market outcomes is small, especially in the 1994–2016 period. Finally, they find no significant relationship between the stock market and updates to Fed growth expectations before 1994, going back to 1982. That is, the Federal Reserve grew more sensitive to the stock market after 1994. It was in 1994 that the Federal Reserve, under Greenspan, had embarked on a series of aggressive and sustained rate hikes that pushed bond yields higher. His large rate hikes and his subsequent musing, two years later, on whether the stock market was irrationally exuberant drew criticisms. Probably, these events resulted in the heightened sensitivity of the Federal Reserve to the sentiment of stock market participants and to stock prices too.

Several concerns arise from the importance monetary policy accords asset prices. Foremost of the concerns is that the importance assigned is asymmetric.

---

[14] Anna Cieslak and Annette Vissing-Jorgensen, 'The Economics of the Fed Put,' April 2017, available at https://papers.ssrn.com/sol3/papers.cfm?abstract_id=2951402.

Policy is more sensitive to falling asset prices and indifferent to rising asset prices. Monetary policy stance towards asset prices is asymmetric because the principle that underpins it is inconsistent. When asset prices rise, the Federal Reserve adopts the policy of 'market knows best' and non-interference. When asset prices decline, it cuts interest rates and increases money supply to counteract it because its models suggest (somewhat wrongly, as per Cieslak and Vissing-Jorgensen) that the economy is more sensitive to falling asset prices. 'Laissez faire' no longer applies. That is, according to its models, output, employment growth and inflation rates decline when asset prices dive but the inflation rate does not rise when stock prices rise. Inflation does not rise because, as we had seen in earlier sections, political economy and real economy developments had broken the wage–price link. But rising asset prices bring with them other undesirable consequences such as resource misallocation and economic and social inequality.

Further, when bubbles burst, they leave a trail of destruction. Collateral values shrink. The quality of lenders' balance sheets deteriorates. Unemployment rises, undoing the job creation of the boom era. More importantly, as we have seen in the post–2008 period, monetary policy is unable to undo much of the consequences and restore vigour to the real economy. For the real economy, monetary policy is not as effective as central bankers think it is. It only succeeds in restoring asset price booms, which sets up the conditions for the repeat of the boom–bust cycle all over again. That is the second concern. That is why the recommendation that Stephen King, economic advisor to HSBC, made to central banks in November 2017 makes a lot of sense. He said that central banks should raise rates when inflation is above target and when inflation is below target too 'because central banks that focus on price stability alone may only be stoking the next financial bubble'.[15]

The third concern is that attention to asset prices can lead to monetary policy being captured by the interests of the financial sector in benign and not-so-benign ways. Willem Buiter, a former external member of the Monetary Policy Committee of the Bank of England (1997–2000), was probably the first to write[16] openly about the capture of policymakers by the regulated. He

---

[15] Stephen King, 'Why Interest Rate Decisions Are Deliberately Ambiguous?' *Financial Times*, 3 November 2017, available at https://www.ft.com/content/9a0bee2c-bf28-11e7-823b-ed31693349d3 (accessed on 30 July 2018).

[16] Willem Buiter, 'The Role of Central Banks in Financial Stability: How Has It Changed?' Discussion Paper No. 8780, Centre for Economic Policy Research, January 2012, available at https://voxeu.org/sites/default/files/file/DP8780.pdf (accessed on 30 July 2018).

termed it regulatory capture but it could also be policy capture. He identified two channels for the capture: direct and cognitive. Direct capture refers to 'inducing regulators and supervisors to act in the interest of the industry they supervise or regulation rather than in the public interest they are committed to serve, by offering financial or positional rewards or by creating the expectation that such rewards may be forthcoming in the future'. Cognitive capture refers to 'blind faith in the self-regulating properties of financial markets. It is the triumph of market fundamentalist religion over science'.

Another example of benign cognitive capture is the transparency and predictability of monetary policy that central bankers repeatedly promise the financial sector. They promise no surprises. Well, no negative surprises. That is the topic of the next section. But there is also scope for less-than-benign (or, direct) capture.

Systematic informal communication between Federal Reserve officials and financial market participants can erode and has eroded trust in the financial system and the credibility of the Federal Reserve. In March 2017, Jeff Lacker, the president of the Federal Reserve Bank of Richmond, resigned, admitting to his role in the leaking of confidential market-sensitive information to an outside agency.[17] His resignation statement alluded to the possibility that the source of leak was another Federal Reserve Official.

In the United Kingdom, a BBC Panorama tape produced details of the conversation between employees at Barclays Bank on the low-balling of the London Interbank Offer Rate (LIBOR) by financial institutions that alluded to pressure from the Bank of England to do so.[18] The matter is under investigation. Earlier, a deputy governor of the Bank of England had to resign because she failed to disclose that her brother worked for Barclays Bank.[19] Central banking is in need of reform, as monetary policy framework is.

---

[17] Antoine Gara, 'Richmond Fed President Lacker Resigns after Admitting to 2012 Leak and Cover-Up', *Forbes*, 4 April 2017, available at https://www.forbes.com/sites/antoinegara/2017/04/04/richmond-fed-president-lacker-resigns-after-admitting-to-2012-leak-and-cover-up/#4c16b1bd20fb (accessed on 30 July 2018).

[18] See 'Barclays Blamed BoE over Lowering of Libor Rate, Claims BBC', *Financial Times*, 10 April 2017, available at https://www.ft.com/content/f7b6b39a-1dcf-11e7-a454-ab04428977f9 (accessed on 30 July 2018).

[19] See 'BoE's New Deputy Governor Resigns after Damning TSC Report', *Financial Times*, 14 March 2017, available at https://www.ft.com/content/461802b0-512b-3f02-a1cd-e83785e9c626 (accessed on 30 July 2018).

## 4.4 Transparency and predictability in the service of finance

One of us wrote in March 2008 – well before Lehman Brothers collapsed:

> 'Transparency' and 'openness' are normative words that have a positive ring to them. It is hard to declare oneself against transparency and openness. Therefore, the onus is on those who call for transparency and openness to be sure of the purposes behind their call.[20]

In February 2008, David Greenlaw, Jan Hatzius, Anil Kashyap and Hyun Song Shin presented a paper at the US Monetary Policy Forum. The paper was dedicated to arriving at a quantitative assessment of the impact on economic growth of the ongoing and expected defaults in sub-prime mortgages.[21] The bulk of the subprime origination, on a scale never seen before, started in 2004. That was the year the Federal Reserve, under Chairman Alan Greenspan, started its transparent and measured rate increases from a low 1 per cent. The transparent normalization of monetary policy caused credit creation to accelerate instead of slowing it down. 'Instead of tighter cost of capital leading to reduced risk-taking, it saw leveraged institutions expand their balance sheets aggressively.'[22]

William White, former deputy governor of the Bank of Canada, later chief economist at the BIS, said in an interview published in March 2015 that central banks got drawn into this 'transparency' thing, sort of. Without much discussion, it morphed from 'trust me to do the right thing' to 'I am going to tell what I am going to do in the future'. He pointedly noted that BIS, of which he was a part then, started taking notice of Greenspan's 'measured' rate increases from 2004.[23]

---

[20] V. Anantha Nageswaran, 'Transparent Harm', *Livemint*, 11 March 2008, available at http://www.livemint.com/Opinion/v0ncBwUn7vJ33nvwuhz8WL/Transparent-harm. html (accessed on 5 March 2018).

[21] Available at https://research.chicagobooth.edu/~/media/5831dfaf05624aecb83f08776 7e72dd3.pdf (accessed on 30 July 2018).

[22] Cieslak, Morse and Vissing-Jorgensen, 'Stock Returns Over the FOMC Cycle'.

[23] 'An interview with William White – Part II: the Former Economic Adviser for the Bank of International Settlements (BIS) speaks with Sean Corrigan, Cobden Centre contributor and its Editor Max Rangeley, available at https://www.cobdencentre. org/2015/04/interview-with-dr-william-white-former-head-of-the-monetary-and-economic-department-at-the-bis-part-2/ (accessed on 30 July 2018).

In our view, transparency and predictability of policy became respectable covers for policymakers to camouflage their fears that the leveraged edifice that they had helped create would fail to withstand even moderate tightening of policy. Hence, they wanted to soften and cushion the impact as much as possible and give time for financial institutions, non-financial businesses and investors to unwind their leverage. But the law of unintended consequences operates unfailingly. Far from inducing a gradual unwind of leverage, it led to a gradual or more rapid ratcheting up of leverage!

In his working paper on the subject of monetary policy transparency, Daniel Thornton of the Federal Reserve Bank of St Louis wrote: 'Transparency is desirable if it enhances the effectiveness of policy and is not if it does not.'[24] On that basis, transparency had failed the Federal Reserve again more recently too. As mentioned earlier, the Federal Reserve began to raise interest rates rather tentatively from 2014. Since then, at least until the end of 2017 if not longer, financial conditions in the United States had become substantially easier, conclusively defeating and nullifying the policy intent.

Claudio Borio explained [25] how central bankers' atheoretical fetish for transparency and predictability has undermined their own policy tightening by easing financial conditions:

> The very mix of gradualism and predictability may also have played a role. The pace of tightening has slowed across episodes, and it is now expected to be the slowest on record. And, scorched by the outsize reaction in 1994 – not to mention the 'taper tantrum' in 2013 – the central bank has made every effort to prepare markets and to indicate that it will continue to move slowly. Indeed, today's experience is reminiscent of the repeated reassurance of the 2000s' 'measured pace,' except that the adjustment has been, if anything, even more telegraphed. If gradualism comforts market participants that tighter policy will not derail the economy or upset asset markets, predictability compresses risk premia. This can foster higher leverage (debt) and risk-taking. By the same token, any sense that central banks will not remain on the sidelines should market tensions arise simply reinforces those incentives. Against this backdrop, easier financial conditions look less surprising.

---

[24] Daniel Thornton, 'Monetary Policy Transparency: Transparent about What?' Working Paper no. 2002-028B, November 2002, revised May 2003, available at https://files. stlouisfed.org/files/htdocs/wp/2002/2002-028.pdf (accessed on 6 March 2018).

[25] Claudio Borio, 'Introductory Remarks for the Quarterly Review (December 2017) of the Bank for International Settlements,' 3 December 2017, available at https://www. bis.org/publ/qtrpdf/r_qt1712_ontherecord.htm.

When policymakers swear to underwrite the downside by doing whatever it takes – as Mario Draghi promised in the summer of 2012 – and by offering explicit forward guidance, they are interfering with the very nature of capitalism. In the process, central bankers administer euthanasia for capitalism for there is no capitalism without births and deaths for enterprises. On the face of it, Draghi's explicit underwriting of the downside had rescued the Eurozone economy, putting it on a road to recovery, and saved the monetary union itself from collapsing. But policy has long lags and consequences appear after a considerable delay.

Part of the central banks' solution of encouraging more borrowing and risk-taking is their reliance on forward guidance to shape interest rate expectations. Central banks promise to keep policy rate lower than their policy rules suggest. Accordingly, the Federal Reserve and central banks across the Atlantic have communicated their commitment to keep interest rates very low for a long period, even indicating the time horizon until economic recovery and job creation are fully entrenched.

Policymakers fail in their quest to defy the law of nature as the promise of permanent stability invites an eventually inevitable, larger and more debilitating attack of instability. Ski slope operators and forest rangers knew this simple logic. Mini avalanches, deliberately set off, avert major ones and small bushfires lessen the chances of a major conflagration.[26]

Whatever its empirical outcome, it is fair to argue that in a real world political economy, it may be difficult, even impossible, to ensure central bankers adhere ex-post to what they promised ex-ante. Further, any reneging on the commitment would seriously dent their credibility – arguably the most important weapon in their armoury. More importantly, forward guidance, by promising full policy transparency on the path forward, is further encouragement to reckless and excessive risk-taking. We cannot put it better than Charles Goodhart.

In his speech to the Federal Reserve Bank of New York on 12 March 2012, James Grant exhorted them to read Charles Goodhart's book, *The New York Money Market and the Finance of Trade, 1900–1913*:[27]

---

[26] James G. Rickards, 'A Mountain, Overlooked', *Washington Post*, 2 October 2008, available at http://www.washingtonpost.com/wp-dyn/content/article/2008/10/01/AR2008100101149.html (accessed on 6 March 2018).

[27] Tyler Durden, 'Must Read: Jim Grant Crucifies the Fed; Explains Why a Gold Standard Is the Best Option', 30 March 2012, available at http://www.zerohedge.com/news/must-read-jim-grant-crucifies-fed-explains-why-gold-standard-best-option (accessed on 6 March 2018).

In the pre-Fed days with which the history deals, the call money rate dove and soared. There was no stability—and a good thing, Goodhart reasons. *In a society predisposed to speculate, as the US was and is, he writes, unpredictable spikes in borrowing rates kept the players more or less honest.* 'On the basis of its record,' he writes of the Second Federal Reserve District before there was a Federal Reserve, 'the financial system as constituted in the years 1900–1913 must be considered successful to an extent rarely equalled in the United States.' And that notwithstanding the Panic of 1907. (Emphasis ours)

## 4.5 Macroprudential and monetary policies – the twain shall meet

Unable to shake off the calls for paying heed to financial stability, central banks and multilateral policy bodies like the IMF began looking around for an escape route. They found it in 'macroprudential regulation and supervision'. After all, once central banks get the economy overfed with debt on a diet of low interest rates, the economy is trapped and so is the Federal Reserve. Rate increases have to be slow and small. That does nothing to improve financial stability as risk-taking continues. It is a game of chickens and the Federal Reserve usually swerves.

In 2015, having counselled the US Federal Reserve Board to resist the temptation to move the federal funds rate off its six-year-long zero base, the IMF suggested that the Federal Reserve fall back on the ill-defined macroprudential framework to handle those risks.

This is nothing new. This is a replay of what happened a year earlier. The only difference was that a multilateral institution was at the receiving end of the advice from central bankers. In its annual report published in July 2014, BIS made the point that interest rates might be, arguably, too high for the real economy but they were too low for the financial sector and global financial markets and, consequently, encouraged excessive risk-taking. At that time, three central bankers pounced on the BIS – Mario Draghi of the European Central Bank, Janet Yellen of the Federal Reserve and Mark Carney of the Bank of England.[28]

Do macroprudential policies work? What exactly are they? Simply put, they refer to quantitative restrictions imposed by the central bank (regulator) on the

---

[28] See blog post by Gavyn Davies, 'Keynesian Yellen versus Wicksellian BIS', 6 July 2014, available at https://www.ft.com/content/57c3c845-9215-3a06-81a1-21e9cb877ebc (accessed on 6 March 2018).

amount of credit extended by banking (regulated) institutions collectively to different sectors of the economy. These measures have been in vogue in many emerging economies before they came to be labelled 'macroprudential'. India is a noteworthy example. Developed nations used to balk at them charging such methods as inefficient means of managing the amount of money supply and credit supplied to the economy. They were deemed arbitrary and porous. Regulated entities and borrowers could always circumvent them. Now, the shoe is on the other foot. Unable or unwilling to raise interest rates – and we will discuss shortly the reasons behind them – western policymakers and their academic cheerleaders have been spouting the mantra of macroprudential measures. But they have very little history, if at all, of application and effectiveness in recent times in the western context.

A working paper[29] published by the Bank of Spain in 2011 helpfully clarifies the approach to macroprudential policy:

> A macroprudential policy should have a preventive nature in orientation and should provide the economy with specific tools and instruments so that in case of crisis its impact on the financial and real sector is minimised. Broadly speaking, a macro-prudential policy should rest on helping the financial system to withstand shocks and to continue functioning in a stable way without receiving emergency support in the form of public aid. In articulating this objective, two aims can conceptually be distinguished: on the one hand, emphasis should be placed on reinforcing the overall resilience of the financial system.

> On the other hand, importance should also be placed on establishing the grounds for moderating the financial cycle, something commonly known as to lean against the financial cycle.

In April 2015, IMF hosted a conference[30] on 'Rethinking Macropolicy', which was co-organized by two former research directors of the IMF. Unfortunately, not much light was shed on what macroprudential regulation meant in practice. Olivier Blanchard, the then research director of the

---

[29] Enrique Alberola, Carlos Trucharte and Juan Luis Vega, 'Central Banks and Macroprudential Policy: Some Reflections from the Spanish Experience', Occasional Paper no. 1105, 2011.

[30] 'Rethinking Macro Policy III: Progress or Confusion?' IMF, 15–16 April 2015, available at http://www.imf.org/external/np/seminars/eng/2015/macro3/ (accessed on 6 March 2018).

Fund, noted[31] that political economy dimensions were involved in determining the specific form and duration of macroprudential regulation.

Gavyn Davies wrote a good analysis in his blog[32] of the conference and the learnings from the crisis. Unsurprisingly, he found that many questions remained unanswered. He noted that unorthodox economists were largely unrepresented at the conference.

Few years ago, Jeremy Stein, then in the Federal Reserve Board, had pointed[33] out that macroprudential tools worked best in conjunction with conventional monetary policy tools. He said that they were a complement and not a substitute for conventional monetary policy. Among other things, he noted that interest rates got in through all the cracks because they are common for a commercial bank, a hedge fund, a broker-dealer and a special purpose vehicle. To the extent that interest rates influence risk appetite and the incentives to engage in maturity transformation (simply put, borrow short and lend long), interest rates have the ability to reach into the corners of the market that regulation and supervision would not. More importantly, macroprudential regulation, just on its own, far from eliminating risk, might simply cause risk migration to non-regulated areas.

A recent staff report[34] from the Federal Reserve Bank of New York highlights this risk based on the behaviour of banks and non-banks to guidance and clarifications issued by regulators on leveraged lending (loans extended

---

[31] Olivier Blanchard, 'Rethinking Macroeconomic Policy: Introduction', 20 April 2015, available at http://www.voxeu.org/article/rethinking-macroeconomic-policy-introduction (accessed on 4 June 2017).

[32] Gavyn Davies, 'Has the Rethinking of Macroeconomic Policy Been Successful?' *Financial Times*, 31 May 2015, available at http://blogs.ft.com/gavyndavies/2015/05/31/has-the-rethinking-of-macro-economic-policy-been-successful/ (accessed on 4 June 2017).

[33] 'Overheating in Credit Markets: Origins, Measurement, and Policy Responses', speech delivered by Jeremy Stein at the 'Restoring Household Financial Stability after the Great Recession: Why Household Balance Sheets Matter' research symposium sponsored by the Federal Reserve Bank of St. Louis, St. Louis, Missouri, 7 February 2013, available at http://www.federalreserve.gov/newsevents/speech/stein20130207a.htm (accessed on 4 June 2017).

[34] Sooji Kim, Matthew C. Plosser and João A. C. Santos, 'Macroprudential Policy and the Revolving Door of Risk: Lessons from Leveraged Lending Guidance', Staff Report no. 815, Federal Reserve Bank of New York, May 2017, available at https://www.newyorkfed.org/medialibrary/media/research/staff_reports/sr815.pdf (accessed on 4 June 2017).

to already leveraged borrowers). It found that after the clarifications issued by the regulators, banks subject to close supervision by regulators reduced their leveraged lending significantly. However, the slack was picked up by non-banks. In turn, these non-banks financed their leveraged lending by increasing their borrowing from banks! If the intention was to reduce systemic risk arising out of leveraged lending, it is not clear that macroprudential regulation achieved that.

Jeremy Stein was not making an original point, however. At least a couple of others had made the same point before. Spain was singled out for praise before the global financial crisis for its counter-cyclical macroprudential policies. Bank of Spain had urged its banks to employ dynamic provisioning against credit losses, as credit growth was rapid in the boom years before the 2008 crisis. Dynamic provisioning meant that provisions for non-performing assets rose faster as new loans rose, even though the ratio of bad and non-performing loans to overall bank loans usually dropped as banks disbursed more loans. Despite that, bank credit growth was very high. Without macroprudential policies, credit growth might have been higher. We will not be able to find out for counterfactuals are an impossibility in economics. Equally, we will not know if higher interest rates would have been more effective. There are limits to what such a policy alone could achieve.

---

**Box 4.2  The IMF and the macroprudential**

In the years after the financial crisis of 2008, particularly when Oliver Blanchard was the chief economist at the Fund, there was a fresh air and intellectual openness in certain crucial policy areas, such as income inequality, capital flows, public investments and fiscal policy. In the past, the Fund would have been satisfied with homilies about economic growth being more important than inequality, on the importance of maintaining free entry and exit for external capital and on the virtues of private over public investment and the limitations of fiscal policy. However, in all these areas, the Fund has come around to accepting that there can be other views than these.

However, it has not spilled over into the usefulness of macroprudential vs. monetary policy. Despite the eloquent case against the 'stand-alone' usefulness of macroprudential policies, the Fund continues to stress its deployment for achieving financial stability and cautions against using monetary policy.

In 'Selected Issues' – a report that usually accompanies the Fund's Article IV annual economic assessment of member countries – on China issued in August 2017, the Fund has clearly articulated its institutional view on monetary policy and financial stability:

*In principle, monetary policy should deviate from its traditional objective of price and output stabilization only if costs are smaller than benefits. Costs of raising interest rates arise in the short term from lower output and inflation. Benefits materialize mainly in the medium term, as financial risks are mitigated, though effects are more uncertain.*

*The case for leaning against the wind to counter financial risks is generally limited. Even if benefits outweigh costs, implementation remains challenging, including detecting vulnerabilities and predicting crises in real time and calibrating monetary with prudential policies.*

*Macroprudential policies should be the key instrument in preventing financial instability. These measures, when well targeted and effective, can target imbalances and market imperfections much closer to their source than monetary policy. Also, they could allow monetary policy to focus on its price stability mandate.*

The Fund has provided two exceptions to its institutional position above. That is, it concedes that monetary policy could be useful in achieving financial stability goals if credit transmission mechanisms were clear and if financial systems were large and interconnected. One is not sure if the Fund is discussing interconnectedness nationally or internationally. Internationally, it is clear that financial systems are highly interconnected and crisis costs could be potentially very large, exceeding the costs of deploying monetary policy for financial stability purposes.

Andrew Haldane had documented the complex and homogeneous network that finance had become in a speech in 2009. In his speech, he did not discuss using monetary policy to achieve stability in the complex financial network although he included deregulation as one of the causal factors that enhanced the fragility of the financial network.

If the network had become complex and, by definition, a network is interconnected, then the case exists for the use of monetary policy to achieve financial stability goals.

That is the conclusion that two IMF researchers reached in a working paper they published in 2017. Indeed, the paper published in November 2017 directly contradicts the Fund's 'institutional view on monetary policy and financial stability' as captured in the 'Selected Issues' report. The papers speak from our hearts:

*... to the extent that regulation and supervision are insufficient, central banks may need to use monetary policy tools to reduce the incidence of financial crises as well as to stabilize inflation and output directly. Indeed, if overly accommodative monetary policy – responding to low inflation risk – contributes*

> *to the boom and bust cycles that end in financial crises and output losses, then central banks would certainly need to incorporate financial cycles in their policy modelling and analysis.*

At last, Jeremy Stein stands vindicated. Now, we will be on the lookout for changes in the Fund's official view on monetary policy and financial stability. Not that we are holding our breath.

**References**

Cerra, Valerie and Sweta C. Saxena, 'Booms, Crises, and Recoveries: A New Paradigm of the Business Cycle and Its Policy Implications', IMF Working Paper no. WP/17/250, November 2017.

Haldane, Andrew, 'Rethinking the Financial Network', speech delivered at the Financial Student Association, Amsterdam, The Netherlands, April 2009.

'People's Republic of China – Selected Issues,' IMF Country Report no. 17/248, August 2017.

'The Blanchard Touch', *Francesco Saraceno's Blog*, April 2015, available at https://fsaraceno.wordpress.com/2015/04/15/the-blanchard-touch/ (accessed on 17 March 2017).

The 'Bank of Spain' occasional paper cited earlier was quite clear on the limitations of macroprudential policy:[35]

> ... dynamic provisioning is not the macro-prudential panacea, since the lending cycle is too complicated to be dealt with using only loan loss provision policies. Indeed the Spanish experience shows that even well targeted and calibrated instruments cannot cope perfectly with the narrow objective for which they are designed, among other things because the required size to fully achieve its goals would have inhibited and distorted financial and banking activity. Thus, the management of the lending cycle and more in general the reinforcement of financial stability should be consistently complemented with other instruments, either within the macro-prudential sphere – tighter control over lending standards and concentration of risks, countercyclical capital buffers or provisions, for instance – with microprudential policies *and in the broader context of macroeconomic management, including monetary policies.* (Emphasis ours)

---

[35] Enrique Alberola, Carlos Trucharte and Juan Luis Vega, 'Central Banks and Macroprudential Policy: Some Reflections from the Spanish Experience', Occasional Paper no. 1105, 2011.

These observations have salience in the broader global context and not just with respect to the circumstances that prevailed in Spain. A Staff Note[36] prepared by researchers at the IMF observed:

> Using interest rates to counter financial imbalances may risk increasing macroeconomic volatility and thus impose collateral damage to the real economy and, in some cases, it may even lead to an increase in capital inflows. Still, the high cost of systemic financial instability shown by the crisis strengthens the case for 'leaning against the wind' as a supplement to macroprudential policies oriented towards preserving financial stability. The lack of understanding of transmission suggests that, for now, central banks should best utilize judgment. *The combination of rising asset prices and rapid credit growth may warrant a higher policy rate than otherwise.* (Emphasis ours)

Perhaps, Fund executives and researchers inhabit parallel universes or they do not talk to each other. Other considerations too should make central bankers temper their enthusiasm for macroprudential measures over interest rate decisions. Since interest rates are prices, official changes to interest rates can be as granular as desired. Macroprudential measures are lumpier. In fact, the argument that interest rates are blunt instruments whereas macroprudential measures could be targeted needs to accommodate this important difference between the two. Second, while all economic policy decisions – including monetary policy decisions on interest rates – have distributional consequences, macroprudential controls have more direct and possibly greater distributional consequences because of their more discretionary nature than interest rate decisions. Hence, the question of whether central banks are the right and sole authority to impose macroeconomic regulation on the economy remains unsettled.

In a speech[37] on the myths and facts relating to the Swedish monetary policy after the financial crisis, Per Jansson, the deputy governor of the Swedish Riksbank urged caution on the exclusive reliance on macroprudential policies. He posed several questions for advocates of macroprudential policy. He wanted to know the specific macroprudential measures that should be taken, their dosage and their duration and if other measures were needed.

---

[36] 'Shaping the New Financial System', IMF Staff Position Note (SPN/10/15), 3 October 2010.

[37] 'Swedish Monetary Policy after the Financial Crisis – Myths and Facts,' speech delivered at the SvD Bank Summit 2014, Stockholm, 3 December 2014, available at http://www.riksbank.se/Documents/Tal/Jansson/2014/tal_jansson_141203_eng.pdf (accessed on 15 April 2017).

His counterpoint was Lars Svensson, a Princeton academic (where Bernanke was teaching) and a former member of the MPC of the Swedish Riksbank. Svensson had been an enthusiastic votary of macroprudential tools while arguing against interest rate increases to deal with issues of financial instability. He had resigned[38] from the Swedish Riksbank in April 2013 because his call for further monetary easing went unheeded in the executive committee.

With reference to Sweden, he had shown that the costs of the policy of leaning against the wind by raising interest rates to deal with financial instability risks far exceeded the benefits of job losses saved through a crisis averted.[39] The problem is a classic one in economic policy-making as in real life. Both are faced with the impossibility of the counterfactual scenario. Leaning against the wind has costs that can be seen and estimated but the costs it avoids – a crisis or a serious meltdown in housing and other markets – cannot be seen. The estimates that Mr Svensson makes of such avoided or averted costs can vary hugely and carry a wide margin of error. Despite Mr Svensson's caveats that his cost–benefit analysis – with all its possible limitations – is only applicable to the specific context of Swedish monetary policy decisions since 2010, Olivier Blanchard, the outgoing research director of IMF, wrote that he found Lars Svensson's cost–benefit analysis 'convincing',[40] leaving the world with the impression that it was a good template for all. It was both unfortunate and misleading. He did not mention that there existed equally persuasive contrarian evidence.

Indeed, one such evidence came from within the IMF itself. In their Staff Position Note, IMF researchers have noted recent empirical work that suggested that the trade-off was nearly absent if the large output costs of financial crises were taken into account.[41]

---

[38] Johan Carlstrom, 'Riksbank's Svensson Leaves after Failing to Gain Support,' *Bloomberg*, 22 April 2013, available at http://www.bloomberg.com/news/articles/2013-04-22/riksbank-s-svensson-leaves-after-failing-to-gain-support (accessed on 15 April 2017).

[39] Lars E. O. Svensson, 'Inflation Targeting and Leaning against the Wind', paper presented at the conference on 'Fourteen Years of Inflation Targeting in South Africa and the Challenge of a Changing Mandate', South African Reserve Bank, Pretoria, 30–31 October 2014.

[40] Olivier Blanchard, 'Ten Takeaways from the 'Rethinking Macro Policy: Progress or Confusion?' 25 May 2015, available at http://www.voxeu.org/article/rethinking-macro-policy-ten-takeaways (accessed on 15 April 2017).

[41] 'Shaping the New Financial System', IMF Staff Position Note (SPN/10/15), 3 October 2010.

There is an interesting postscript to the Swedish debate on the relative effectiveness of macroprudential vs. interest rate tools in helping to maintain financial stability. Per Jansson lost and Svensson won in influencing the Swedish monetary policy. The Riksbank policy rate was lowered from around 1.0 per cent in 2014 to –0.5 per cent in early 2016 and for the last two years, it has remained there. For this 'unprecedented' policy response, Sweden's inflation rate rose from –0.5 per cent to little over 2 per cent and it had dropped to 1.6 per cent in February 2018. In the meantime, Sweden's house price inflation rate had risen rapidly. Figure 4.9 below tells its own tale without us having to rub it in.

**Figure 4.9 Sweden succeeds in creating inflation of the wrong kind!**

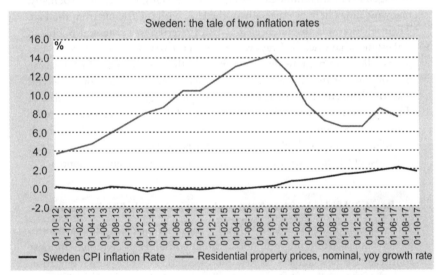

*Source*: Organisation for Economic Co-operation and Development via FRED for inflation data. BIS for data on nominal residential property prices.

In the meantime, Swedish households' debt to GDP ratio has gone up from around 69 per cent in December 2008 to 86 per cent by June 2017. The household debt to disposable income is estimated at 180 per cent. An independent money manager has included Sweden in the list of five fragile countries (Australia, New Zealand, Canada and Norway are the other four) as the Federal Reserve in the US has come under the leadership of a new chairperson who appears inclined to abandon the policy framework of the last three decades.[42]

Indeed, from these and other experiences of recent financial-market-induced economic crises, the costs of not 'leaning against the wind' can no longer be underplayed. In his remarks at the Bundesbank Symposium on Financial Stability and the Role of Central Banks held in February 2014, Ottmar Issing, former chief economist of the ECB, alluded precisely to this cost–benefit analysis:[43]

> One argument was that monetary policy is too blunt a tool. I think this argument has lost its credibility. We know from many studies that even small early increases in interest rates would have an impact on interest rate structure, risk-taking, etc. In the context of an asymmetric approach and 'risk management', I am reminded writing these few pages, I'm reminded of many, many meetings here or especially in the U.S. with my friends from the Fed. Their reaction was absolutely clear: when I referred to a potential Bubble in real estate, what I heard always was 'never in the last 50 years have real estate prices fallen on a nationwide aspect'. For me, this was not a comfort. Because in economics – and this was before the 'black swan' became popular – and once this happens their reaction to my critique or argument was very relaxed: 'In the meantime, we have had much higher GDP, higher employment, more houses, etc. So compared to the cost of raising interest rates would be much too high – much too high.' I have never seen so far the comparison of the high cost of the mess we are in if we take this 'risk management' approach.

---

**Box 4.3  Hedonic pricing and the law of unintended consequences**

The 'elephant in the room' with respect to the evolution of inflation dynamics in the western world might be the fact that consumer price indices in most countries are now subject to hedonic calculations while actual inflation continues to hurt households.

Western governments have become victims of their own success in wringing inflation out of all statistics – an effort that was first made in the United States in the late 1990s and quickly adopted elsewhere in the western world.

---

[42] See Aimee Kaye, 'Cracks Appearing in Five Highly Leveraged Economies', 27 February 2018, available at http://blog.loomissayles.com/cracks-appearing-in-five-highly-leveraged-economies (accessed on 1 April 2018).

[43] Doug Noland, 'Bundesbankification', *Credit Bubble Bulletin*, 28 February 2014, available at http://creditbubblebulletin.blogspot.sg/2014/12/02282014-bundesbankification_14.html (accessed on 1 April 2018).

Far too little attention has been paid on the role that hedonic price adjustments have played in the distortion of inflation numbers in the US. This methodology has been adopted with the aim of understating inflation, by making egregious assumptions about households substituting goods whose prices are rising with goods whose prices are stable or falling. In addition, hedonic price calculations make adjustments for quality improvements such that a normal price increase is reversed in statistical indices by taking improvements in quality into account.

Let us look at one example of how the computation of consumer prices is badly distorted by hedonic price adjustments. The Bureau of Labour Statistics Index of prices for new vehicles was at 146.735 in February 2015 against 144.6 in January 1997. Hence, it has gone up by a cumulative 1.14 per cent over 18 years from January 1997 to February 2015. Try telling that to someone who shops for a new car in the US. According to readily available public information, the average new car price in 1997 was USD 17,000 compared to about USD 33,000 today. As David Stockman, former budget director under President Ronald Reagan, put it, it is 'hedonics gone haywire'.

By squeezing all inflation out of statistics but not in reality, all that the American government has achieved is less inflation-adjusted growth in pensions and lower social security contributions than otherwise. The average worker finds his actual real wages growing more slowly because official inflation is lower while his disposable income based on actual inflation is a lot lower. On the other hand, officially measured inflation being low enables monetary policymakers to pursue looser monetary policy and enrich asset owners since low interest rates precipitate and nurture asset bubbles.

There are laws of unintended consequences to human decisions and actions. They occur over infinitely long horizons whereas our comprehensions and horizons are far too limited. Policymakers have been guilty and continue to be guilty of ignoring this basic fact of life.

Another argument against the use of monetary policy – interest rates – to ensure financial stability is that an instrument should not be burdened with more than one objective. 'One instrument, one objective' is the argument. Hence, monetary policy can and should deal with the aftermath of bubbles rather than be deployed to counter the formation of bubbles in asset prices proactively. It is troubling to note that policymakers are prepared to use monetary policy to address financial instability when asset prices are falling but they become reluctant to address financial instability risks arising from asset price booms that turn into bubbles.

In his seminal paper published in 2012, William White notes that the price stability goal of monetary policy and financial stability are not in conflict if the relevant policy horizon is longer. 'To lean against a credit bubble is to lean against some combination of possible near term inflationary pressures and/or the possibility of excessive disinflation (or even deflation) over the medium term'.[44] White, therefore, prefers that central banks lean against asset prices because they may not be able to clean up after an asset price bubble bursts. However, as Stephen Golub and others point out, this is in contrast to the view of Bernanke and Gertler 'that identifying bubbles is very difficult, pre-emptive bursting may be harmful, and that central banks could limit the fallout from systemic financial disturbances through ex post interventions'.[45]

Alas, his voice is among the rare ones in the monetary policy pantheon in advanced nations. Fixated on the absence of retail inflation and ignoring credit booms and asset bubble risks, central banks in the West unleashed UMP and negative interest rates, after the 2008 crisis. The unintended consequences of such an unprecedented policy experiment are still unfolding, 10 years after the crisis. That is the subject of the next chapter.

---

[44] William White, 'Ultra-Easy Monetary Policy and the Law of Unintended Consequences', Working Paper no. 126, Federal Reserve Bank of Dallas Globalization and Monetary Policy Institute, August 2012, available at http://www.dallasfed.org/assets/documents/institute/wpapers/2012/0126.pdf (accessed on 30 July 2018).

[45] Stephen Golub, Ayse Kaya and Michael Reay, 'What Were They Thinking? The Federal Reserve in the Run-Up to the 2008 Financial Crisis', September 2014, available at https://voxeu.org/article/federal-reserve-run-global-crisis (accessed on 30 July 2018).

# 5 | Consequences of Unconventional Monetary Policy

The Global Financial Crisis (GFC) of 2008 and the long and deep recession that followed it left a deep scar on all developed economies. After Lehman Brothers collapsed in September 2008, asset prices plunged and fear gripped the financial markets, forcing credit markets to dry up. Spooked by uncertainties about counter-party risks, lenders shut shop. The liquidity squeeze made even solvent institutions face the threat of insolvency.

Businesses, governments and households were left with bruised balance sheets. Credit markets froze, consumption and investment tanked, and economies contracted. Since governments had limited fiscal space to indulge in pump priming, the onus of containing the damage and leading the economic recovery efforts fell on the shoulders of central banks. Central banks assumed centre stage in this context (see Box 5.1).

---

**Box 5.1 The false dawn of being the only game in town**

The extraordinary monetary accommodation that started in the aftermath of the global financial crisis had a very justifiable rationale. The turmoil and its impact on the economy were devastating. Households, corporates and financial institutions needed the space and time to deleverage in a gradual and orderly manner. Keeping borrowing costs low was critical to this. Besides, this would also provide the time for governments to get their acts together with both fiscal policies as well as certain deep-rooted structural reforms so as to restore the economy to its pre-crisis levels.

Unfortunately, this had two flawed assumptions. One, governments would get their acts together. Two, we had to regain pre-crisis growth path. But both of these stood on flimsy foundations. Political considerations meant that governments were reluctant to bite the bullet with hard choices. In any case, governments in most developed economies had limited fiscal space available to prime the pump any more. In contrast, the likes of quantitative easing appeared a free lunch. And, as Larry Summers has written in the context of secular stagnation, the pre-crisis growth was itself built on unsustainable excesses. Regaining that was neither desirable nor possible without inflating more bubbles.

The resulting abdication by governments paved the path for central banks to assume leadership of the fight to restore growth. And the quest for pre-crisis growth necessarily meant prolonging the monetary accommodation and creating the conditions for another bubble.

Soon monetary accommodation and central banks became the only game in the town.[1] After all who would not want to occupy a power vacuum? The extended monetary accommodation suited everyone. The massive volume of credit sloshing around meant that corporates could borrow plentiful and cheap, household mortgage costs went lower (with attendant wealth effect) and the rising stock markets (buoyed by share buybacks) kept the C-suite executives and plutocrats happy. There was also the reluctance to take away the punch bowl when the party is in full swing, something that central banks commit to do ex-ante but have consistently preferred to renege ex-post.

Governments were not the only ones to abdicate on their responsibilities. Central banks had the opportunity to communicate the limits of monetary accommodation and draw the line of how far they would go and throw the policy ball back in the court of the elected governments. After all, monetary policy was only supposed to do the holding job to buy time to help governments and others undertake the more serious repairs. It was no substitute for these other measures. But captivated by their own new found power and attendant profile, instead of exercising restraint and signalling intent, central bankers allowed governments to cop out.

This brings us to the role of central banks in the modern economy. The narrative around them is one of technocrats making objective decisions free from political expediencies. But on any meaningful yardstick, it is hard to deny that QE has been a deeply political choice, and that too one not made by a democratically elected government. It cannot be denied that by keeping rates low for an extended period, central banks have benefitted the richest people at the cost of the savings of the vast majority of common citizens. It is not for nothing that QE has been described as the largest wealth transfer from savers to borrowers in modern history.[2]

Such trends are unsurprising. After all, when plutocrats and other elites have captured the entire establishment, central banks could not have escaped the trend. As we discussed in Section 4.3, financial markets have become the cart that drives monetary policy. Independence from political control did not immunize central banks from being in the thrall of financial market narratives.

In summary, while succeeding in establishing independence from their political masters, central banks were captive to the interests of financial markets. Such trends, apart from invariably generating backlash, also end up eroding the credibility of central banks among the public. In democracies, in the medium term, this credibility matters more than anything else.

[1] Paul Tucker, 'The Only Game in Town: Central Banking as False Hope', *ProMarket*, 14 May 2018, available at https://promarket.org/game-town-central-banking-false-hope/ (accessed on 7 May 2018).

[2] Michael McAlary, 'Greatest Wealth Transfer in History', *LinkedIn*, 20 September 2016, available at https://www.linkedin.com/pulse/greatest-wealth-transfer-history-michael-mcalary (accessed on 7 May 2018).

As the crisis response gathered pace, it soon became evident that the dominant strand of policy influencing thinking among central banks and governments across developed economies was that monetary accommodation could help provide the conditions for restoring economic growth. It was believed that, at the very least, it would provide the time for businesses, households and governments to repair their balance sheets, pave the way for consumption and investment recovery, and thereby restore economic growth.

Accordingly, in the aftermath of the GFC, central banks, led by the US Federal Reserve, pursued extraordinary monetary accommodation. Once the interest rates hit the zero lower bound (ZLB), they unveiled a series of UMP responses aimed at increasing money supply, bringing down bond yields and lowering real interest rates.

Modern central banks have been using interest rates as their instruments. They lower interest rates – usually overnight interest rates – to signal that they want banks to lower the cost of borrowing across the maturity spectrum. It is also a signal for capital markets to lower yield expectations. When they wish to make money dearer, they raise the overnight interest rate. In this world, it is only borrowing that drives spending – both consumption and investment, although textbooks would intone gravely that savings drives investments. The use of interest rates denotes conventional monetary policies.

What is an unconventional monetary policy (UMP)? After central banks had already lowered interest rates to zero per cent and were still not happy with the results, they decided to turn unconventional. Instead of targeting the overnight interest rate, they decided to target interest rates along the yield curve. Under conventional monetary policy, the central bank sets the overnight interest rate – the rate at which banks lend to each other overnight from their Reserve accounts held at the central bank. Under UMP, the central bank directly influences the interest rate by buying bonds from primary dealers and directly credits their accounts held with the central bank. QE was part of UMP. QE is a misnomer because it did not target a particular growth rate for money supply. In that sense, it was not about the quantity of money. QE was about asset purchases with a view to bringing down interest rates across the yield curve, mostly on government bonds and also quasi-government bonds. QE was still about the price of money! In some cases, asset purchases included corporate bonds too. Even though QE did not involve a money supply growth target, it increased the monetary base at a rapid pace to levels not seen before. It was not exactly 'running the printing press', no doubt, because the QE programme did not involve printing new currency notes and distributing them to the public through banks by buying assets from banks. But QE was about 'printing' digital money. Deposits held by depository institutions (we know them as banks) shot up, for example, in the Federal Reserve when it began to buy assets from them.[1]

It started with direct credit injection through unlimited liquidity auction windows, lowering collateral requirements, rescheduling tenures, and so on. Then, QE policies sought to leverage the central bank's balance sheet by purchasing securities, government and even private, undertaking maturity transformations in government securities and so on, thereby 'rebalancing portfolios' to lower real interest rates. Finally, through forward guidance, central banks sought to shape market expectations by credibly communicating a commitment to remain accommodative over a long enough time horizon to keep lowering real interest rates and restore normalcy in the economy.

UMP was a trap – a trap that was easy to walk into but difficult to exit. When the Federal Reserve warned in the summer of 2013 that it would start to reduce its monthly asset purchases of around USD 85 billion, financial markets reacted too nervously. The Federal Reserve blinked. Against expectations that the Federal Reserve would start reducing its monthly asset purchases from September that year, Ben Bernanke, the then chairman of the Federal Reserve

---

[1] For an explanation that is accessible to non-economists, see Richard G. Anderson, 'The Curious Case of the U.S. Monetary Base', *Regional Economist*, Federal Reserve Bank of St. Louis, July 2009, available at https://www.stlouisfed.org/~/media/Files/PDFs/publications/pub_assets/pdf/re/2009/c/monetary_policy.pdf (accessed on 7 May 2018) and William T. Gavin, 'More Money: Understanding Recent Changes in the Monetary Base', *Review*, Federal Reserve Bank of St. Louis, March/April 2009, available at https://files.stlouisfed.org/files/htdocs/publications/review/09/03/Gavin.pdf (accessed on 7 May 2018).

Board, desisted from announcing the 'tapering' of monthly asset purchases. Commenting on the decision, Gillian Tett of the *Financial Times* wrote,[2] 'Faced with a choice of curbing the addiction or providing more hits of the QE drug, in other words, it chose the latter.' The IMF recommended that the Federal Reserve keep up the liquidity supply to the addicts. To use a different analogy, it wanted the Federal Reserve to keep filling up the punch bowl regardless of whether the party was already too long and too rowdy.

On 4 June 2015, the IMF (or 'The Fund') placed a statement on its website after the conclusion of its Article IV consultation with the US.[3] It exhorted the US Federal Reserve Board to postpone its planned rate hikes to 2016, for fear of destabilizing financial markets. That was a breathtaking recommendation in the context of the federal funds rate having been held at 0.0 per cent for about six years at that time.

It was breathtaking because the Fund was not counselling caution and 'go slow' approach to a rampaging Federal Reserve that was willing to raise rates swiftly and sizeably. The Federal Reserve had repeatedly reassured financial markets that, even after the Federal funds rate got off the zero base, further rate increases would be gradual; that monetary policy would remain accommodative for a long period and that the average level of the Federal funds rate would be well below the levels seen in previous expansions.

To reiterate, the federal funds rate hovered at around 0.0 per cent to 0.25 per cent since December 2008 until the Federal Reserve made a first rate hike after seven years in December 2015. Since then, over 25 months of economic recovery, there have been only five small increases, with the most recent being a rate hike of 25 basis points in March 2018. The federal funds rate is still only 1.75 per cent. The Federal Reserve is behind the curve. Indeed, it has moved from being 'recklessly ultra loose' to being 'somewhat recklessly loose' in the last two years.

Doug Noland had put it very well in his weekly credit bulletin on 4 March 2017:

> The current remarkable cycle has brought new meaning to the phrase "Behind the Curve." Rates were cut from 5.25% starting back in September 2007. By December 2008, they had been slashed to zero (to 25bps), with the DJIA

[2] Gillian Tett, 'West's Debt Explosion Is Real Story behind Fed QE Dance', *Financial Times*, 19 September 2013, available at http://www.ft.com/intl/cms/s/0/76b6f332-2133-11e3-8aff-00144feab7de.html (accessed on 4 June 2017).

[3] 2015 Article IV Consultation with the United States of America Concluding Statement of the IMF Mission, http://www.imf.org/external/np/ms/2015/060415.htm.

ending the year at 8,876. Now, with the DJIA at 21,000, Fed funds sit at only 0.75%. Rates have budged little off zero despite record securities prices, record corporate bond issuance, record home prices and a 4.8% unemployment rate.

While Q4 data will be out soon, it appears that 2016 posted the largest Credit growth since 2007. Through the first three quarters of 2016, non-financial Credit expanded at an annualized pace of just under $2.4trillion, not far off 2007's record $2.503trillion.

For comparison, non-financial debt expanded $1.259trillion in '09, $1.589trillion in '10, $1.309trillion in '11, $1.916trillion in '12, $1.545trillion in '13, $1.807trillion in '14 and $1.931trillion in '15.

U.S. Credit growth and economic activity had attained sufficient self-sustaining momentum by 2014 and 2015 for the Fed to have launched so-called 'normalization.' It was a major policy blunder not to have this process well underway by 2016. The Fed basically disregarded domestic considerations as it postponed rate adjustments after its single December 2015 baby-step.

If the exclusion of financial stability considerations from the monetary policy framework was a first-order consequence of financialization, then UMP was its second-order consequence.

The trillion dollar question is if QE or UMP worked. The answer remains inconclusive. Some argue that economic conditions would have worsened resulting in a severe economic contraction like the world witnessed between 1929 and 1935. That may be true and, in any case, it is unverifiable. Some would argue that it did not make the world better off as much as the champions of UMP (like Ben Bernanke) expected or claimed. Recall Figure 4.7 which showed that the post-2009 recovery in the United States was the weakest in five decades. This is despite the Federal Reserve balance sheet expanding more than five times between 2008 and 2013 and interest rates remaining at zero until 2014 and rising rather gingerly thereafter. Nearly a decade after the QE began, the inflation rate is still below 2.0 per cent in the US. In the previous section, we saw the inflation rate in Sweden that tightly hugged the zero line even after the policy rate was slashed to 0 per cent.

In a paper[4] presented at the Monetary Policy Forum in 2018, Greenlaw, Hamilton and others do an event study on the behaviour of long-term interest

---

[4] David Greenlaw et al., 'A Skeptical View of the Impact of the Fed's Balance Sheet' (US Monetary Policy Forum, 23 February 2018, New York), available at https://goo.gl/xKHPaF (accessed on 7 March 2018).

rates around the time of the announcement of QE by the Federal Reserve. The hypothesis is that the long-term interest rate (represented by the 10-year US Treasury yield) should decline around the announcement of QE programmes. They found that, instead, the long-term interest rate went up. That may be a limited impact study of the QE programme.

Stephen Williamson of the Federal Reserve wrote[5] that there was no theory that linked QE to either inflation or real economic activity – the two underlying goals of monetary policy. That is important. It is one thing to point to recovery in the prices of financial assets as proof of success of UMP but what the economy needed was improvement in growth and capital formation and, of course, policymakers wanted to see an improvement in inflation expectations. Nearly a decade after the commencement of UMP, as of 2018, the core personal consumption expenditure inflation in the United States is below 1.7 per cent. A determined central bank is not guaranteed to succeed in generating inflation.

Although the impact of UMP on the real economy – where it mattered – has been underwhelming, it has worked tremendously well in financial markets, in creating even more debt and in widening inequality. Some even attribute the rise in populism in Europe to UMP.[6] That is not entirely without merit. If real economic impact were small and impact on asset prices much bigger, then clearly that would have been a recipe for widening inequality. In turn, it has made people turn to politicians who promise both extreme and easy-sounding remedies.

In sum, there is a compelling case to argue that UMP has succeeded in

- fostering excessive risk-taking and speculation
- creating more indebtedness and preventing de-leveraging of the indebted global economy
- engendering resource misallocation and impeding capital formation
- de-coupling asset prices from economic fundamentals
- diminishing future growth prospects and
- widening income and wealth inequality

---

[5] Stephen Williamson, 'Current Federal Reserve Policy under the Lens of Economic History: A Review Essay', Working Paper no. 2015-015A, July 2015, available at http://research.stlouisfed.org/wp/2015/2015-015.pdf (accessed on 7 March 2018).

[6] See 'Germany Blames Mario Draghi for Rise of Right-Wing AfD Party', *Financial Times*, 11 April 2016, available at https://www.ft.com/content/bc0175c4-ff2b-11e5-9cc4-27926f2b110c (accessed on 7 March 2018).

Needlessly to say, these were not the intended consequences. Yet, central bankers persisted with their UMP far longer than they should have. The next few sections examine these unintended consequences.

## 5.1 Speculation and risk-taking

Why did low interest rates not encourage borrowing for real investment but for speculative investments in financial markets? Why did central bankers not see it or refuse to see it? We abstain from exploring less-benign explanations. We would like to put this down to a basic cognitive error that acclaimed economists and policymakers have forgotten. It is that low interest rates result in higher investment, *other things held constant*. In the real world, other things are never constant. They are constantly on the move. That is why economic theories are never points of destination to an immutable, fixed and inviolable destination. They are approximations, points of departure for exploration into reality.

Interest rates reflect future scarcity of goods and services relative to the money that is used to buy them. That is why interest rates are positive. When interest rates are low, it sends a signal that future scarcity will not arise or that there will be a surplus. Capital investment for production of goods takes place to address the relative scarcity of goods vs. money. Low interest rates send a different signal to prospective investors. There is no scarcity to address. Hence, low interest rates do not encourage investment. They encourage speculation instead.

Other things being equal, low interest rates are a disincentive for savings through bank deposits. The opportunity cost of not saving is lower. With bank fees sometimes higher than interest rates, keeping money in the bank will even reduce the stock of savings. Hence, it makes sense to take it out to spend or speculate in search of higher return. Researchers from the Massachusetts Institute of Technology and Harvard University have shown[7] that is what indeed happens when interest rates are 'too low'. What is interesting is that they found that reaching for yield was significant among financially well-educated individuals and it did not appear to diminish with wealth, investment experience, or work experience in finance.

---

[7] Chen Lian, Yueran Ma and Carmen Wang, 'Low Interest Rates and Risk Taking: Evidence from Individual Investment Decisions', Massachusetts Institute of Technology and Harvard University, January 2017, available at http://economics.mit.edu/files/12105 (accessed on 4 June 2017).

Thus, low interest rates induce savers to seek higher yielding investments because their targeted returns from savings are likely to be lower with low interest rates. They may have a fixed return in mind to supplement their earnings and to provide for their retirement or for bulk expenses. Hence, they seek higher yielding investment options. When they seek a yield unmindful of risk, it is not investment. It is speculation.

One of the signs of speculation is the sudden burst in popularity of exotic products that have no proven history of stability or performance. Before 2008, it was CDSs. In the last few years, financial products that bet on the persistence of low volatility and exchange traded funds (ETFs) that invest in illiquid underlying assets have taken its place. VIX, short for volatility index, used to be a measurement of implied volatility extracted from the prices of at-the-money CALL and PUT options on the S&P 500 stock index. It informed investors of the option markets' expectations of volatility. In the last few years, it had morphed into a product of its own. Investors began betting on the direction of the VIX. As the S&P 500 kept rising relentlessly from 2009, the VIX index kept drifting lower. A sign of investor complacency. Therefore, with 'excellent' judgement, investors bet that it would continue to drift lower. In February 2018, the tide receded. Those who were swimming naked were caught out. Volatility spiked. Short volatility funds lost and two were almost wiped out. Drop in asset prices wipes out the entire net worth only when debt is deployed to build up long positions in assets. That is what had happened.

An article[8] in Reuters manages to give us a sense of the complexity that is inserted into these products:

> The VIX itself measures market expectations of how choppy the S&P 500 might be over the coming month. With the U.S. index becoming the most widely-traded in the world, the VIX is seen by many as a key barometer of investment sentiment.
>
> Investors trade volatility through VIX futures contracts, reflecting bets on future stock swings.
>
> Inverse exchange-traded products (ETPs) based on the VIX add another element of complexity, allowing investors to take short positions on volatility futures, hence betting on fading volatility.
>
> Add in leveraged products, which enable the buyer to multiply the scale of their bet many times over, and the possibility for market havoc becomes clear.

---

[8] See Helen Reid and Alasdair Pal, 'Meltdown Raises Fears of 'financial Innovation the Planet Doesn't Really Need,' 8 February 2018, available at https://goo.gl/sS4HTj.

This is as good an illustration of the effects of low interest rates on speculation as any. To the extent that low interest rates fail to result in higher capital formation but end up fuelling speculation, they cause a divergence or de-coupling between asset prices and the real economy. Financial assets are ultimately claims on real assets and their cash flows. With low or no capital formation, fewer real assets are created and thus fewer new financial claims are created. Existing financial assets are marked up in value because less of them are created. Bubbles result.

## 5.2   Low interest rates do not boost capital formation

Lower interest rates cannot generate 'wealth', if an increase in wealth is appropriately defined as the capacity to have a higher future standard of living. From this perspective, higher equity prices constitute wealth only if based on higher expected productivity and higher future earnings. This could be a by-product of lower interest rates stimulating spending, but this is simply to assume the hypothesis meant to be under test.[9]

Data bear out that elegant demolition by William White of the notion that lower interest rates generate wealth through higher equity prices. Capital formation and productivity have been conspicuously missing in the American economic recovery from the crisis of 2008. Figure 5.1 shows the evolution of durable goods orders (non-defence excluding aircraft). Although the federal funds rate was reduced to zero in 2008 and kept at zero for the next seven years, orders for durable goods picked up only briefly in 2010–2011 and then faded away for a long time. Nor did QE that lowered long-term interest rates help. Orders for durable goods recovered in the course of 2017 but it would be quite a stretch to attribute it to monetary policy. Too many other forces were at work such as the deregulation agenda of the new administration. Figure 5.2 tells the same story with respect to real output per hour has stagnated in the last six years. There is much hand wringing today about declining productivity globally.[10]

---

[9] White, 'Ultra-Easy Monetary Policy and the Law of Unintended Consequences'.

[10] See, for example, a press release by the Conference Board dated 16 June 2015 on its report 'Global Productivity: Drifting into Crisis', available at https://www.conference-board.org/press/pressdetail.cfm?pressid=5479 (accessed on 4 June 2017).

## Figure 5.1 Non-response of investment spending to low rates

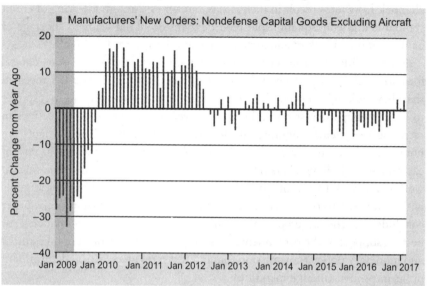

Source: FRED database of the Federal Reserve Bank of St. Louis (data through February 2017).

## Figure 5.2 Fading productivity follows sluggish capital formation

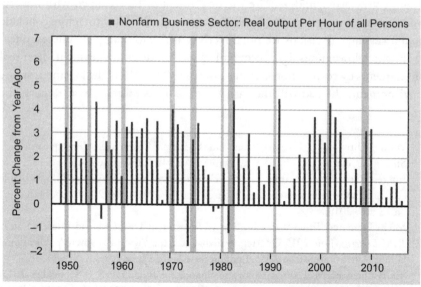

Source: FRED database of the Federal Reserve Bank of St. Louis (data through 2016).

William White warns that UMP impedes capital formation through another channel. Low rates result in incipient boom times through lowering of credit standards and consequent rapid credit expansion. That leads to shortage of bank capital and lack of adequate reliable and long-term funding.[11]

Micro evidence from corporate behaviour offers clues to poor capital formation. A survey of chief financial officers (CFOs) in the US revealed that they seldom lower their hurdle rate for approving investments in response to lower policy interest rates. Therefore, even as cost of funding declines in response to a weak economy, hurdle rates do not and real investments are not undertaken. However, CFOs do raise their hurdle rates when the cost of capital rises.[12] Policymakers have failed to grasp the behavioural dynamics at work here. No CFO wants to be held responsible for approving investments with lower returns than what the company is used to. The authors of the paper conclude that the large body of empirical research offers mixed evidence, at best, in support of the fundamental tenet of traditional theories of investment and monetary policy transmission that interest rates are a critical determinant of business investment expenditure.

Kevin Lane and Tom Rosewall of the Reserve Bank of Australia come to similar conclusions using survey data of Australian firms.[13] They find that Australian firms tend to 'require expected returns on capital to exceed high "hurdle rates" of return that are often well above the cost of capital and do not change very often' and 'require the investment to be recouped within a few years, requiring even greater implied rates of return'. They therefore conclude that investment decisions are 'not directly sensitive to changes in interest rates'.

Further, lower rates signal economic malaise – one more reason to deter real investments by corporations. 'If the cost of capital reflects the low interest rate environment, then so will the cash flows.'[14] In its 86th Annual Report, the

---

[11] White, 'Ultra-Easy Monetary Policy and the Law of Unintended Consequences'.

[12] Steven A. Sharpe and Gustavo A. Suarez, 'Why Isn't Investment More Sensitive to Interest Rates: Evidence from Surveys', Federal Reserve Board, August 2015, available at https://www.federalreserve.gov/econresdata/feds/2014/files/201402r.pdf (accessed on 13 June 2018).

[13] Kevin Lane and Tome Rosewall, 'Firms' Investment Decisions and Interest Rates,' *RBA Bulletin*, June 2015 Quarter, available at https://www.rba.gov.au/publications/bulletin/2015/jun/pdf/bu-0615-1.pdf (accessed on 13 June 2018).

[14] 'ECB Quantitative Easing: Failure to Spark', *Financial Times*, 8 September 2015, available at https://www.ft.com/content/619b139c-3ce4-11e5-8613-07d16aad2152 (accessed on 13 June 2018).

BIS noted, 'Despite exceptionally easy financial conditions, firms in advanced economies have been unwilling to invest. A major reason for this appears to be uncertainty about future demand and thus profitability.'[15] Interest rates do not matter. Underlying demand conditions matter.

It added, 'Likewise, households' confidence may be shaken by the prospect of negative nominal interest rates, given the widespread attention paid to nominal variables (i.e., "money illusion") and the sense of direness that adopting negative rates may convey.'

Unfortunately, UMP is rather effective in the wrong areas. Low interest rates, especially when in place for long periods, are likely to engender massive resource misallocation. The extraordinary monetary accommodation has predictably unleashed perverse incentives among borrowers who seek to cash in on the ultra-low interest rates.

### 5.3 Low interest rates encourage resource misallocation

According to Danielle Booth, former advisor to the president of the Federal Reserve Bank of Dallas, a funny thing happens when monetary policy provides a floor under asset prices:[16]

> Recessions fade from the norm. Over the past 25 years, the economy has contracted one-fourth as often as it did in the 25 years that preceded this benign era. Hence, the illusion of prosperity, one that has rendered investors complacent to the point of being comatose. That's what happens when entire industries are able to run with more capacity than demand validates simply because the credit to remain in operation is there for the taking. To take but one example, capacity utilization is at 78.1 percent, shy of the 30-year average of 79.6 percent some six years into the current recovery. The downside is that the cathartic cleansing that takes place when recession is allowed to play out all the way to the bitter end of a bankruptcy cycle never occurs – winners and losers alike stay in business.

> The savvy fellows in the C-suites are not blind to reduced competitiveness. As such, they are remiss to expand their core businesses too much, that is, until the time they can truly assess the operating environment in a post-easy money world. The tricky part is that the credit is still there for the taking.

---

[15] See footnote 12, chapter 3 of the BIS Annual Report (no. 86) for more citations that offer evidence in support of the thesis.

[16] Danielle DiMartino Booth, 'The Great Abdication,' 15 June 2018, available at http://tlrii.typepad.com/thelisicioreport/.

What's to be done? In the words of one of the wisest owls on Wall Street, UBS's Art Cashin, such environments raise the not-so-fine art of financial engineering to a 'botox state'. It's no secret that companies have been gorging themselves on share buybacks and mergers and acquisitions, non-productive but highly lucrative endeavours. When combined the results are magnificent – costs are cut, profits juiced and bonus season becomes the most wonderful time of the year.

The allusion to the linkage between UMP and the rising tendency towards financial engineering pursued with the aim of boosting executive compensation is unmistakable. One of the most pernicious forms of QE-induced distortion is the spurt in share buybacks.

Consider the case of Apple. With interest rates low and expected to remain so for the foreseeable future, Apple with nearly USD 200 billion of cash surplus has borrowed billions to finance share buybacks that would boost its share price.[17] It served the purpose of avoiding the repatriation of foreign profits and payment of US taxes, as well as claiming tax deductions on debt repayments. Apple is not alone in this game. The largest US corporates are piling up debt to finance share buybacks, though currently sitting on USD 2.0 trillion in cash reserves.

In fact, between 2005 and 2015, S&P 500 companies in the US have spent USD 4.0 trillion on buybacks and USD 2.5 trillion on dividends, representing 52.5 per cent and 37.5 per cent, respectively, of their net earnings. In other words, capital investments and R&D, the determinants of corporate growth, took up just 10 per cent of the net earnings! Share buybacks and dividends were 105 per cent and 115 per cent of net earnings of listed US companies in 2014 and 2015, respectively.[18] In the year ending March 2016, S&P 500 companies spent a record USD 589.4 billion on share repurchases, beating the previous record of USD 589.1 billion set in 2007.[19] Between 2014 and 2016,

---

[17] Claire Boston, 'Apple's Embrace by Bond Market Prompts Calls for Sanity Check', *Bloomberg*, 29 July 2016, available at http://www.bloomberg.com/news/articles/2016-07-29/apple-s-embrace-by-bond-market-prompts-calls-for-sanity-check (accessed on 18 March 2017).

[18] Rana Foroohar, *Makers and Takers: Rise of Finance and Fall of American Business* (New York: Crown Business, 2016), 131.

[19] Aaron Kuriloff, 'S&P 500 Firms Spend $161.4 billion on Share Buybacks in the First Quarter', *Wall Street Journal*, 22 June 2016, available at http://www.wsj.com/articles/s-p-500-firms-spent-161-4-billion-on-share-buybacks-in-the-first-quarter-1466618520 (accessed on 18 March 2017).

S&P 500 companies had bought back roughly USD 1.6 trillion of stocks (Figures 5.3 and 5.4).

**Figure 5.3 S&P 500 index and buyback ETF**

**Figure 5.4 NASDAQ composite index and buyback ETF**

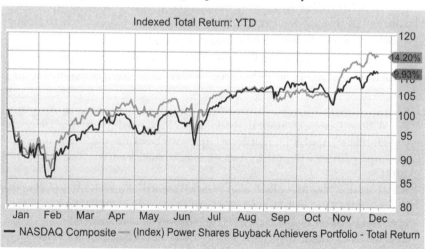

*Source*: Buyback Quarterly, *Factset*, 19 December 2016.

William Lazonick has described that corporates have embraced buybacks with gusto, moving from a model of 'retain-and-reinvest' to 'downsize-and-distribute'.[20] It appears that monetary policy supports financial market speculation and asset prices through several routes. Worse, stock buyback is one of the conduits through which recent monetary policy actions have facilitated widening income and wealth inequality in societies.

Unfortunately, share buybacks are not the only game in town:[21]

> American firms today make more money than ever before by simply moving money around, getting about five times the revenue from purely financial activities, such as trading, hedging, tax optimisation and selling financial services, than they did in the immediate post-war period. No wonder share buybacks and corporate investment into research and development have moved inversely in recent years. It is easier for chief executives with a shelf life of three years to try to please investors by jacking up short-term share prices than to invest in things that will grow a company over the long haul.

As an example, Zoltan Pozsar of Credit Suisse has documented USD 1.0 trillion of off-shore savings of 150 US corporates belonging to the S&P 500.[22] 80 per cent of this belongs to the largest and most IP-rich 10 per cent of companies, who can easily move their IPs across borders. Almost all of this money is invested in high-yielding corporate bonds, turning some of these corporates into as influential bond market players as some investment banks.[23] Hardly any of this money, even if repatriated back to US, is likely to finance new investments in factories or be paid out as higher wages.

All this has created what Claudio Borio, the BIS chief economist, has described as the spiral of 'ugly three' – high debt contributes to resource

---

[20] See William Lazonick, 'Stock Buybacks: From Retain-and-Reinvest to Downsize-and-Distribute', April 2015, available at http://www.brookings.edu/~/media/research/files/papers/2015/04/17-stock-buybacks-lazonick/lazonick.pdf (accessed on 18 March 2017).

[21] Rana Foroohar, 'Too Many Businesses Want a Piece of the Financial Action', *Financial Times*, 15 May 2016, available at http://www.ft.com/intl/cms/s/0/ed421ea4-1925-11e6-b197-a4af20d5575e.html#axzz48go0TAtJ (accessed on 18 March 2017).

[22] Zoltan Pozsar, 'Repatriation, the Echo-Taper, and the €/$ Basis', Global Money Notes #11, Credit Suisse Global Strategy, 29 January 2018, available at https://goo.gl/FXdQZx (accessed on 18 March 2017).

[23] Rana Foroohar, 'Tech Companies Are the New Investment Banks', *Financial Times*, 11 February 2018, available at https://www.ft.com/content/0ee3bef8-0d87-11e8-8eb7-42f857ea9f09 (accessed on 18 March 2017).

misallocation which in turn leads to lower productivity growth[24] and less policy room to manoeuvre. Abundance of credit encourages entrepreneurs to invest both their efforts and capital in projects with 'higher pledgeability but lower productivity' like those in construction.[25] In contrast, projects that require higher skilled workers are unlikely to be able to load up with debt due to their 'low pledgeability', like with R&D intensive manufacturing. The result is an equilibrium where entrepreneurs leverage up in lower productivity but high collateral sectors, while finance crowds-in the skilled workers. Greater financialization, therefore, leads to reduced productivity growth.[26]

In addition, research by BIS economists using a sample of 21 advanced economies since 1969 has shed more evidence that financial crisis which follows a debt binge amplifies the effect of labour misallocation that took place during the boom.[27] They find that slightly less than two-third of the just over a quarter of a percentage-point annual productivity loss during a typical credit boom reflects the shift of labour to low productivity growth sectors like construction and real estate (Figure 5.5). More importantly, the 'average loss per year in the five years after a crisis is more than twice that during a boom, around half a percentage point per year'. This means that over a 10-year episode, the cumulative productivity loss is about four percentage points.

Finally, declining productivity growth erodes profitability. In an already heavily leveraged ecosystem, this in turn has the effect of increasing the firm's indebtedness and pushing it into a downward debt spiral.[28] Leverage becomes a substitute for productivity in boosting profitability. At policy level, fiscally strapped governments force monetary policy to do the heavy lifting. As interest rates touched the zero-bound in the aftermath of the GFC, central banks were

---

[24] Claudio Borio et al., 'Labour Reallocation and Productivity Dynamics: Financial Causes, Real Consequences', BIS Working Paper no. 534, December 2015, available at http://www.bis.org/publ/work534.pdf (accessed on 18 March 2017).

[25] Stephen G. Cecchetti and Enisse Kharroubi, 'Why Does Financial Sector Growth Crowd Out Real Economic Growth?' BIS Working Paper no. 490, February 2015, available at http://www.bis.org/publ/work490.pdf (accessed on 21 March 2017).

[26] Stephen G. Cecchetti and Enisse Kharroubi, 'Reassessing the Impact of Finance on Growth', BIS Working Paper no. 381, July 2012, available at http://www.bis.org/publ/work381.pdf (accessed on 21 March 2017).

[27] Borio et al., 'Labour Reallocation and Productivity Dynamics'.

[28] Claudio Borio, 'The Movie Plays On: A Lens for Viewing the Global Economy', *FT Debt Capital Markets Outlook*, 10 February 2016, available at http://www.bis.org/speeches/sp160210_slides.pdf (accessed on 18 March 2017).

egged on into expanding the boundaries of monetary policy. In fact, as Figure 5.6 shows, this has been a secular trend since the mid-1980s with debt and policy rates reinforcing their respective moves in opposite directions.

**Figure 5.5 Credit booms sap productivity**

Credit booms sap productivity growth through labour reallocation1
Percentage points
0.5
0.4
0.3
0.2
0.1
0.0
Annual cost during credit boom...
... and over a five-year window post-crisis
Productivity loss due to labour reallocation2
Productivity loss due to other reasons3

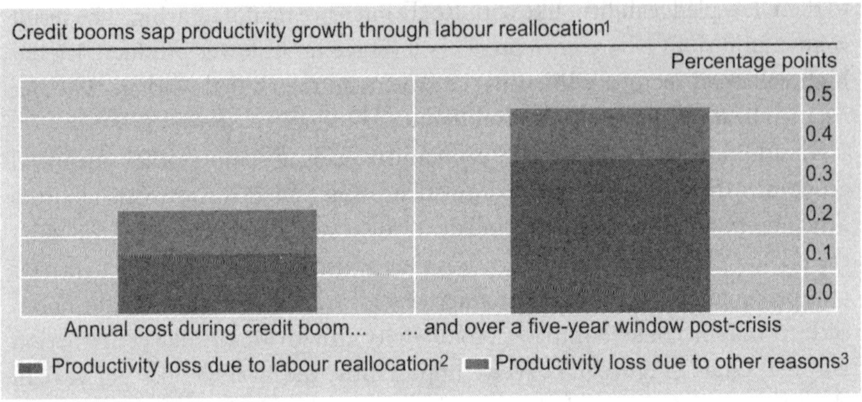

*Source*: Claudio Borio et al., 'Labour Reallocation and Productivity Dynamics: Financial Causes, Real Consequences,' BIS Working Paper no. 534, December 2015, available at http://www.bis.org/publ/work534.pdf (accessed on 18 March 2017).

**Figure 5.6 Downward debt spiral since the 1980s even as interest rates sink**

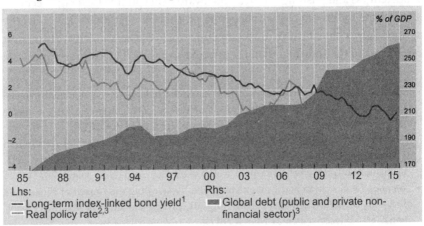

% of GDP
6
4
2
0
–2
–4
270
250
230
210
190
170
85
88
91
94
97
00
03
06
09
12
15
Lhs:
Long-term index-linked bond yield1
Real policy rate2,3
Rhs:
Global debt (public and private non-financial sector)3

*Source*: Claudio Borio, 'The Movie Plays On: A Lens for Viewing the Global Economy,' *FT Debt Capital Markets Outlook*, 10 February 2016, available at http://www.bis.org/speeches/sp160210_slides.pdf (accessed on 18 March 2017).

## 5.4 Low interest rates create scarcity of safe assets and subvert market mechanisms

Arguably, the biggest asset misallocation caused by QE has been in the market for long-term safe assets. As Avinash Persaud wrote,[29] if the last financial market crisis was triggered by unsafe and exotic assets, the next could be caused by the safest of assets. Through QE, central banks have sucked up massive volumes of sovereign bonds, estimated at over USD 5.0 trillion[30] so far. Once the ECB announced its version of QE in early January 2015, sovereign bond yields of even weaker peripheral economies, which were tethering on the verge of losing market access, dropped dramatically converging with the German Bund.

This vacuuming of safe assets has coincided with a period of increased regulatory standards, which simultaneously mandate banks to increase their holdings of safe assets, insurers to raise the risk weights associated with their more volatile assets and everyone to hold more safe and liquid collateral than earlier. The net result of this has been an unprecedented scramble for an already scarce pool of safe assets, driving their prices over the roof and inflating the great safe asset bubble. So much so that bond yields have entered negative territory and at least some banks are even forcing depositors to pay them. The liquidity problem has been strangling the corporate bond market as much as that in Treasuries.[31] As an illustration, the daily US Treasury trading volume collapsed by 70 per cent between 2007 and 2017 from 13 per cent of the market size to just 4 per cent. In the same period, investment grade corporate bonds too have suffered a 50 per cent decline in daily trading volumes.

Further, in their attempt to shift portfolio preferences and encourage risk-taking by their asset purchases, central banks have not only absorbed the collateral needed to liquefy private markets, but have also reduced the signal value of market prices for policymaking. The recent concerns about the lack of liquidity in many sovereign bond markets can be traced to central banks

---

[29] Avinash Persaud: 'The Assets Made Combustible When Regulators Call Them "Safe"', *Financial Times*, 1 June 2015, available at http://www.ft.com/intl/cms/s/0/924460dc-085c-11e5-85de-00144feabdc0.html (accessed on 18 March 2017).

[30] Ewen Cameron Watt, 'Investors on "Safe" Assets Starvation Diet', *Financial Times*, 20 May 2015, available at http://www.ft.com/intl/cms/s/0/a54d8124-f347-11e4-8141-00144feab7de.html (accessed on 18 March 2017).

[31] Robin Wigglesworth, 'Liquidity Pitfalls Threaten Parched Markets', *Financial Times*, 18 June 2015, available at http://www.ft.com/intl/cms/s/0/fac4ae4c-146d-11e5-ad6e-00144feabdc0.html (accessed on 18 March 2017).

becoming the sole market maker for bonds at all points along the yield curve in major sovereign bond markets. More importantly, this dilutes whatever market discipline that could have been exerted on policymakers. It is no secret that investors in equities had been seduced by policy puts. By capturing vast segments of bond markets, central bankers have ensured that prices in these markets too would be determined by central bank actions. Consequently, 'the information normally provided to central banks by market movements, information which ought to help in the conduct of monetary policy, will be increasingly absent'.[32] The result is excessive risk-taking, including more debt accumulation, by market participants and inappropriate monetary policy for an inordinately long period by central banks.

## 5.5　Low interest rates beget more debt

Low interest rates render borrowers insensitive to the ultimate cost of borrowing. They lull them into borrowing more. Borrowers tend to look at the interest rate and not at their overall debt servicing costs in absolute dollar terms. Hence, low interest rates encourage excessive borrowing (that is, accumulate debt) which is not only a threat to systemic stability but also drains future income of the borrowers. It is hard not to come away with the conclusion that while the Federal Reserve still appears reluctant to embrace financial stability as a legitimate and explicit goal of monetary policy, it seems to have embraced medium-term financial instability as a goal of monetary policy!

In spite of weak global economic cues and limited investment opportunities, the extraordinary and extended period of monetary accommodation has encouraged firms to undertake financial engineering and load up on debt. Sovereigns too, especially in the emerging economies, have not been far behind in splurging on debt. History is replete with examples which show that finance loses its disciplining powers when credit is sloshing around. This time has been no different.

The global stock of debt – households, non-financial corporates and governments – has surged from about USD 105 trillion to USD 145 trillion in the 2008–15 period.[33] As a share of global nominal GDP, it has risen from

---

[32] See Aimee Kaye, 'Cracks Appearing in Five Highly Leveraged Economies', 27 February 2018, available at http://blog.loomissayles.com/cracks-appearing-in-five-highly-leveraged-economies (accessed on 5 June 2018).

[33] At the time of writing this (19 March 2018), BIS data on non-financial debt is available up to the end of second quarter 2017. For all the reporting countries to this data, the

180 per cent to about 215 per cent in the same period, with the largest increase from corporates and governments in that order[34] (Figure 5.7).

**Figure 5.7  Debt rises after debt-induced crisis of 2008!**

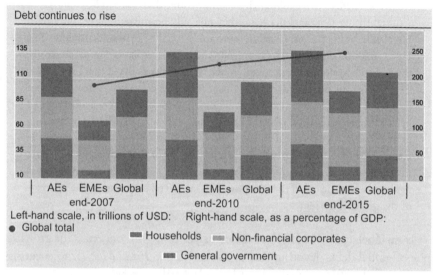

*Source:* Graph I.3, Annual Report 2016, Bank for International Settlements (BIS).

On a recent historical note, this rise has been stunning in its pace since the GFC. As the BIS data till end-2017 shows, the outstanding dollar denominated debt of non-banks in developing economies has more than doubled since end of 2009.[35] For the world as a whole the increase has been only slightly less.

That debt has increased consequent to actions taken in response to a global financial and economic crisis caused by excessive debt is a severe indictment of the intellectual and moral bankruptcy of the global policymaking elite.

---

total value of non-financial (households, non-financial businesses and governments) debt has risen to USD 168.9 trillion. As a percentage of GDP, it was 243 per cent. Readers should note that data even for earlier periods are revised as and when new data are added.

[34] Claudio Borio, 'The Movie Plays On: A Lens for Viewing the Global Economy', *FT Debt Capital Markets Outlook*, 10 February 2016, available at http://www.bis.org/speeches/sp160210_slides.pdf (accessed on 5 June 2018).

[35] 'BIS Global Liquidity Indicators at End-December 2017', BIS, 30 April 2018, available at https://www.bis.org/statistics/gli1804.htm (accessed on 5 June 2018).

Even the usually pro-establishment Martin Wolf of the FT was moved to observe thus:[36]

> The economic, financial, intellectual and political elites mostly misunderstood the consequences of headlong financial liberalisation. Lulled by fantasies of self-stabilising financial markets, they not only permitted but encouraged a huge and, for the financial sector, profitable bet on the expansion of debt. The policy-making elite failed to appreciate the incentives at work and, above all, the risks of a systemic breakdown. When it came, the fruits of that breakdown were disastrous on several dimensions: economies collapsed; unemployment jumped; and public debt exploded. The policy-making elite was discredited by its failure to prevent disaster. The financial elite was discredited by needing to be rescued. The political elite was discredited by willingness to finance the rescue. The intellectual elite – the economists – was discredited by its failure to anticipate a crisis or agree on what to do after it had struck. The rescue was necessary. But the belief that the powerful sacrificed taxpayers to the interests of the guilty is correct.

Even if belatedly, the IMF too joined in expressing its concern at the growing pile of global debt, devoting half of its April 2018 *Fiscal Monitor* to covering the issue.[37] In 2016, global debt at USD 164 trillion reached 225 per cent of GDP, with public debt alone in advanced economies reaching 105 per cent, levels not seen since World War II. A whopping 43 per cent of the increase since 2007 came from China. The irony of this cautionary note by the IMF on debt accumulation could not have been missed, for it was the same organization which contributed to the debt build-up with its insistence on the continuation of the extraordinary monetary accommodation. Recall the discussion earlier in the chapter on the Fund advising the United States to stick to monetary accommodation in 2015.

Several countries saw negative rates as a great opportunity to borrow very long. Spain, France and Belgium sold 50-year bonds in 2016. On 12 April

---

[36] Martin Wolf, 'Failing Elites Threaten Our Future', *Financial Times*, 14 January 2015, available at http://www.ft.com/intl/cms/s/0/cfc1eb1c-76d8-11e3-807e-00144feabdc0. html (accessed on 5 June 2018).

[37] IMF, 'Capitalising on Good Times', *Fiscal Monitor*, April 2018, available at https://www.imf.org/en/Publications/FM/Issues/2018/04/06/fiscal-monitor-april-2018 (accessed on 5 June 2018).

2016, France sold its 2066 bond at a 1.75 per cent coupon.[38] Investors would have to experience a very long period of deflation or low inflation for such assets to be rewarding long-term investments in delivering real returns. In fact, the average yield on the benchmark 10-year bond of the Group of Ten industrial countries had fallen precipitously from 4.3 per cent in mid-2007 to 0.5 per cent in July 2016![39]

However, as mentioned earlier, more than advanced economies, emerging economies have led the post-2008 debt binge. This should count as the most pernicious spillover of the post-crisis monetary policies in the developed world.

## 5.6 Cross-border capital flows, spillovers and instability

It would be an understatement to say that the extraordinary monetary accommodation in developed economies has affected emerging economies. In deeply integrated global financial markets, it is inevitable that monetary policy actions of the larger developed economies have external 'spillover' effects.

A large share of the flood of capital unleashed by QE, instead of stoking investment activity in their home countries, has found their way into EMs in their search for yield. This endangers their macroeconomic stability by inflating asset market bubbles and introducing foreign exchange volatility. As the taper tantrum of mid-2013 showed, external shocks can have hugely destabilizing effects on markets exposed to such capital inflows. Asset bubbles are pricked, credit freezes up, banking crisis ensues, currencies fall sharply and economies tank. No country is safe from these risks and the adverse effects vary only in degrees. While weakening currencies boost external competitiveness, as they did for all the economies that resorted to QE, they also generate resentment and threaten retaliatory responses from trading partners.

The contagion from cross-border flows operates through multiple channels. Surging inflows, apart from unleashing inflationary pressures and adversely affecting local manufacturing and other tradable, also cause exchange rate appreciation, which in turn lowers export competitiveness and generates current account imbalances. Simultaneously, in the financial markets, it

---

[38] 'Italy Plans to Follow European Trend with 50 Year Bond,' *Financial Times*, 17 May 2016, available at http://www.ft.com/intl/cms/s/0/034d6a2a-1c17-11e6-a7bc-ee846770ec15.html#axzz49gVL16hl (accessed on 5 June 2018).

[39] Felix Martin, 'There Is Life in Sovereign Bonds If You Know Where to Look', *Financial Times*, 12 July 2016, available at http://www.ft.com/cms/s/0/ef961f30-475a-11e6-8d68-72e9211e86ab.html#axzz4ECnkXv4t (accessed on 5 June 2018).

engenders resource misallocation manifested in asset bubbles and reckless corporate leveraging.

In the 2009–15 period, non-financial private debt in EM economies has climbed steeply from about 75 per cent to 125 per cent of GDP (Figure 5.8).[40] Further, by 2013, non-financial corporate debt as a share of GDP of EMs had exceeded that of advanced economies.[41]

**Figure 5.8 Non-financial private sector debt growth**

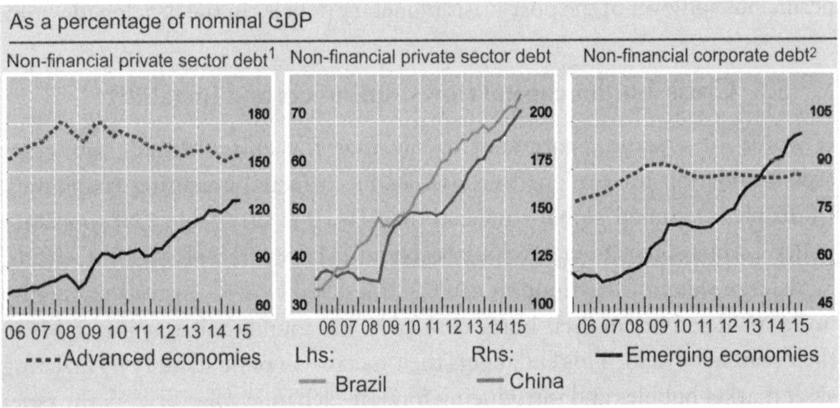

As a percentage of nominal GDP

Non-financial private sector debt[1] · Non-financial private sector debt · Non-financial corporate debt[2]

06 07 08 09 10 11 12 13 14 15

----Advanced economies    Lhs:    Rhs:    ——Emerging economies

—— Brazil    —— China

*Source*: Jaime Caruana, 'Credit, Commodities, and Currencies', Lecture at the LSE, 5 February 2016, available at http://www.bis.org/speeches/sp160205.pdf (accessed on 17 March 2017).

An examination of a sample of 280 EM companies reveals certain disturbing signs. For one, indebtedness has increased faster among the non-tradeable sector companies than tradeable sector ones (Figure 5.9). Further, the scale of bond issuance by non-financial companies has been higher among the non-tradables.[42] This raises concerns of currency mismatches and attendant vulnerabilities in case of external borrowings. More worryingly, the increased

---

[40] As of mid-2017 (latest data available at the time of writing), the ratio has gone up to 142 per cent.

[41] Jaime Caruana, 'Credit, Commodities, and Currencies', Lecture at the LSE, 5 February 2016, available at http://www.bis.org/speeches/sp160205.pdf (accessed on 17 March 2017).

[42] Michael Chui, Emese Kuruc and Philip Turner, 'A New Dimension to Currency Mismatches in the Emerging Markets: Nonfinancial Companies', BIS Working Paper no. 550, March 2016, available at http://www.bis.org/publ/work550.pdf (accessed on 17 March 2017).

leverage has coincided with declining profitability among corporates, both in EM and advanced economies.[43]

**Figure 5.9 Non-financial international bond issuances**

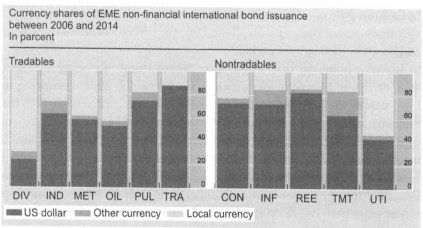

Currency shares of EME non-financial international bond issuance between 2006 and 2014
In parcent

*Source*: Michael Chui, Emese Kuruc and Philip Turner, 'A New Dimension to Currency Mismatches in the Emerging Markets: Nonfinancial Companies', BIS Working Paper no. 550, March 2016, available at http://www.bis.org/publ/work550.pdf (accessed on 17 March 2017).

The most striking manifestation of the expansion of credit risk boundaries in sovereign borrowing was the spurt in bond issuances among frontier markets.[44] After hovering in the range of USD 3–5 billion every year for much of last decade, it touched a record USD 23 billion in 2014.[45] Ivory Coast was able to borrow for 10 years at a rate of 5.63 per cent and Vietnam at 4.8 per cent. The problem now is that having already borrowed, most of these countries have no choice but to borrow again to refinance their loans as they mature. That comes at an even higher cost, thereby pushing them down the

---

[43] Jaime Caruana, 'Credit, Commodities, and Currencies', Lecture at the LSE, 5 February 2016, available at http://www.bis.org/speeches/sp160205.pdf (accessed on 17 March 2017).

[44] Belarus, Belize, Dominican Republic, Ecuador, Egypt, El Salvador, Gabon, Georgia, Ghana, Iraq, Ivory Coast, Jamaica, Jordan, Nigeria, Pakistan, Senegal, Sri Lanka and Vietnam.

[45] 'Higher Frontier Debt Yields Test Issuers,' *Financial Times*, 22 October 2015, available at http://www.ft.com/intl/cms/s/0/8c1d3206-7896-11e5-933d-efcdc3c11c89.html#axzz3qDNApC00.

slippery slope. The poor history of macroeconomic management and stability only amplifies the risks.

The initiation of QE has been followed by large-scale capital flows into EM economies. These capital flows have been motivated by search for yields by investors from developed to emerging economies. BIS economists estimated that an amount of USD 9 trillion flowed into the EM economies as bank loans and bonds in the 2009–14 period.[46]

It is also estimated that a significant proportion of private capital flows were driven by leveraged 'carry trades'. 'Carry trade' is about borrowing in low-interest rate currencies to lend or invest in high-yield currencies, with the exchange rate risk unhedged. Creditworthy firms in EM economies that are able to access cheap long-term credit abroad borrow to accumulate financial assets in domestic currency to take advantage of the interest rate differential between the domestic currency and the funding currency. One study has estimated that 23 cents out of each dollar bond issue by EM corporates in recent years have ended up on the firm's balance sheet as cash.[47] This has naturally increased the credit available in these markets.

One of the abiding lessons of cross-border capital flows is that what comes as a flood also leaves as a flood. An example of this was the so-called 'taper tantrum' of mid-2013, following the Federal Reserve Chairman Ben Bernanke's Congressional testimony on 22 May 2013, where he hinted at the possibility of tapering the Fed's USD 85 billion a month securities purchase programme. This set off strong speculation that the taper would start sometime in 2014 and led to sudden stop in capital inflows into emerging economies and reversal of capital flows, ravaging many currencies and adversely affecting economic activity.

When this tide reversal happens, the risks of over-leveraged corporate balance sheets and aggressive bank lending become evident, with devastating consequences. Sudden stop follows and capital rushes out. Interestingly, and this is important, the trigger for a reversal of capital flows can happen due to exogenous events which have little to do with the host country. This is a reflection of the deep global financial linkages and necessitated by liquidity and portfolio rebalancing among global financial market participants.

[46] 'Emerging Markets: Deeper into the Red', *Financial Times*, 6 November 2015, available at http://www.ft.com/cms/s/0/46f42c36-8965-11e5-90de-f44762bf9896.html?siteedit ion=intl#axzz4DMXOimqZ (accessed on 17 March 2017).

[47] V. Bruno and H. S. Shin, 'Global Dollar Credit and Carry Trades: A Firm-Level Analysis', BIS Working Paper no. 510, August 2015.

Unfortunately, by this time, the country's current account imbalances would have approached unsustainable levels, thereby amplifying the country risk perceptions and hastening the capital flight. De-leveraging and banking crisis invariably follow, accompanied by recession and prolonged slowdown. A decade or so is lost.

Several studies have shown that such capital flow reversals do not distinguish between economies and their adverse effects are felt universally, including by the fiscally prudent and economically stable ones. Barry Eichengreen and Poonam Gupta had this to say about the consequences[48] based on their analysis of the 'taper tantrum'-induced crisis:

> We find that emerging markets that allowed the real exchange rate to appreciate and the current account deficit to widen during the prior period of quantitative easing saw the sharpest impact. Better fundamentals (the budget deficit, the public debt, the level of reserves and the rate of economic growth) did not provide insulation. A more important determinant of the differential impact was the size of the country's financial market: countries with larger markets experienced more pressure on the exchange rate, foreign reserves and equity prices. We interpret this as investors being able to rebalance their portfolios better when the target country has a relatively large and liquid financial market.

They found that measures of policy fundamentals and economic performance – budget deficit, public debt, current account deficit, level of reserves and GDP growth rate – provided no insulation for exchange rate, reserves and stock market when the tide turned. In the light of what Eichengreen and Gupta write on countries that saw real exchange rate appreciation suffering more than others, Dani Rodrik's suggestion for emerging economies to maintain a slightly undervalued currency makes sense. However, that has its own costs. That would entail foreign exchange reserve accumulation, which, in turn, would distort domestic prices. Further, exchange rate intervention invariably leads to easier domestic credit conditions causing capital misallocation, presaging troubles in the banking system down the road. It simply shows that spillovers entail substantial economic costs for developing economies that are not easily avoided.

---

[48] See Barry Eichengreen and Poonam Gupta, 'Tapering Talk: The Impact of Expectations of Reduced Federal Reserve Security Purchases on Emerging Markets', 12 December 2013, available at http://eml.berkeley.edu/~eichengr/tapering_talk_12-16-13.pdf (accessed on 17 March 2017).

From a policy perspective, these spillovers significantly shrink the policy space for other countries, especially the emerging economies. A BIS paper found significant monetary policy spillovers.[49] A 100 basis point change in US interest rates, depending on the chosen interest rate and specification, is associated with a 26–59 basis point change on average in the respective rate elsewhere (Figure 5.10). In the end-2007 to end-2014 period, US policy and short-term rates fell by 440 and 480 basis points, respectively, which had a major impact on rates across the world. As Figure 5.10 shows, their short-term and policy rates declined by 280 and 290 basis points, respectively, of which the US changes contributed 160 and 200 basis points, respectively, suggesting 'broad spillover effects' of US monetary policy actions.

**Figure 5.10  Spillover effects of US interest rate changes**

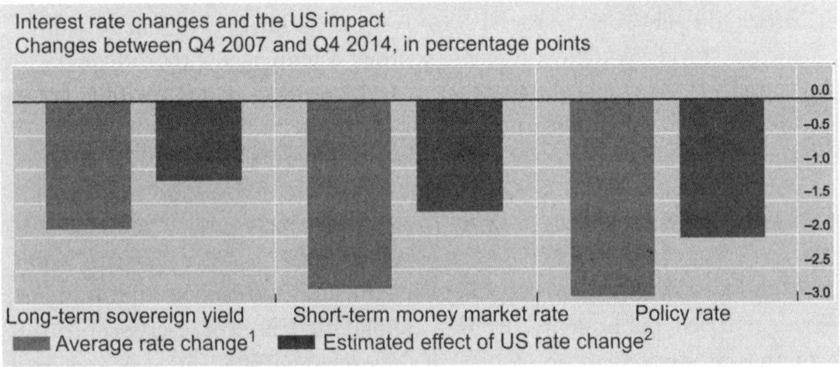

Interest rate changes and the US impact
Changes between Q4 2007 and Q4 2014, in percentage points

Long-term sovereign yield    Short-term money market rate    Policy rate
■■■ Average rate change[1]    ■■■ Estimated effect of US rate change[2]

*Source*: Boris Hofmann and Előd Takáts, 'International Monetary Spillovers', *BIS Quarterly Review*, 13 September 2015 available at http://www.bis.org/publ/qtrpdf/r_qt1509i.htm (accessed on 17 March 2017).

Stephen G. Cecchetti and co-authors find similar spillover effects. In fact, they find that the impact of monetary easing in the US is much larger, nearly four times bigger (Figure 5.11), than a country's own monetary easing.[50]

---

[49] Boris Hofmann and Előd Takáts, 'International Monetary Spillovers', *BIS Quarterly Review*, 13 September 2015, available at http://www.bis.org/publ/qtrpdf/r_qt1509i. htm (accessed on 17 March 2017).

[50] Stephen G. Cecchetti, 'On Spillovers and Policy Co-ordination', Presentation, Brandeis Business School, available at http://www.mas.gov.sg/~/media/MAS/Monetary%20 Policy%20and%20Economics/AMPF/2016/profcecchetti_load.pdf (accessed on 17 March 2017).

**Figure 5.11 US monetary policy effects trump domestic policy effects**

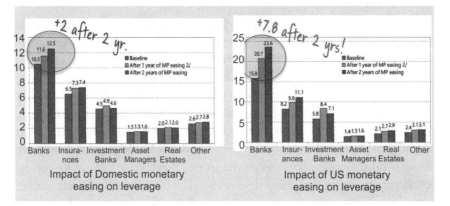

*Source*: Stephen G. Cecchetti, 'On Spillovers and Policy Co-ordination', Presentation, Brandeis Business School, available at http://abfer.org/docs/2016/prof-cecchetti.pdf (accessed on 17 March 2017).

Echoing the discussion in Section 2.5, they attribute the outsized impact to the massive size of the Global Dollar system that operates outside the US, which is possibly larger that the liabilities of banks operating within the US. Since it dominates the currency, trade and broader global financial transactions, it is unsurprising that any change in US monetary policy affects all the dollar-related financial intermediaries.

In another paper, BIS economists Peter Hordahl, Jhuvesh Sobrun and Philip Turner find that contrary to conventional wisdom, the spillovers are most pronounced from changes in the US long-term interest Treasuries than the short-term federal funds rate.[51] From a sample of 6 developed and 12 developing economies, for the 2005–16 period, on average they find that a 100 basis points rise in US 10-year Treasury Bond yields is associated with a 79 basis points rise in the yields in developed economies and 69 basis points rise in EM yields. This correlation has been increasing in recent years.

They also find that 'central banks in small economies have only a very limited ability to influence the long-term interest rate in their own currencies'. In other words, taken together, the monetary policy autonomy of small open economies has been progressively declining. They not only have less ability

---

[51] Peter Hordahl, Jhuvesh Sobrun, and Philip Turner, 'Low Long Term Interest Rates as a Global Phenomenon,' BIS Working Paper No 574, August 2016, http://www.bis.org/publ/work574.pdf (accessed on 17 March 2017).

to influence their own interest rates but their long-term interest rates are also vulnerable to shifts in US long-term yields.

Another paper by Robin Koepke of the Institute of International Finance (IIF) examined the impact of changes in US monetary policy in 27 emerging economies, specifically in terms of currency and banking crises and sovereign defaults.[52] The paper studied 154 such crises over the 1973–2014 period and claimed that 'US monetary policy is often just as important as domestic factors in explaining the incidence of EM crises, if not more important'. In other words, US monetary policy is not just a trigger, but one of the underlying factors that amplify EM vulnerabilities. More specifically, it finds that the 'probability of crises is substantially higher when the federal funds rate is above its natural level (stance), during Fed policy tightening cycles (direction), and when market participants are surprised by signals that the Fed will tighten policy faster than previously expected (surprise)'.

These adverse consequences, specifically the collateral damage that it inflicted on emerging economies, persuaded Raghuram Rajan, former governor of the RBI, to caution against excessive pursuit of QE, beyond repairing markets. He claimed, 'Spillovers from such policies were fuelling currency and asset-price volatility in both the home economy and emerging countries', thereby causing 'unintended collateral damage'.[53] He also argued that if developed economies resorted to unrestrained QE, unmindful of its consequences on emerging countries, it would become legitimate for the latter's central banks to follow 'quantitative external easing' where they would hold down their currencies to build up foreign exchange reserves as well as not lose their external competitiveness. Competitive QE would be just as legitimate, or illegitimate, as competitive currency devaluations.

Fundamentally, QE is currency devaluation by stealth, different from direct foreign exchange market interventions of central banks only in degree. QE in the US led to depreciation of dollar between 2009 and 2011, and much the same has happened to the Yen and Euro as Bank of Japan and European

---

[52] Robin Koepke, 'Determinants of Emerging Market Crises: the Role of US Monetary Policy', Institute for International Finance Working Paper, 26 July 2016.

[53] Raghuram Rajan, 'Containing Competitive Monetary Easing', *Project Syndicate*, 28 April 2014, available at http://www.project-syndicate.org/commentary/raghuram-rajan-calls-for-monetary-policy-coordination-among-major-central-banks (accessed on 4 June 2017).

Central Bank (ECB) initiated their respective QE programmes.[54] Underlining the thin line between QE and currency manipulation, in just a few months of initiation of the QE by the ECB, the Euro fell sharply from under USD 1.40 to USD 1.10, an over one-fifth decline. America got a taste of its own medicine.

The charge of currency manipulation is compelling in the light of the 'exorbitant privilege' enjoyed by the US due to the dollar's dominant role as the global reserve currency. It gives the US a carte blanche to run up deficits without suffering any of the attendant costs. It encourages (or at least contributes to) other countries (say, China) to consume less and run up large surpluses, makes them park their savings in low-yield US assets, amplifies the risks arising from cross-border capital flows, and so on. More disconcertingly, irrespective of its economic fundamentals, it privileges America to print money and borrow very cheap, more than any other country, and at the cost of the savers in other countries.

Conventional wisdom on capital flows has been that prudent and stable macroeconomic management, flexible exchange rates and open capital account provide ample cushions against vulnerabilities engendered by cross-border capital flows and exogenous shocks. However, as a mounting array of empirical evidence shows, no country is safe from the forces unleashed by capital flood, sudden stops and capital flight. As credit becomes plentiful, finance loses its traditional disciplining powers. Economic agents indulge in greedy lending and reckless borrowing, thereby fuelling asset bubbles. When the tide turns, markets respond by over-reacting, causing asset prices to fall and exchange rates to collapse far more dramatically than they should. This over-shooting is the natural response of cognitively biased human agents who populate the markets.

In the Andrew Crockett Memorial Lecture that he delivered in June 2013, Raghuram Rajan said, 'In a world integrated by massive capital flows, monetary policy in large countries serves as a common accelerator pedal for the globe'.[55] Finally, spillovers have consequent spillbacks that hurt the developed economy. But even without this self-interest, the dominance of the dollar means that the Federal Reserve has an obligation to limit the resultant instability and also ensure stable dollar intermediation.

---

[54] Jeffrey Frankel, 'The Chimera of Currency Manipulation', *Project Syndicate*, 10 June 2015, available at http://www.project-syndicate.org/commentary/trade-negotiations-currency-manipulation-by-jeffrey-frankel-2015-06 (accessed on 8 June 2018).

[55] Raghuram Rajan, 'A Step in the Dark: Unconventional Monetary Policy after the Crisis', First Andrew Crockett Memorial Lecture, 23 June 2013, available at https://www.bis.org/events/agm2013/sp130623.htm (accessed on 8 June 2018).

It is with a mix of sadness and, admittedly, some pride that we draw attention to the fact that one of us anticipated this as early as in 1998, purely based on the personal experience of working for a Swiss private bank and observing as an insider–outsider the world of investment banking, the incentives in that world that facilitated gains for its inhabitants and costs for all others, particularly in developing countries which were innocent to the ways of investment banking 20 years ago (see Box 5.2).

---

**Box 5.2  LETTERS TO THE EDITOR:**
**Too high a price paid in financial crises**

Financial Times; Jun 15, 1998

From Mr. V. Anantha-Nageswaran.

Sir, Your leader, "The banks in east Asia" (June 10), in the wake of the Bank of International Settlements annual report, on the role of banks in international financial crises has not come a day too soon. The blame for the "vigorous" lending activity that sows the seeds of an eventual blow-out should, of course, be apportioned between home-country borrowers, regulators and international lenders. However, the risk-return distribution in this game is painfully skewed. The home country pays for its sins with asset price erosion and economic contraction. But international lenders get away virtually scot-free.

The problem lies not just with multilateral agencies' bail-out. Anomalous incentive systems that banks adopt also play an equally important role.

The world of investment banking is glamorous – a jet-set luxurious life, a high media profile and vulgarly high levels of incentives linked to business creation and income generation. Loss prevention is barely recognised. It is therefore no surprise that risk considerations play little or no part in an investment bank's priorities. When economists get paid by the sales force, research can comes up short on objectivity sometimes.

Actually, banks' commercial credit departments can benefit from in-house research that supports asset acquisitions (known in the industry as buy-side research) and hence pays more attention to risk issues. Unfortunately, this is being de-emphasised in the squeeze on margins that is generated by intense competition.

If these are not reversed, it could have serious repercussions for the world economy. The impoverishment of developing countries that have made considerable progress on catching up with western standards of living, and its implicit income and wealth redistribution effects in favour of the west could set back, by decades, attempts to create globally open financial and trade systems. Furthermore, social disruptions caused by large-scale immigration and security risks from disgruntled youths of the developing world would inevitably follow. Indifference to the broad social picture would eventually negate attempts to maximise shareholder wealth.

V. Anantha-Nageswaran, General Wille Strasse 46, Feldmeilen, 8706 Switzerland

The letter to *Financial Times* in the box above was in the context of the ongoing Asian crisis then. The letter warned of widening inequality between nations as a result of the sudden starts and stops in the flow of international capital in which all the downside is borne by borrowers with creditors bailed out. More often than not, the bailout of the borrower is nothing but a disguised bailout of the creditor institutions – banks and others. There is much resistance and public consternation towards bailing out delinquent and profligate borrowers. But the truth is that it takes two to arrange finance and to ignore the embedded risks in the transaction. In order to assuage the public outcry, bailouts come attached with humiliating conditions that impinge on the sovereign rights of nations to pursue economic policies at a pace and sequence suited to their history and context, prompting the conservative economist Martin Feldstein to write in *Foreign Affairs* (March/April 1998) that IMF, as a creditor, had no business dictating economic policies to sovereign nations. It was particularly galling for South Korea to accept humiliating conditions in return for IMF assistance in 1998 for it had just been admitted to the OECD, the club of rich nations, in 1997.

The setting up of the Independent Evaluation Office (IEO) at the Fund was a fallout of the severe backlash to the Fund's conditionalities imposed on Asian nations in 1997–98. Developed nations skipped the economic orthodoxy that the Fund mandated to Asian nations when they were faced with their own crisis in 2008. They cut rates, boosted fiscal spending and flooded the economy with liquidity – all of which were denied to countries in Asia during the crisis of 1997–98. Of course, hindsight is 20/20; Asian countries had dollar borrowings and hence the haemorrhaging of their currencies had to be stopped whereas developed nations borrow in their own currencies which makes it easier for them to print and repay their creditors! Nonetheless, the fact remains that the policy prescriptions of the Fund worsened the economic fallout.

The collapse of the GDP in dollar terms in several crisis-affected Asian nations was of a shockingly high magnitude (Figure 5.12).

**Figure 5.12  The impact of Asian currency crisis**

| Currency | Exchange rate (per US$1) | | | Currency | GNP (US$ 1 billion) | | |
|---|---|---|---|---|---|---|---|
| | June 1997 | June 1998 | Change | | June 1997 | June 1998 | Change |
| Thai baht | 24.5 | 41 | ▼ 40.2% | Thailand | 170 | 102 | ▼ 40.2% |
| Indonesian rupiah | 2.380 | 14,150 | ▼ 83.2% | Indonesia | 205 | 34 | ▼ 83.4% |
| Philippine Peso | 26.3 | 42 | ▼ 37.4% | Philippines | 75 | 47 | ▼ 37.3% |
| Malaysian ringgit | 2.48 | 4.88 | ▼ 45.0% | Malaysia | 90 | 55 | ▼ 38.9% |
| South Korean won | 850 | 1,290 | ▼ 34.1% | South Korea | 430 | 283 | ▼ 34.2% |

*Source*: https://en.wikipedia.org/wiki/1997_Asian_financial_crisis.

Further, such debt crises served as a useful pretext for opening markets and finding opportunities for investors in developed countries to snap up assets in debtor nations at distressed prices. That is how inequality between nations widens and nations at the top of the food chain maintain their affluent status and rankings. The Asian crisis of 1997–98 set nations back considerably as did the crisis of 2008 prompting the World Bank to write in 2015 that convergence (between nations) was derailed.

By the time the crisis in Greece rolled in at the end of the first decade of the new millennium in 2010, the lessons of the Asian crisis had been forgotten. Greece, the debtor sovereign was seemingly bailed out to bail out the financial institutions in creditor nations. The International Monetary Fund picked up the courage eventually to break with the European Commission and the ECB (they constituted the 'troika') and to recommend a cancellation of some of Greece's debt. But the other two would have none of it and managed to thrust down the throat of a young and inexperienced Alexis Tsipras, the Greek prime minister, both the loan and the conditions attached to them in 2015, despite the Greek people voting in a referendum that they would rather be ejected out of the Eurozone than to accept humiliating conditions in the name of a bailout.

In the process, they claimed the scalp of Yanis Varoufakis, the Greek finance minister, who resisted it. He remained the finance minister of Greece precisely for 151 days. He predicted that the bailout would worsen economic conditions in Greece and would further alienate public in other European nations from the European project. He was prophetic.[56] In 2018, Italians voted to power parties that rejected the European single currency and the economic policies, dear to Germany, championed by the European Commission.

In good times, capital flows across borders freely and copiously. Financial institutions help arrange them in ways that may conform to the letter but not the spirit of law and conventions. But when things turn for the worse for borrowing nations, the pain falls disproportionately on them. Unless nations resist the shortcut of debt to goose economic growth in good times, this cycle will keep repeating and with each cycle, growth potential will keep diminishing and bulk of the citizens will face income and wealth squeeze.

Reforms to the architecture of the international monetary system and monetary policy frameworks in the US and Europe would substantially attenuate the effects of spillovers on vulnerable economies in the developing world. In a speech[57] in New York in May 2015, Raghuram Rajan called for new international rules of the game, stronger well-capitalized multilateral institutions with widespread legitimacy, some of which can provide patient capital and others that can monitor new rules of the game. He also called for better international safety nets. These measures are as important as they are difficult to achieve. Who has the incentive and the vision to initiate them?

Let us recall that the Bretton Woods conference followed the devastating Great Depression of the 1930s and the destruction of World War II. Arranging catastrophes of such magnitude such that a reform of the international monetary regime will be undertaken is neither our preference nor within our ability. We will limit ourselves to appealing to human reason much as it might be both naïve and in vain, most of the time. We offer our proposals – some of them have been in public domain already – in Chapter 6.

Before that, we have to deal with the two most important spillovers – ultimate consequences – of the post-crisis policy framework – diminished growth prospects around the world and widening inequality. That should not surprise us. They are inevitable in a world of resource misallocation, diminished productivity growth and asset price bubbles powered by debt.

---

[56] We cannot recommend Yanis Varoufakis' 'Global Minotaur' and 'Adults in the Room' strongly enough.

[57] Raghuram Rajan, 'Going Bust for Growth', Remarks to the Economic Club of New York, available at https://www.rbi.org.in/Scripts/BS_SpeechesView.aspx?Id=957#F8 (accessed on 8 June 2018).

## 5.7  Low interest rates diminished growth prospects

From around April 2016, global economic growth apparently turned the corner. The International Monetary Fund had projected a growth rate of 3.1 per cent for the world economy. It is estimated to have grown at a rate of 3.2 per cent. Similarly, in January 2016, the expectation for 2017 world growth was 3.6 per cent. Now, it is estimated that the world economy had grown at 3.7 per cent in 2017. In January 2018, IMF had boldly projected a growth rate of 3.9 per cent each for 2018 and 2019. To be sure, IMF had upgraded its global growth assessment in April 2007 for 2007 and 2008, months before the cookie crumbled. The Federal Reserve Bank of Atlanta has a 'nowcast' model for real economic growth in the current quarter in the United States. In late January, growth estimate for the first quarter was 5.0 per cent (annualized growth rates). As of 16 March 2018, it had declined to 1.8 per cent. Economies are no longer able to sustain high growth rates for long. Even the global economic growth 'turnaround' in 2016 and 2017 owes (pun intended) a lot to China's recourse to its traditional medicine of pumping credit.

Further, the optimistic growth projections of the Fund assume 'business as usual' in asset markets which are overvalued, across the world. Notwithstanding how things turn out in the short term, average economic growth around the world had seen its best days. Developing economies that have a lot of catching up to do have been struggling to maintain their growth rates, despite (or because of) record rise in debt.

Global economic growth witnessed in the twentieth century (especially in the second half) and in the first decade of the twenty-first century has been more anomalous than normal. Just the growth in the first decade of the new millennium is estimated to have exceeded the growth in the preceding nineteen centuries.[58] One may argue that there may be errors in growth calculations for the past and even the present, especially as the calculation of growth rates over periods of changing consumption baskets is not a trivial issue and the subject of much debate among statisticians. However, the sheer enormity of the difference is such that it clearly outweighs such measurement issues. It is clear that growth has been running at extraordinarily high levels. This surely must have consequences and not all of them will be pleasant, to put it mildly. The assumption that characterizes the UMP post-GFC – that more finance will lead to more growth – may thus run into this constraint.

---

[58] See http://www.economist.com/blogs/graphicdetail/2012/06/mis-charting-economic-history.

While it is human nature to extrapolate the most recent trend into the future, the course of history often runs differently and things are often more circular than linear. Mean reversion may be more valid and relevant than linear extrapolation. The higher growth rates of the last few decades may have been an extraction 'from the world for the world', using finance. The global crisis of 2008 is a reminder of the folly of attempting to push the growth frontier through the relentless use of debt, facilitated by the unrestrained creation of money. Even if they produce a temporary growth spurt above the sustainable level, it may be brought back to trend by a crisis. Much of the growth, witnessed before the crisis, will turn out to have been a chimera. Indeed, lower growth will not only be inevitable but may also be desirable. In that sense, the 2008 global economic, financial and banking crisis was one down payment. The response to the crisis – restoring growth through zero interest rates and more debt – means that more bills for the artificially induced growth spurt will become due in future. Those who do not learn life's lessons are condemned to repeat them.

In his book *The End of Alchemy*, Mervyn King, the former governor of the Bank of England whose tenure straddled the years before and after the crisis of 2008, echoes our argument above:

> The case for pessimism concerns prospective demand growth. In the wake of a powerful shock to confidence, monetary and fiscal stimulus in 2008 and 2009 was the right answer. But, it exhibits diminishing returns. In recent years, extraordinary monetary stimulus has brought forward consumption from the future, digging a hole in future demand.[59]

If insanity was about expecting different results for doing the same thing over and over, policymakers are very much guilty of insanity. Debt-funded recovery efforts will meet with the same fate as the debt-fuelled expansion that preceded it. Debt borrows economic growth from the future and consequently lowers its prospects. It does so by promoting malinvestment, which diminishes potential growth rates. The decline in America's potential growth rate in the new millennium is, perhaps, because of and not despite the unusually accommodative monetary policy that it has maintained in this period.

We could not have put it better than William White:[60]

---

[59] Mervyn King, *The End of Alchemy: Money, Banking and the Future of the Global Economy* (UK: Little, Brown Book Group, 2016), Kindle edition.

[60] White, 'Ultra-Easy Monetary Policy and the Law of Unintended Consequences'.

By mitigating the purging of malinvestments in successive cycles, monetary easing thus raised the likelihood of an eventual downturn that would be much more severe than a normal one. Moreover, the bursting of each of these successive bubbles led to an ever more aggressive monetary policy response. In short, monetary policy has itself, over time, generated the set of circumstances in which aggressive monetary easing would be both more needed and also less effective.

He is right that the monetary policy stances of advanced nations have become self-reinforcing as each successive round of rate cuts aims to revive growth but by stimulating unproductive borrowing, it is only bringing growth forward at the expense of the future. In his book cited earlier, Mervyn King summed up the fallacy of the post–2008 monetary policy aptly:

> Monetary stimulus via low interest rates works largely by giving incentives to bring forward spending from the future to the present. But, this is a short-term effect. After a time, tomorrow becomes today. Then we have to repeat the exercise and bring forward spending from the new tomorrow to the new today. As time passes, we will be digging larger and larger holes in future demand. The result is a self-reinforcing path of weak growth in the global economy.

Indeed, the perfect analogy for this is that of a dog chasing its own tail. As growth slows, interest rates are cut and that induces more borrowing and as debt loads become large, interest rates cannot raise much further. Low rates beget lower interest rates and after a while, debt ceases to stimulate because there is already a mountain of it that needs to be serviced. So, in turn, low growth begets low growth. Stagnant growth and rising debt reinforce each other. Central banks have brought the world economy to this pass and no one has the courage to risk personal reputation and future to break the vicious grip of debt on the global economy and the spell that low interest rates have cast on monetary policy framework in many advanced nations. Sustainable economic growth requires that the world economy be weaned off its addiction to debt. That will be painful in the short term but no addiction withdrawal has been achieved painlessly. Without that, there is no redemption.

In short, there are limits to monetary policy and there are limits to economic growth too. Recognition of both the limits is the beginning of sensible monetary policy and sustainable economic growth. We are far from both.

**Box 5.3  Secular Stagnation Is a Matter of Time**

We could do worse than reflecting on the responses of Dennis Meadows, author of the book *Limits to Growth* published in 1970, to a couple of questions in an interview with *Format*:[1]

*FORMAT: Could a major technological development to save the earth?*

*Meadows: Yes. [But] Technologies need laws, sales, training, people who work with them – see my above statement. Moreover, technology is just a tool like a hammer or a neoliberal financial system. As long as our values are what they are, we will [try to] develop technologies that meet them.*

*FORMAT: All the world currently sees salvation in a sustainable green technology.*

*Meadows: This is a fantasy. Even if we manage to increase the efficiency of energy use dramatically, use of renewable energies much more, and painful sacrifices to limit our consumption, we have virtually no chance to prolong the life of the current system. Oil production will be reduced approximately by half in the next 20 years, even with the exploitation of oil sands or shale oil. It just happens too fast. Apart from that, you can earn more than non-oil with alternative energy. And wind turbines can be operated, with no planes.* **The World Bank director (most recently responsible for the global airline industry) has explained to me, the problem of peak oil is not discussed in his institution, it is simply taboo. Whoever will try to anyway is fired or transferred. After all, Peak Oil destroys the belief in growth. You would have to change everything.** (Emphasis ours)

*FORMAT: Do you have solutions to these mega miseries?*

*Meadows: This would change the nature of man. We are basically now just as programmed as 10,000 years ago. If one of our ancestors could be attacked by a tiger, he also was not worried about the future, but his present survival. My concern is that for genetic reasons we are just not able to deal with such things as long-term climate change. As long as we do not learn that, there is no way to solve all these problems.*

As long as our values are what they are, technological advancements are not going to be answers to problems but would turn out to be ones that compound our problems in ways that we would never know or comprehend.

The great biologist E. O. Wilson once observed:[2]

'*The real problem of humanity is the following: we have paleolithic emotions; medieval institutions; and god-like technology. And it is terrifically dangerous, and it is now approaching a point of crisis overall.*'

Our brains have, more or less, stopped evolving after the Stone Age, and most of its instincts were honed in the days when we were just hunter-gatherers. Life expectancy was short. Danger lurked around every corner. Resources were in short supply or had not been discovered. Hence, skills that provided for the day and that helped the species ward off attacks and survive were most needed. If rats and pigeons knew what a stock market is, they might be better investors than human beings because they seem to be able to stick within the limits of their ability to identify patterns, giving them a natural humility in the face of random events.[3]

[1] Dennis Meadows, 'There Is Nothing That We Can Do', 31 March 2013, available at https://damnthematrix.wordpress.com/2013/03/31/there-is-nothing-we-can-do-meadows/ (accessed on 8 June 2018).

[2] Tim Price, 'The Only Thing We Have to Fear...', 22 June 2015, available at http://thepriceofeverything.typepad.com/the_price_of_everything/2015/06/the-only-thing-we-have-to-fear.html (accessed on 8 June 2018).

[3] V. Anantha Nageswaran, 'In Short, We Are Doomed', *Livemint*, 4 May 2009, available at http://www.livemint.com/Opinion/IpYc4wjhL4Q8e2DofESKGO/In-short-we-are-doomed.html) (accessed on 8 June 2018). The quote has been slightly paraphrased from Jason Zweig's *Your Money and Your Brain: How the New Science of Neuroeconomics Can Help Make You Rich* (Simon & Schuster, 2008).

## 5.8 Low interest rates drive widening inquality

Apart from its indirect contribution to inequality through facilitating the rise of finance, does monetary policy contribute directly to inequality? This question has acquired some salience in light of the divergence between buoyant asset markets and sluggish real economies in the advanced world, post-2008. Our view is that the inequality consequence UMP is an extension of the role it has been playing already in reducing labour surplus and augmenting capital surplus. Given the extraordinary persistence and pervasiveness of the practice of UMP across the developed world and its dramatic effect on asset markets in contrast to its faint impact on the real economies, probably and hopefully, the impact of UMP on inequality is climatic and final.

We explore two channels of UMP contributing to widening inequality. The first by way of penalizing savers and the second by way of resource misallocation towards equity markets which predominantly benefits a small proportion of the richest.

Discussion on the role played by UMP in fomenting income and wealth inequality has begun only lately.[61] Arguably, the biggest losers from the persistent low rates have been savers, the vast majority of citizens who rely

---

[61] See, for example, Makoto Nakajima, 'The Redistributive Consequences of Monetary Policy', *Business Review*, Federal Reserve Bank of Philadelphia, 2nd Quarter, 2015 and Grégory Claeys et al., 'The Effects of Ultra-Loose Monetary Policies on Inequality', *Bruegel Policy Contribution*, Issue 2015/09, June 2015.

largely on fixed income assets invested through their retirement accounts. A world with low yields for the foreseeable future compounds the problems for pension funds across the world. In recent years, the dynamics of demographics – rising share of aging populations – has already been exerting pressure on these pension funds, many of which are grappling with massive underfunded liabilities. They now have to not only earn sufficient returns from their assets, but also make incremental returns to bridge their deficits. But the low-return environment leaves them without enough to meet even the first objective. The Hoover Institution, a Stanford University think tank, estimates the underfunded US public pension liabilities to be USD 3.85 trillion.[62]

Danielle DiMartino Booth, former advisor to Richard Fisher, the president of the Federal Reserve Bank of Dallas, presents clinching evidence on the culpability of monetary policy in the pension underfunding crisis in her article written for Bloomberg in March 2017 (Figure 5.13). Debt of state and local pension funds (liabilities) has soared since 2007. It is no accident. That is when the Federal Reserve slashed interest rates. It brought the policy rate down to zero in 2008. That explains the big leap in the liabilities of US state and local pensions.

**Figure 5.13 Monetary policy and pension liabilities – a direct link**

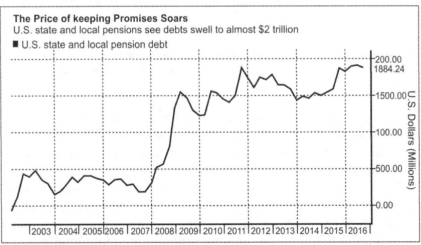

*Source*: Danielle DiMartino Booth, 'Pension Crisis Too Big for Markets to Ignore', *Bloomberg*, 24 March 2017, available at https://www.bloomberg.com/view/articles/2017-03-24/pension-crisis-too-big-for-markets-to-ignore (accessed on 4 June 2017).

---

[62] 'US Faces Crisis as Pension Funding Hole Hits $3.85 tn', *Financial Times*, 15 May 2017, available at https://www.ft.com/content/f2891b34-3705-11e7-99bd-13beb0903fa3 (accessed on 4 June 2017).

If they discount their liabilities at a more realistic rate – the rate of return on their investments – their unfunded liabilities would be much higher than what they report. Only one state, Kentucky, had shown the courage to map out the underfunding of pension plans in different scenarios (Figure 5.14). In all monetary policy calculus, post-crisis, the pension funding crisis never figures.

**Figure 5.14  Pension underfunding in Kentucky – four dire scenarios**

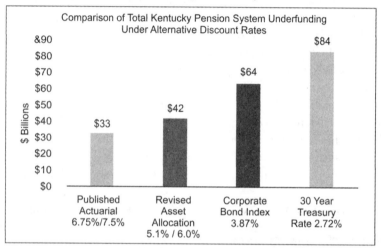

*Source*: Commonwealth of Kentucky Pension Performance and Best Practices Analysis Interim Report #2, Historical and Current Assessment: Summary Presentation to the Public Pension Oversight Board, 22 May 2017, available at https://goo.gl/qtavbk (accessed on 4 June 2017).

The consequence of low returns on their savings is that these people will now have to cut back on their consumption to save at least enough to maintain the same level of post-retirement income. Its impact on economic growth cannot be salutary.

The second channel is through the encouragement for speculation in assets and malinvestment rather than capital formation that UMP had contributed to widening wealth inequality. Further, their indirect encouragement to financial engineering and executive compensation widens income inequality.[63]

---

[63] It is instructive to listen to Stanley Druckenmiller, legendary hedge fund manager and a billionaire, talk about the Federal Reserve making it easy for the rich to become richer with its policies. Robert Frank, 'Druckenmiller: Fed Robbing Poor to Pay Rich, *CNBC*, 19 September 2013, available at http://www.cnbc.com/id/101046937 (accessed on 4 June 2017).

Monetary policy in recent years has boosted stock buybacks by companies through issuance of debt. That is financial engineering. Companies borrow cheaply, thanks to UMP, and use the proceeds to buy back stock. As stock prices rise, executives, whose compensation is tied to stock prices, benefit. Although the precise quantification of the impact of this on income inequality is impossible, clearly, stock buyback has played a bigger role in supporting stock markets post-2008. Consequently, it has boosted the incomes of the top 1 per cent of the labour force.

Separately, the Bank of England had acknowledged in a paper published in 2012[64] that its asset purchases, post-2008, had disproportionately favoured the wealthy. Between 2009 and 2012, the Bank of England bought GBP 325 billion of assets translating into a wealth effect of GBP 600 billion, based on financial market reaction (higher prices of corporate bonds, gilts and stocks). These wealth effects accrue, naturally, only to those who hold financial assets. The paper noted based on a survey cited that close to 80 per cent of the financial assets were held by those above the age of 45 and that the median household only had an average of only GBP 1,500 of gross assets. Further, the top 5 per cent of the households held an average of GBP 175,000 of gross assets or around 40 per cent of the financial assets of the household sector as a whole (Figure 5.15). So, it does not need a Sherlock Holmes to figure out the beneficiaries of asset prices and UMP, in general, and the magnitude of benefits that have accrued to them. In contrast, vast majority of the households held deposit rates and they would have been hurt by the lower rates. In other words, the Bank's asset purchases favoured a few and hurt many.

Bank of England's confessions did not stop with this. It went further. A Centre for Economic Policy Research (CEPR) discussion paper published in October 2015[65] showed that the Bank of England's QE programme did not create a bank lending channel because the QE programme gave rise to 'flighty deposits' – deposits held by other finance corporations. They are subject to frequent withdrawals. Indirectly, it confirms that the QE programme aimed to operate through the asset price channel rather than through the bank lending channel. That begs the question of whether stimulus is more effective and better for the households if it is through real economic activity than through

---

[64] See 'The Distributional Effects of Asset Purchases', Bank of England, July 2012, available at http://www.bankofengland.co.uk/publications/Documents/news/2012/ nr073.pdf (accessed on 4 June 2017).

[65] Nick Butt et al., 'QE and the Bank Lending Channel in the United Kingdom', Discussion Paper no. 10875, Centre for Economic Policy Research, October 2015.

asset prices. The latter relies on the assumption that asset price gains diffuse to real output and employment. Further, there is the risk that asset price gains only accrue to those who own assets.

**Figure 5.15  Distribution of household assets in the UK**

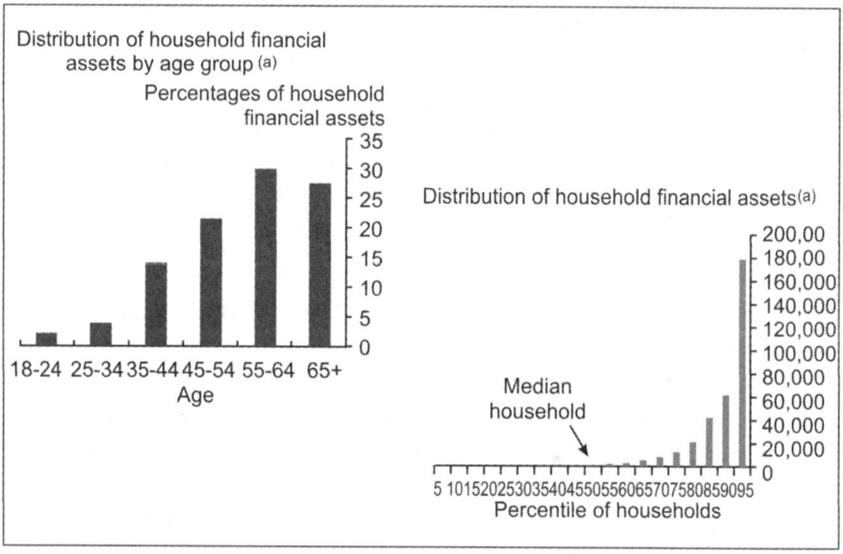

*Source*: 'The Distributional Effects of Asset Purchases', Bank of England, July 2012, available at http://www.bankofengland.co.uk/publications/Documents/news/2012/nr073. pdf (accessed on 4 June 2017).

A BIS paper finds that wealth inequality has risen in advanced economies since the GFC. It finds that rising equity prices have been the 'key driver of inequality'.[66] A recent OECD policy note finds that financial expansion fuels greater income inequality.[67] Underlining the skewed nature of its effect, a 10 per cent of GDP expansion of financial sector credit has a positive effect on incomes of only the top decile of households (Figure 5.16).

---

[66] Dietrich Domanski, Michela Scatigna and Anna Zabai, 'Wealth Inequality and Monetary Policy', *BIS Quarterly Review*, March 2016.

[67] OECD, 'How to Restore a Healthy Financial Sector That Supports Long-Lasting, Inclusive Growth?', OECD Economics Department Policy Notes, no. 27, June 2015, available at http://www.oecd.org/eco/How-to-restore-a-healthy-financial-sector-that-supports-long-lasting-inclusive-growth.pdf (accessed on 4 June 2017).

**Figure 5.16 Impact of financial sector growth on household incomes**

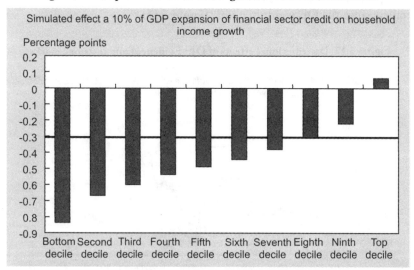

*Source:* 'How to Restore a Healthy Financial Sector That Supports Long-Lasting, Inclusive Growth?' OECD Economics Department Policy Notes, no. 27, June 2015, available at http://www.oecd.org/eco/How-to-restore-a-healthy-financial-sector-that-supports-long-lasting-inclusive-growth.pdf (accessed on 4 June 2017).

*Note:* Household income growth is household disposable income growth per capita. The horizontal line indicates the change in household income growth for the economy as a whole.

The channels of inequality transmission are clear. Businesses have preferred to return the accumulated surpluses to shareholders as dividends, rather than make capital investments. In fact, the largest US companies have capitalized on the low rates to borrow heavily to even finance share buybacks. The net result has been a boom in the equity market, which is dominated by a very small minority.[68] In fact, in 2010, the top 1 per cent wealthiest Americans owned 35 per cent of the stock market, and the bottom 80 per cent owned just 8.4 per cent.[69] A fascinating anecdotal evidence, one that reflects this redistributional

---

[68] Kevin Warsh and Stanley Druckenmiller, 'The Asset-Rich, Income-Poor Economy', *Wall Street Journal*, 19 June 2014, available at http://www.wsj.com/articles/warsh-and-druckenmiller-the-asset-rich-income-poor-economy-1403220446 (accessed on 4 June 2017).

[69] G. William Domhoff, 'Wealth, Income, Power, Who Rules America?' *Who Rules America?* February 2013, available at http://www2.ucsc.edu/whorulesamerica/power/wealth.html (accessed on 4 June 2017).

consequence, is the striking divergence in the stock prices of regular and luxury retailers since the QE was initiated[70] (Figure 5.17).

**Figure 5.17  Distributional effects of QE: Evidence from the stock market**

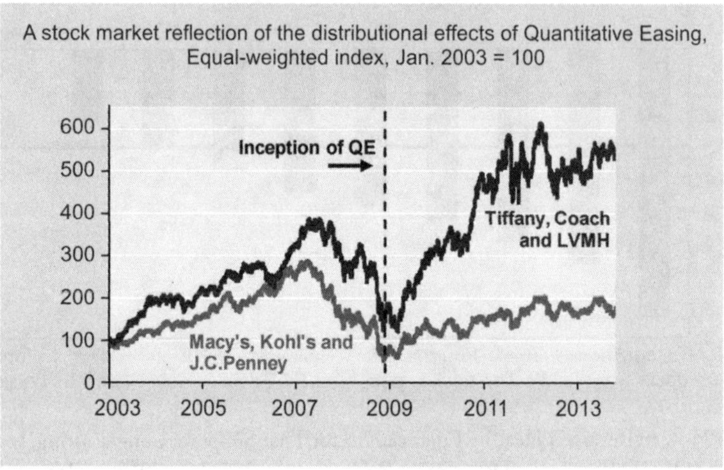

A stock market reflection of the distributional effects of Quantitative Easing, Equal-weighted index, Jan. 2003 = 100

*Source*: JPMorgan Chase Newsletter, 'Eye on the Market', 18 November 2013.

Given these facts and admission of the negligible positive effects to sizeable ill effects of UMP on the majority of the households, it should really come as no surprise that UMP had undermined confidence and hurt consumer sentiment. Poorer households have a higher propensity to consume than richer households do. That their savings have been eroded and incomes on savings lowered would not do much to boost their spending. That is why economic growth in advanced economies trailed forecasts almost every year until 2015 when a fresh round of credit infusion by China revived short-term growth outcomes in 2016 and 2017.

Given the distributional consequences of UMP, it is unsurprising that monetary policy is becoming politicized. When the next asset price crash comes (it is a matter of WHEN and not IF), central banks will have no tools to address it. The more they dip into their tool kit and become even more unconventional, the more likely that they risk losing their independence and pre-eminence. Not entirely an unwelcome prospect if that results in a better

---

[70] 'Eye on the Market', JPMorgan Chase Newsletter, 18 November 2013, available at http://www.aei.org/wp-content/uploads/2013/11/-eyeonthemarketcourseofempi re_114209483876.pdf (accessed on 4 June 2017).

balance between the priorities of the real economy and real people and that of financial markets, asset holders and speculators.

In a simple and effective post[71] for *FT Alphaville*, Victor Xing of Kekselias examined how monetary policy in advanced nations is fast becoming a political liability because of their distributional consequences. He notes that the chief executive of the Hong Kong Monetary Authority (HKMA) made the following points in his remarks at the Jackson Hole Economic Symposium in August 2017:

- There needs to be more research and study by economists, central bankers and policymakers on the distributional effects of unconventional policy
- Policymakers need to understand more on the trend of rising income and wealth inequality and its economic, social and political impact
- Policymakers also need to study more on the labour-displacing impact of technological innovations
- Governments are generally more equipped to tax income but less so in wealth.
- Policymakers must consider what can and should be done to deal with the rising concentration in the distribution of income and more so in wealth. It is also not too early for policymakers to consider what should be done to pre-distribute income by helping those displaced workforce to retrain or adapt to the new environment

Central bankers must be sensitized to the concerns of the public and not that of financial market participants. Their ultimate responsibility is to the public. While they will not dispute this, their actions speak otherwise for they hurt the public while rewarding speculators. There is much talk of the new normal of 'secular stagnation' denoting lower economic growth than before the crisis of 2008 and diminished growth expectations. Secular stagnation is absent in returns to capital – returns generated in stock and real estate markets and corporate profit margins having been rising at disproportionately high rates despite mediocre and moderate economic growth and wage growth. Returns to capital are bulked up by monetary policies that have helped capitalists lever up their gains with enormous but cheap debt. This is deepening and worsening economic and social schisms. Politically, it has contributed to the

---

[71] Victor Xing, 'Central Bank Quantitative Easing as an Emerging Political Liability,' *FT Alphaville*, 20 September 2017, available at https://ftalphaville.ft.com/2017/09/19/ 2193960/guest-post-central-bank-quantitative-easing-as-an-emerging-political-liability/.

rise of economic populism and nationalism. It is futile to blame populists for the problems that preceded them.

---

**Box 5.4  The Diverging Fortunes of Wall Street and Main Street**

On 2 February 2018, in the latest sign of a slow economic recovery in the US, the monthly jobs report from the Labour Department indicated that average hourly earnings had risen 2.9 per cent in January from a year earlier.[1] This came on top of separate data released earlier in the week pointing to wages and salaries having risen 2.8 per cent in the final three months of 2017 compared with a year earlier.

This good news from Main Street, far from bringing cheer among investors, spooked Wall Street. The following Monday, the Dow Jones Industrial Average index plunged 4.6 per cent or 1175 points, its largest ever absolute decline in a day.[2] The spillovers across global equity markets were equally devastating.[3] Over the Friday and the Monday week, nearly USD 5.0 trillion was shaved off global stock market wealth, compared to the USD 500.0 billion (USD 1.1 trillion in today's dollars) decline on Black Monday of 19 October 1987.[4]

Sajjid Chinoy, chief India economist of JP Morgan, highlighted the irony that this turmoil occurred not because of any bad news such as Chinese hard landing, Euro area unravelling or North Korean breaking point.[5] In fact, as he pointed out, given that expectations of the US wage growth were 2.6 per cent, the impact of an additional 0.3 percentage points was stunning. Of course, this sell-off and turmoil was precipitated by investors suddenly realizing that an economic recovery may be on its way to stoking off inflation and prompting more rate hikes by the Federal Reserve. This represented a potential double whammy for market participants. For heavily leveraged entities and corporates, the spectre of rising rates posed serious dangers. It also sounded a warning about the possible end of the bond rally with the threat of inflicting huge losses on a bond market with historically high durations.[6]

In simple terms, the medicine of extended monetary accommodation had driven financial markets into a territory where market participants had suspended belief in the most standard principles of economics – persistent lower rates would lead to overheating, and the resultant inflation and rate hikes cannot be escaped. Financialization had not only distorted incentives big time but had also hallucinated the markets!

The turmoil was only the latest example of how the fortunes of Wall Street and Main Street have diverged dramatically to a point that what hurts Main Street is good news for Wall Street.

[1] Ben Casselman, 'Job and Wage Gains Deliver a Promising Start for the Year,' *New York Times*, 2 February 2018, available at https://www.nytimes.com/2018/02/02/business/economy/jobs-report.html (accessed on 7 May 2018).

[2] BBC, 'US Stock Plunge Sparks Global Sell-Off', *BBC News*, 6 February 2018, available at http://www.bbc.co.uk/news/business-42942921 (accessed on 7 May 2018).

[3] Alanna Petroff, 'The Biggest Losers – Global Stock-Market Edition', *CNN Money*, 9 February 2018, available at http://money.cnn.com/2018/02/09/investing/stock-markets-biggest-losers/index.html (accessed on 7 May 2018).

[4] *Daily Sabah*, 'Nearly $5 Trillion Wiped Out in Global Market Meltdown', 10 February 2018, available at https://www.dailysabah.com/finance/2018/02/10/nearly-5-trillion-wiped-out-in-global-market-meltdown-after-dows-biggest-point-drop-in-history (accessed on 7 May 2018).

[5] Sajjid Chinoy, 'Plunging to Reality', *Indian Express*, 9 February 2018, available at http://indianexpress.com/article/opinion/columns/stock-markets-volatility-global-finance-markets-bse-sensex-union-budget-indian-economy-5056600/ (accessed on 7 May 2018).

[6] Emma Wall, 'Bond Market Rally Has Further to Run', *Morningstar*, 26 January 2018, available at http://www.morningstar.co.uk/uk/news/164621/bond-market-rally-has-further-to-run.aspx (accessed on 7 May 2018).

Finance, financial markets and financial assets are transmission mechanisms, instruments or means to achieve public policy ends/goals of enhanced economic welfare, employment and higher standard of living for the people. As is the case with human beings, tragically, 'means' have displaced 'ends' and become ends in themselves.

How can central bankers free themselves of this confusion and do what they have to do? That forms the subject of the next chapter.

# Part C | The Cure

# 6 | The Way Forward

## 6.1 Treating the disease at its roots

This is the third and final part of the book where we discuss the cures to the 'Rise of Finance'. To cure something, one has to establish that what we are attempting to cure is a disease. We hope we have done that at least adequately in the first two parts of the book. Now is the time to propose remedies.

As we write this in 2018, the world is approaching the tenth anniversary of the peak of the financial crisis that culminated in the collapse of Lehman Brothers in September 2008. Financial crises are acute events whereas financialization is a chronic condition. In that sense, the world remains as unsafe as it was before the crisis of 2008. Much work has been done but, equally, much remains to be done.

Many proposals have been put forward for making the world's banking system safer in the aftermath of the crisis of 2008. Several of those proposals are in different stages of implementation. Some are facing resistance and delays.[1] The process of approvals of banks' living wills that outline how they should be wound up in the event of failure is inordinately delayed. There are also proposals for banks to pay into an insurance fund that could be used to bail them out in case of failure. Banks are expected to create contingent capital to deal with capital shortage during liquidity and solvency crises. Risk-weighted capital adequacy ratios for banks are expected to go up gradually in the coming years in accordance with the Basel III commitments.

Then, there are counter-cyclical capital buffers that are activated during excess credit growth and deactivated during credit downturns. Each national

---

[1] See, for example, Charles Levinson, 'How Wall Street Captured Washington's Effort to Rein in Banks,' *Reuters*, 9 April 2015, available at http://www.reuters.com/investigates/specialreport/usabankrulesweakening/); Gary Rivlin, 'How Wall Street Defanged Dodd-Frank,' *The Nation*, 20 May 2013, available at http://www.thenation.com/article/174113/how-wall-street-defanged-dodd-frank?page=full.

central bank sets the parameters with regard to local circumstances. Banks undergo regular stress tests. Banks are restricted from undertaking proprietary trading with depositors' money ('Volcker Rule').[2] Central banks name certain institutions as systemically important financial institutions (SIFIs) and subject them to extensive monitoring. Of course, far from making these institutions behave more responsibly, this might make them take on more risks as they are systemically important and cannot be allowed to fail!

In an interesting exercise conducted in 2016, Thomas Hsieh, senior legal editor for the Practical Law division of Thomson Reuters, asked financial industry experts including policy veterans of the last crisis for their views on the roots of the next financial crisis. One of the experts said that TBTF institutions could be the next source of crisis as the implicit government guarantee encourages them to take on more risk than is socially desirable.[3] Further, the Richmond Fed's bailout barometer, which estimates the explicit and implicit bailout guarantees of the government reading stood at 61.6 per cent at the end of 2015 versus 44.8 per cent in 1999. Of course, it is slightly lower than the estimate of 65 per cent for 2009.[4] The bigger the number, the bigger the likely taxpayer bill and the incentive for risk-taking on the part of private sector participants.

Finally, there have been proposals to claw back bonuses from traders and executives. It has happened with Wells Fargo Bank recently. International financial institutions and central banks publish reports on global and national financial stability, respectively, twice a year.

It is clear that a lot has been done. It is equally clear that humans are very good at taking preventive action against the last crisis. It is not in our nature

---

[2] In a lecture delivered in April 2017, Paul Volcker, former chairman of the Federal Reserve Board, acknowledged that big banks have adjusted to the requirements of the new rules on proprietary trading (2017 Annual Meeting of the Bretton Woods Committee, 19 April, available at https://www.volckeralliance.org/sites/default/files/attachments/Paul%20Volcker_Bretton%20Woods%20Speech_19Apr2017.pdf, accessed on 29 May 2017).

[3] See Lawrence Hsieh, 'Roots of the Next Financial Crisis: The Last One's Veterans Give Views', Financial Regulatory Forum, 19 April 2016, available at http://blogs.reuters.com/financial-regulatory-forum/2016/04/19/column-roots-of-the-next-financial-crisis-the-last-ones-veterans-give-views/ (accessed on 29 May 2017).

[4] See https://www.richmondfed.org/publications/research/special_reports/safety_net (last updated on 12 January 2017) and https://www.richmondfed.org/publications/research/special_reports/safety_net/bailout_barometer_previous_estimates (accessed 29 May 2017).

to be able to anticipate crises. Indeed, evidence has accumulated that risks have now accumulated in the commercial credit segment after the securitization of subprime residential mortgages triggered the last crisis in 2007.[5] Risks are neither eliminated nor avoided but they simply find homes elsewhere as memories of previous episodes of pain of risks gone wrong fade. The reason is that remedies do not address root causes but treat symptoms as modern medicines do. To have lasting effect, cures must try to attack the root causes of the disease and help cope with the consequences of the disease.

What were the root causes of the problem? In Chapter 2, we argued that the economic choices of the US in the 1970s facilitated by intellectual developments in economics and finance were two of the important causes. The third one is the establishment of the pre-eminent role of the US dollar in global trade and financial flows. It is difficult to propose direct answers to reverse the choices the US made in the 1970s. In fact, such a reversal may happen as a consequence of curbing and capping the rise of finance. How about the hegemony of the US dollar?

The dominance of the US dollar has certainly facilitated the rise of finance as it originated in the US and spread elsewhere. It is the invoicing currency for global trade and the funding currency in global finance. These two have ensured a dominant role for American monetary policy and American financial markets globally. For all practical purposes, the world has a single currency (US dollar), single monetary policy (that of the Federal Reserve) and a single financial market (American bond and equity markets).

It would certainly help the cause of global financial and economic financial stability to have multipolarity in currencies. Regardless of one's political leanings, one can support the idea of more than one currency that underpin the global economy. It will enable diversification, reduce dominance of one country and introduce limits on their policy choices and the spillover effects of such choices. The global economic cycle will not be synchronized – waxing and waning everywhere simultaneously. Financial markets too will not be correlated. There will be genuine diversification.

But how realistic are the chances of that happening in the near future? The answer is simple. Very unrealistic. Potential alternatives to the US dollar have

---

[5] V. Anantha Nageswaran, 'Unelected Policymakers Brew Another Debt Cocktail', *Livemint*, 29 May 2018, available at https://www.livemint.com/Opinion/ 84RUhbR9HXbuq AINcQZaYO/Unelected-policymakers-brew-another-debt-cocktail.html (accessed on 5 June 2018).

far bigger problems than the US has. The Euro was touted and it was hoped that it would emerge as a counterweight to the US dollar. But in the nearly two decades of its existence, the Eurozone has encountered far too much turbulence. The Eurozone economy is sclerotic; its population is aging and its banking system is fragile, at best, and a source of global instability at worst. It has become clear that the Eurozone is not an optimal currency area and that there is unbridgeable chasm between its Northern and Southern members.

China has desire, nay, burning ambition, for its currency to become an alternative to the US dollar or join it at the top of the table. Unfortunately, China's ambitions are inconsistent with its preference for tight control over the economic affairs of the country. One cannot have an international currency and want to control who buys what with it in China. In October 2015, John Williams, president of the Federal Reserve Bank of San Francisco, summed up the situation pretty well:

> As long as they have the threat and reasonable expectation that in a moment of panic or crisis that they would clamp down on the movement of capital so it doesn't disrupt their economy, there is no way that anyone would view the RMB as a reserve currency.[6]

What he said is true in general and not just with respect to becoming a reserve currency. Ordinary people around the world will not keep the Chinese yuan in their wallets if they are not sure that Chinese authorities would not take it away – no questions asked.

In short, the US dollar's position is safe for now. Replacing it with a basket of currencies is not a cure to rein in finance that is available to us. We have to turn to next best alternatives. On the top of the list is capital flows. Capital flows are the transmitters of US monetary policy effects across the world. Capital controls allow policymakers in the rest of the world to wrest back policy freedom from the whims of financial flows and safeguard financial stability. That is the subject of Section 6.2.

Next on the list of the forces that fanned and contributed to the rise of finance is the spread of leverage. Banks' untrammelled ability to create credit is the force behind the crime. Contrary to what textbooks tell us, banks do

---

[6] Krista Hughes and Ann Saphir, 'China Makes Fresh Push for Yuan Inclusion in IMF Basket', *Reuters*, 10 October 2015, available at https://www.reuters.com/article/us-imf-china-sdr/china-makes-fresh-push-for-yuan-inclusion-in-imf-basket-idUSKCN0S32K820151009 (accessed on 19 June 2018).

not create out of deposits. They create assets and then create deposits. Banks' asset creation is a function of their risk appetite (or reckless rapacity for profits, depending on one's perspective), capital requirements and the cost of acquiring the reserves that they need to set aside against deposits. Financial crises have arisen when rampant and mispriced credit has stoked asset bubbles. Therefore, several well-meaning economists have resurrected proposals that are nearly a century old from the 1930s on 'full reserve banking' or 'sovereign money' that place strict limits on banks' ability to create money (deposits). We appreciate and applaud the concerns behind such proposals. But we are not sure if it is possible to get 'there' from 'here' or that there will be political will to do so. Somewhat easier (not in any absolute sense) is to insist on higher bank capital and central bankers taking credit growth into consideration in setting interest rates. Section 6.3 is thus dedicated to the topic of banks and their money creation and what to do about them.

For all their credit creation, it is not that banks are funding real investments – investments in capital assets of businesses that generate employment and create ancillary business opportunities. Since the 1980s, most of bank lending has gone towards mortgages. Mortgage loans are collateralized and they carry a lower risk weight under Basel capital adequacy norms. Talk of unintended consequences. Banks' failure and unwillingness to fund real investments has had other consequences. Section 6.4 is about the fading of real investments by businesses. Many things have contributed to it. Our focus here is on the role played by finance. One of the important contributors is the returns available in financial markets, especially at short horizons. That helps nicely with executive compensation arrangements which are tied to performance of the company stock in financial markets. Real investments will be made and banks will fund them if returns available to speculative investment in stock markets, especially in short horizons, cease to exist. That is possible if the Federal Reserve puts its mind to it.

Section 6.5 is the logical follow-up to Section 6.4. It is a plea to the Federal Reserve to stop underwriting asset prices. Not that it is an explicit part of the mandate of the Federal Reserve but it is there. At one level, it is logical. The more the debt, the greater is the need for collateral values. If asset prices tank, debt goes bad. That is a benign explanation for the attention that asset prices get from the Federal Reserve. There are less-than-benign explanations too. Be that as it may, if the Federal Reserve musters the resolve to leash debt creation in the economy, it will also be freed of its excessive concern over decline in asset prices.

If one has to take the fight to debt creation, one has to fight the battle on many fronts. One is capital requirement. The other is the focus on monetary policy. There is a third front. Fiscal policy has privileged debt over equity. Returns to debt (interest payments) are above the line and hence tax deductible. Returns to equity (dividend) are after tax. Section 6.6 is an exhortation to governments to end the tax inducement to debt creation. To their credit, some governments are getting the message.

In Section 6.7, we take up a topic that, on the surface, might be only tangentially linked to the rise of finance. It is not. Technological developments and the power of finance have combined to facilitate the return of the oligopolist. Again, we scarcely need to remind readers that low interest rates boost stock prices. Together, corporations deploy the currency of overvalued stock and borrowings financed by low interest rates to gobble up competition and scuttle them. That is how industry concentration has managed to leap out of economics textbooks into reality. It is a welcome sign that, lately, this topic is gaining attention (let us not confuse that with action, however) from governments.

A recent working paper by the IMF points out that markups have increased by an average of 39 per cent in advanced economies. Higher markups go hand in hand with profits and industry concentration. Investments initially rise with markups but drop later. More importantly, the paper found a negative association in firms between labour shares and markups, implying that the labour share of income declines in industries where market power rises. In other words, with higher market power, the share of firms' revenue going to workers decreases, while the share of revenue going to profits increases.[7]

Section 6.8 is about an international ramification of the rise of finance – spillover on developing economies of the consequences of monetary policy. There are no readymade answers to dealing with spillovers. Advanced economies will only privilege domestic considerations. They will rightly argue that, without their policy actions, the situation might be worse for developing economies. There is no way to falsify this claim. That is the beauty or bane of social sciences. Counterfactuals are impossible, for other things seldom remain constant. Spillovers are inevitable when countries choose to anchor

---

[7] Federico Diez, Daniel Leigh and Suchanan Tambunlertchai, 'Global Market Power and Its Macroeconomic Implications', IMF Working Paper no. 18/137, 15 June 2018, available at http://www.imf.org/en/Publications/WP/Issues/2018/06/15/Global-Market-Power-and-its-Macroeconomic-Implications-45975 (accessed on 19 June 2018).

their currency to the US dollar – formally or otherwise. Minimizing spillovers is not just a plumbing exercise but a wholesale economic renovation exercise for developing countries.

Finally, Section 6.9 proposes an intellectual way forward. It appeals to central bankers to embrace their cognitive limitations as humans and remember them especially when they make policies that have known and immediate costs but unknown and uncertain benefits. The section reminds them of the asymmetric and non-linear relationship between economic variables and between economic and financial variables.

The proposals we have made in this chapter are premised on our firm belief that finance has long gone past its point of usefulness in advanced countries. The onus lies with the United States of America. The recent appointment of Jerome Powell as the Federal Reserve chairperson and the likely appointments of four other governors to the Federal Reserve's Federal Open Market Committee (FOMC) are an opportunity to change the monetary policy regime in the US and, with that, reverse the domination of finance that is about to enter its fifth decade in a few years.

## 6.2 The case for capital controls

The global impact of financialization, and in particular its most recent driver, the unconventional monetary expansion by the central banks of developed economies, has been to engender serious vulnerabilities.

What contributes to the current vulnerability in the global financial system? There are at least four explanations for this.

One view, popularized by former Federal Reserve chairman, Ben Bernanke, revolves around a global 'savings glut'. Its proponents believe that the rising stockpile of foreign exchange accumulated by the emerging economies, led by China, has ushered in an era of cheap capital, inflating asset prices in the process.[8] Chastened by the bitter experience of the East Asian currency crisis of 1997, emerging economies have run up massive foreign exchange reserves in an effort to insulate themselves from the vagaries of cross-border capital

---

[8] Mr Bernanke might not appreciate that Professor Barry Eichengreen thought that the credit boom and housing bubble in the West were created primarily by the West. He, however, added that it was hard to imagine that the boom and bubble would have scaled such extreme heights absent the enabling role of emerging markets. He made these observations in a discussion of the paper, 'Great Leveraging' by Alan Taylor, presented at a conference on the future of financial globalization held in Lucerne, Switzerland in June 2012.

flows. The undisputed role of dollar as the global reserve currency and the safety and liquidity offered by US government Treasuries have meant that the vast majority of these reserves are invested in them.

As of December 2017, foreign governments and all foreigners, respectively, held USD 4.024 trillion and USD 6.21 trillion worth US Treasuries.[9] With US public debt, or outstanding marketable Treasury securities reported at USD 14.65 trillion in February 2018,[10] foreigners hold around 43 per cent of the US public debt. This 'exorbitant privilege' has doubtless contributed to enabling the Federal Reserve to indulge in excessive monetary accommodation for a prolonged period while leaving the dollar relatively stable. No other country can expect to have the monetary accommodation cake and eat it too!

The second set of views holds the 'excess demand for safe assets' and 'search for yield' responsible for global vulnerability. The uncertainty surrounding the Eurozone and economic weakness in Japan increased the risk premium associated with their assets, thereby further entrenching the dollar's position as global reserve currency. More importantly, as we have seen, while the QE policies have had the effect of sharply shrinking the global supply of safe assets, the increased regulatory standards have increased the demand for safe assets. This has created an artificial scarcity for safe assets, driving US Treasury yields further down.

On the other hand, the ultra-low interest rates forced institutional investors into financial assets of emerging economies in search of yields. The massive inflows into these economies have left them vulnerable to the risks of sudden stops and flow reversals when the tide turns, that is, when US monetary policy tightens and capital flows back to the United States.

Therefore, we would argue that the search for yield and the excess demand for safe assets were intermediate factors. They are consequences of the UMP pursued in Europe, America and Japan.

A third view anchored on international capital flow risks was made in a 2014 essay[11] by Claudio Borio, the chief economist of BIS. He argued that 'the Achilles heel of the international monetary and financial system is that it amplifies the "excess financial elasticity" of domestic policy regimes, i.e., it

---

[9] See http://ticdata.treasury.gov/Publish/mfhhis01.txt (updated regularly; so figures will change).

[10] See https://www.treasurydirect.gov/govt/reports/pd/mspd/2018/opds022018.pdf.

[11] Claudio Borio, 'The International Monetary and Financial System: Its Achilles Heel and What to Do about It', BIS Working Papers no. 456, August 2014, available at https://www.bis.org/publ/work456.pdf (accessed on 23 October 2017).

exacerbates their inability to prevent the build-up of financial imbalances, or outsized financial cycles, that lead to serious financial crises and macroeconomic dislocations'. One can say that Borio is referring to the amplified international spillover risks of domestic policies of advanced nations, mainly.

A fourth view is that the inherent procyclical nature of the financial services industry makes the financial system vulnerable, not just now but always, except that leverage and cross-border capital flows amplify the impact and spread it globally much more than before. Fabrizio Saccomanni, former economics and finance minister in Italy, captured the procyclicality of the financial industry very well in his remarks at the Special Governors' Meeting in Manila in February 2015:[12]

> But, what is the main cause of pro-cyclicality? ... Although global financial intermediaries operate in a highly competitive environment, they have uniform credit allocation strategies, risk management models and reaction functions to macroeconomic developments and credit events. Thus, competition and uniformity of strategies combine, in periods of financial euphoria, when the search for yield is the dominant factor, to generate underpricing of risk, overestimation of market liquidity, information asymmetries and herd behaviour; in periods of financial panic, when the search for safe assets is predominant, they combine to produce generalised risk aversion, overestimation of counterparty risk and, again, information asymmetries and herd behaviour.

Global financial markets have become one giant procyclical market!

In response to the *procyclicality* of the financial sector, Borio advocates policies 'that would lean more deliberately against booms and ease less aggressively and persistently during busts'. In other words, policy should be *countercyclical* given the strong tendency of the financial sector and financial markets towards procyclicality. However, political economy considerations dictate that such counter-cyclicality and moderation may be difficult, if not impossible, to pull off for even mature economies. More importantly, the public and politicians would fail to comprehend that crisis averted is better than effective post-crisis responses. If counter-cyclical policies prevent financial

---

[12] Fabrizio Saccomanni, 'Monetary Spillovers? Boom and Bust? Currency Wars? The International Monetary System Strikes Back', dinner speech by Fabrizio Saccomanni, former minister of economy and finance of Italy, BIS Special Governors' Meeting, Manila, 6 February 2015, available at http://www.bis.org/publ/othp22.pdf (accessed on 23 October 2017).

meltdowns, then no financial meltdowns will occur and no consequences felt. Then, politicians and the public would accuse that counter-cyclical policies caused needless pain and inconvenience, forgetting their role in forestalling the meltdown! That is human nature for you.

It must be clear to readers that three of these four explanations stem from the inherent deficient and instable features of the financial system and their amplification by the prevailing policy dogma, especially that of monetary policy, in advanced nations, particularly in and led by the United States. We hope that we have made a persuasive and logical case that financialization aka the neoliberal agenda and the monetary policy framework feed off each other. They destabilize emerging economies and, increasingly, the social order in the host countries themselves.

The crisis of 2008 and its aftermath have definitively demonstrated that conventional monetary policy, revolving around inflation targeting, flexible or not, cannot ensure macroeconomic stability. Recourse to UMPs in response to the crisis caused by the failure of conventional monetary policy and the resultant flood of cross-border capital unleashed have only served to complicate the issue of external macroeconomic management. This has made many emerging economies, which have liberalized their capital account considerably in recent years, vulnerable to sudden stops and capital flow reversals.

In the circumstances, conventional response involving interest-rates-based monetary policy and reactive imposition of capital controls are unlikely to be very effective in the pursuit of macroeconomic stability. Central bankers should deploy a larger arsenal of weapons, including capital flow management (CFM) measures and stricter microprudential regulation. Further, these policies should be counter-cyclically deployed to limit the damage that spillovers, represented by unrestricted cross-border capital flows, cause to macroeconomic stability.

The CFM measures include direct capital controls, which involve restrictions on cross-border capital flows, and macroprudential measures, which involve restrictions on cross-border or foreign currency exposure and lending. Macroprudential measures include counter-cyclically increasing capital reserve buffers on systemically important financial institutions, counter-cyclical leverage caps on trading positions and financial intermediaries, systemic liquidity surcharges and regulatory restraints on asset markets (like loan-to-value and debt-to-income ratios in property markets) and external commercial borrowing (say, on short-term unhedged debts) to attenuate credit bubbles.

The microprudential armoury involves higher and counter-cyclical requirements on a host of parameters including capital reserve, loan-to-value (or income) and leverage ratios, coupled with periodic and rigorous stress tests.

In the context of the cross-border capital flows and the indiscriminate damage inflicted by them, in a landmark confession (*The Economist* said[13] that 'it was as if the Vatican had given its blessing to birth control!') and after rigorous examination of the evidence, the IMF, no less, argued that capital controls[14] are 'part of the toolkit'.[15] It also admitted:[16]

> Capital flows can have substantial benefits for countries. At the same time, they also carry risks, even for countries that have long been open and drawn benefits from them.... They are volatile and can be large relative to the size of a country's financial markets or economy. This can lead to booms and busts in credit or asset prices, and makes countries more vulnerable to contagion from global instability.... Global financial market volatility ... has significant spillovers to emerging market economies.... Countries with extensive and long-standing measures to limit capital flows are likely to benefit from further liberalization in an orderly manner. There is, however, no presumption that full liberalization is an appropriate goal for all countries at all times.... For countries that have to manage the risks associated with inflow surges or disruptive outflows, a key role needs to be played by macroeconomic policies, as well as by sound financial supervision and regulation, and strong institutions. In certain circumstances, capital flow management measures can be useful. They should not, however, substitute for warranted macroeconomic adjustment.

In its country report on India, which examined the impact of global finance market volatility on India, the IMF said:[17]

[13] 'Capital Controls Are Back as Part of Many Countries' Financial Armoury', *The Economist*, 12 October 2013, available at http://www.economist.com/news/special-report/21587383-capital-controls-are-back-part-many-countries-financial-armoury-just-case (accessed on 23 October 2017).

[14] 'IMF Develops Framework to Manage Capital Inflows', IMF Survey, 5 April 2011, available at http://www.imf.org/external/pubs/ft/survey/so/2011/NEW040511B.htm (accessed on 23 October 2017).

[15] 'High-Level Seminar on the International Monetary System', Keynote address by Dominique Strauss-Kahn, Managing Director, International Monetary Fund, 31 March 2011, available at http://www.imf.org/external/np/speeches/2011/033111.htm (accessed on 23 October 2017).

[16] 'IMF Adopts Institutional View on Capital Flows', IMF Survey, 3 December 2012, available at http://www.imf.org/external/pubs/ft/survey/so/2012/pol120312a.htm (accessed on 23 October 2017).

[17] 'India: Selected Issues', IMF Country Report No. 15/62, March 2015, available at https://www.imf.org/external/pubs/ft/scr/2015/cr1562.pdf (accessed on 23 October 2017).

We argue that strong fundamentals and sound policy frameworks per se are not enough to isolate countries from an increase in global financial market volatility. This is particularly the case where there is a sudden adjustment of expectations triggered by monetary policy normalization uncertainty in advanced economies ... no country (neither advanced markets nor emerging markets) appears immune from the impact of a surge in global financial market volatility.

In a speech in 2013 at the central bankers' retreat at Jackson Hole,[18] Hélène Rey of the London Business School went so far as to claim that 'independent monetary policies are possible if and only if the capital account is managed directly or indirectly'. In fact, she describes monetary policy autonomy and free capital flows as an 'irreconcilable duo', regardless of the exchange rate regime. In other words, as we discussed in Chapter 4, the impossible trinity is simply reduced to a dilemma. Monetary policy autonomy is impossible in the presence of free capital flows regardless of whether the exchange rate regime is fixed or floating.

Research by the BIS backs her up. As mentioned earlier in Section 5.6, in the third quarter review in 2015, BIS economists Boris Hofmann and Előd Takáts report on their empirical investigation of international monetary spillovers.[19] Spillovers are evident in long-term interest rates, short-term interest rates and even policy rates. They are statistically significant regardless of the exchange rate regimes that the countries had adopted. Flexible exchange rates offer neither protection nor policy autonomy to emerging and smaller economies.

Fabrizio Saccomanni argues that capital controls are a form of financial protectionism and warns that it would hurt the growth prospects of the world economy. But finance is not growth enhancing beyond a point. Second, capital controls need not be a blunt instrument. It can be wielded effectively selectively and for temporary periods. At the minimum, policymakers should have the option to use them without being stigmatized or without having to face political and market opprobrium or sanctions for doing so.

---

[18] Hélène Rey, 'Dilemma not Trilemma: The Global Financial Cycle and Monetary Policy Independence', *Proceedings of the Monetary Policy Symposium*, Jackson Hole: Federal Reserve Bank of Kansas City, August 2013, available at https://www.kansascityfed.org/publicat/sympos/2013/2013rey.pdf (accessed on 29 May 2017).

[19] Boris Hofmann and Előd Takáts, 'International Monetary Spillovers', *BIS Quarterly Review*, 13 September 2015, available at http://www.bis.org/publ/qtrpdf/r_qt1509i.htm (accessed on 29 May 2017).

Another objection is that capital controls would be impossible to enforce and that there would be leakages. This straw man is disingenuous since nobody disputes that capital controls are imperfect. In fact, several studies on the impact of capital controls in recent years, while pointing to a mixed picture, acknowledge the undoubted short-term benefits of CFM measures in limiting capital inflow surges.[20] The best evidence that it has some intended effect comes from no less a person than Mohamed El-Erian, former CEO of world's largest bond trader Pacific Investment Management Company LLC (PIMCO), as quoted in *The Economist*, who has this to say about capital controls:

> They do exactly what they are intended to do: put sand in the market. We think twice, or three times.[21]

But as Adair Turner has argued, CFM has to be complemented with domestic policies to control credit misallocation, especially into sectors like real estate which attract hot money inflows.[22] He advocates combining policies that discourage short-term inflows, including tax instruments and reserve requirements, with counter-cyclical measures, like additional capital requirements, to slow domestic credit creation.

In order to plug gaps, he suggests encouraging global banks operating in a developing country to legally incorporate subsidiaries, with locally regulated capital and liquidity reserves, instead of being branches of the global entity.[23] This would help host countries exercise control over the credit outflows of these banks without any adverse impact in terms of long-term capital inflows.

---

[20] Kristin J. Forbes, Marcel Fratzscher and Roland Straub, 'See Capital Controls and Macroprudential Measures: What Are They Good For?' 1 December 2013, available at http://papers.ssrn.com/sol3/papers.cfm?abstract_id=2364486 (accessed on 29 May 2017); Kristin J. Forbes et al., 'Bubble Thy Neighbour: Portfolio Effects and Externalities from Capital Controls,' MIT Sloan Research Paper no. 4962-12, 27 April 2012, available at http://papers.ssrn.com/sol3/papers.cfm?abstract_id=2056491 (accessed on 29 May 2017).

[21] 'Capital Controls Are Back as Part of Many Countries' Financial Armoury', *The Economist*.

[22] Adair Turner, 'In Praise of Fragmentation', *Project Syndicate*, 18 February 2014, available at https://www.project-syndicate.org/commentary/adair-turner-criticizes-economists--adherence-to-the-belief-that-the-benefits-of-capital-account-liberalization-outweigh-the-costs (accessed on 29 May 2017). India is having trouble persuading foreign banks to convert their operations in India into subsidiaries.

[23] See Manojit Saha, 'Reserve Bank of India Firm on Single Subsidiary for Foreign Banks', *The Hindu*, 27 February 2016, available at http://www.thehindu.com/business/Industry/reserve-bank-of-india-firm-on-single-subsidiary-for-foreign-banks/article8289954.ece (accessed on 29 May 2017).

The parent entity could always increase equity stakes and provide long-term loans to the subsidiary.

We would like to leave the final words for this section to Alan Taylor and Barry Eichengreen. In the paper referred to in footnote 8, Alan Taylor wrote that the crisis (of 2008) problem had been perennial and that it had been with humankind throughout history. He noted that the truly anomalous period was the third quarter of the twentieth century, when crises were rare.

Barry Eichengreen responded thus:

> Why was the third quarter of the 20th century anomalous? According to Alan, the explanation for the singular stability of this period lies in either strict regulation of domestic financial institutions and markets (internal factors) or strict regulation of international capital flows (external factors). Those of us of eclectic temperament will suggest, predictably, that it was both. Indeed one can go further and argue that neither strict domestic regulation nor limits on capital flows would have been effective without the other.

We could not have asked for a better launch pad for the rest of the chapter on what governments should do. They need to regulate financial institutions, financial markets and international capital flows well.

### 6.3  Banks and money creation

The recurrent episodes of banking crises have prompted calls for a return to 'boring banking'.[24] Various alternatives have come up for consideration: 100 per cent reserves, narrow banking, limited purpose banking and sovereign money.

One of the most misunderstood proposals of banking reform to have emerged since the financial crisis of 2008 is the proposal for 100 per cent reserve banking or full reserve banking. If banks were to hold 100 per cent cash reserves against all their liabilities, how would they conduct banking? The proposal is meant to provide a full reserve carve-out or shelter only for specific bank deposits. In other words, the idea was to prevent banks from placing risky bets using depositors' money, especially those covered by deposit insurance. That is why some proposals want to restrict 'full reserve banking' only to sight deposits. Banks would be free to create assets with other forms

---

[24] Paul Krugman, 'Making Banking Boring', *New York Times*, 9 April 2009, available at https://www.nytimes.com/2009/04/10/opinion/10krugman.html (accessed on 29 May 2017).

of banking liabilities.[25] This proposal would 'take away the ability of banks to fund loans through money creation' that has been the hallmark of modern banking.[26]

Starting with the lucid discussion papers published by the Bank of England[27] to the more recent Bundesbank April 2017 monthly report, it is now widely understood that modern banking does not do financial intermediation as expounded in textbooks but engages in money creation. Since under the modern fractional-reserve banking only a portion of deposits are backed by reserves, held either at the bank itself or the central bank, banks are creating new money when they make new loans. Accordingly, the BoE paper estimated almost 97 per cent of money in the United Kingdom to have been created electronically by commercial bank.

This has implications for banking regulation and for the relationship between savings and investment as is conventionally understood. If banks create loans and credit the borrower's account with the loan amount, thus creating a deposit liability, then banks have to create reserves for these deposits under 100 per cent reserve banking. They cannot continue to create money through loans and vice versa.

According to Michael Kumhof and Zoltán Jakab,[28] another implication of modern banking is that the amount of household savings and their deposit into the banking system is no longer the constraint for generating real economy investment spending. The constraint is the willingness of the bank to lend, which is based 'on their own assessment of their future profitability and solvency'. Therefore, the message for policymakers is that they should prioritize an efficient financial system that identifies and finances worthwhile projects.

---

[25] The Chicago Plan, developed in the 1930s, envisaged the banking system's credit assets being funded by non-monetary liabilities that are not subject to runs. For more details, see Jaromir Benes and Michael Kumhof, 'The Chicago Plan Revisited', IMF Working Paper no. WP/12/202, March 2012, available at https://www.imf.org/external/pubs/ft/wp/2012/wp12202.pdf (accessed on 29 May 2017).

[26] Michael Kumhof and Zoltán Jakab, 'The Truth about Banks', *Finance & Development*, March 2016, available at http://www.imf.org/external/pubs/ft/fandd/2016/03/kumhof.htm (accessed on 29 May 2017).

[27] Michael McLeay, Amar Radia and Ryland Thomas, 'Money Creation in the Modern Economy', *Bank of England Quarterly Bulletin Q1*, 2014, available at https://www.bankofengland.co.uk/-/media/boe/files/quarterly-bulletin/2014/money-creation-in-the-modern-economy.pdf (accessed on 29 May 2017).

[28] Kumhof and Jakab, 'The Truth about Banks'.

The hope is that with financing of physical investment projects, savings in the economy would arise, as a consequence. This is a cop-out.

What are the tools that governments and regulators have, in a private sector banking system, to encourage them to lend to real investments rather than for speculative purposes? Almost nothing. If anything, risk weights for collateralized and uncollateralized loans have meant that banks make more mortgage loans than assess business risks and engage in commercial lending (see Section 6.4). Indeed, the realization that banks create their own money rather than lend out of deposits and on the basis of reserves created by the central bank leads to a straightforward regulatory proposal. The only way to rein in banks from being carried away with optimistic assumptions about the safety and profitability of their loan assets is to impose a higher capital requirement and consider some form of full reserve banking. The latter has not gained much traction except in Iceland and Switzerland.

The Iceland proposal is discussed in detail in the Box 6.1.

---

**Box 6.1  Sovereign money system**

In the aftermath of its tumultuous banking crisis, which almost bankrupted the economy, the prime minister of Ireland commissioned Frosti Sigurjonsson, the chairman of the Icelandic parliament's Economic Affairs Committee, to study and make suggestions to reform the banking system. The report[1] submitted in March 2015 has, in a radical departure, suggested that the country move over to a sovereign money system of banking from the currency fractional-reserves-based system.

In the fractional-reserve system, banks take deposits from customers, a small part of which is held as reserve with the central bank and the remaining retained as demand deposit of the consumer. In this system, contrary to conventional wisdom, rather than lend out money that they acquire from customers, banks actually create new money when they lend (and conversely delete money when loans are repaid). They create a deposit in the borrowers' name for the equivalent amount, which in turn increases money supply. Therefore, as commercial banks lend, they create new money, which becomes available for onward lending and further money creation.

The problem arises since this money supply is, for a variety of reasons, again contrary to conventional wisdom, not effectively restrained by the reserve ratio. For a start, since the central bank has no choice but to lend for reserves, most often 'banks extend credit, create deposits, and look for reserves later'.[2] Retained profits, raising of additional share capital, securitization and discretionary internal risk ratings allow banks to increase their lending, often far in excess of what is mandated by the reserve ratio, thereby conferring on banks the effective money creation power and weakening the effectiveness of monetary policy.

As recent events have shown, this system is vulnerable to excessive liquidity and asset bubbles. Monetary policy transmission becomes seriously constrained as commercial banks become money creators. Of course, monetary policy need not be constrained if monetary policymakers allow the federal funds rate to rise as banks' reserve requirements rise in line with the deposits they create. But central banks have chosen to target inflation and in rare cases, employment but not credit growth. Hence, they do not let the interest rate – the federal funds rate, in the case of the US – to rise in response to the rise in reserve requirements.

The sovereign money proposal, originally put forth by Frederick Soddy and Irving Fisher, system seeks to separate the money creation (and payments) and credit allocation (investing and lending) functions of banks. Each customer account would have two parts. The risk-free transaction account, held at the central bank, would be used for storing funds available on demand and used for making payments and transactions. This is not a liability of the bank, which merely acts as an intermediary executing payment orders on the money available in the transaction account in return for an account servicing fee. The transaction account balances represent sovereign money, issued and held by the central bank, and are comparable to electronic safe-deposit boxes. It, therefore, does away with the need for deposit insurance and enables the central bank to control the money supply.

The customer can choose to transfer a part of his deposit to an investment account, with a predetermined maturity, risk sharing and return. The customer cannot use this money to make payments or reassign to a third party. While the investment account too is held at the central bank, it is, unlike the transaction account, a liability of the bank. The bank can lend or invest this money for a return.

The investment account, by prohibiting on-demand payments or transfers to third parties, does not create money. Further, investment accounts being risk- and reward-sharing, align the incentives of the banks and their customers and eliminate the need for tax-payer bailouts in case the bank fails. In case of insolvency, account holders can transfer their transaction account, held at the central bank, from one commercial bank to another without any hassle.

The sovereign money system will have just one type of money creation, the sovereign money held in the transaction account of the customer held at the central bank. This enables the central bank to directly control money creation, thereby ensuring effective control over the monetary policy. Undoubtedly, the sovereign money proposal too retains some of the risks of the fractional-reserve banking system, most notably the asset–liability mismatches between short-term investments and long-term lending. But it offers the possibility of a more incentive-compatible system of banking. It removes the scope for pervasive moral hazard that 'business as usual' entails.

The sovereign money proposal may not only be suited to but also necessary for smaller economies whose banks have assets that dwarf the GDP several times over. Bigger economies may risk a much bigger disruption if they walk that path or similar paths. They may be better off rejigging their monetary policy goals and raising bank capital requirements.

[1] Frosti Sigurjonsson, 'Monetary Reform – A Better Monetary System for Iceland', March 2015, available at http://www.forsaetisraduneyti.is/media/Skyrslur/monetary-reform.pdf (accessed on 29 May 2017).

[2] Alan R. Holmes, 'Operational Constraints on the Stabilization of Money Supply Growth', *Proceedings of the Controlling Monetary Aggregates Conference Series*, Boston, MA: Federal Reserve Bank of Boston, available at https://www.bostonfed.org/economic/conf/conf1/conf1i.pdf (accessed on 5 June 2018).

In a referendum on 10 June 2018, the Swiss voted overwhelmingly against a proposal to abolish fractional-reserve banking. As part of the Vollgeld (or sovereign money) initiative, the Swiss National Bank (SNB) alone, and not the commercial banks, would have had the power to inject money into the economy.[29] The idea was that it would insulate tax payers from risks taken by commercial banks.

Despite being intellectually drawn to these proposals for reasons mentioned earlier, we acknowledge that current proposals for full reserve banking suffer from several uncertainties. It raises important concerns on the commercial viability of banks and impact on the economy.[30] Further, as long as there is deposit insurance that protects retail deposits, full reserve banking might be

---

[29] Ralph Atkins, 'Radical Reform: Switzerland to Vote on Banking Overhaul', *Financial Times*, 29 May 2018, available at https://www.ft.com/content/13b92d86-5810-11e8-bdb7-f6677d2e1ce8 (accessed on 5 June 2018).

[30] V. Anantha Nageswaran, 'A Swiss Referendum for Global Economic Stability', *Livemint*, 5 June 2018, available at https://www.livemint.com/Opinion/LAFMKz5ehzgXxbjhSkzW6L/A-Swiss-referendum-for-global-economic-stability.html (accessed on 5 June 2018).

redundant. Therefore, a prerequisite for full reserve banking might be abolition of deposit insurance. That will strengthen systemic stability for it removes the moral hazard that deposit insurance has engendered.

Second, once deposits are fully backed by reserves, is it realistic to expect that bank creditors will exercise a restraining influence on asset creation? Recent history is that creditors rely on the implicit state guarantee or protection of their debt to banks because banks are too big to fail. So, if the underlying purpose of 'full reserve banking' is to restrain asset creation by banks, it may be necessary to remove the perception that any bank is too big to fail. That is a political economy question. Bankers will typically resist that for their status as being too big to fail is a guarantee against their failure and, therefore, it subsidizes their cost of capital as well.

Third, will it be possible for banks to lend profitably relying on debt financing? That is very unlikely. In fact, if bailouts are explicitly discouraged, banks' cost of funding might raise so much as to make lending unprofitable except at very high rates of interest. In that case, credit intermediation will migrate to the non-banking sector that may not be so constrained.

The only way that banks can lend profitably is to finance themselves more and more with equity. Compensation to equity holders is only contingent and not contractual as in the case of debtholders. But in recent years, equity holders have come to expect lottery-type returns from their investments and banks, constrained from creating assets at will, may not be able to generate the kind of returns that would satisfy equity investors.

Notwithstanding the above, it is possible to rein in runaway credit creation by banks. It requires only two things. One is that monetary policy authorities allow interest rates on reserves to rise, instead of setting them on the basis of inflation developments. That is the real issue. Monetary policy rates must take into account credit growth and policy rates must rise in response to higher reserve requirements necessitated by banks' asset and consequent deposit creation.

The second thing that can slow down the runaway growth in bank assets is higher capital requirements for banks. Mandating higher capital requirement is an important banking sector reform. Unfortunately, higher capital requirements are being phased in too slowly with sufficient scope for banks to manipulate risk weights under Basel norms still intact. That is why Sheila Bair, former chairperson of the FDIC, and Thomas Hoenig, currently the vice chairman of FDIC, favour a high (simple) capital (or tangible equity) ratio and lighter regulation for banks.[31] Even higher capital requirements fall far short of those suggested by the likes of Anat Admati as necessary to provide meaningful enough cushion against the need for bailouts.[32]

In this context, the recent decision by the US Federal Reserve to nearly halve leverage requirements on the eight globally systemically important banks (GSIBs) in the US is baffling. The *Wall Street Journal* criticized the decision, pointing out that their current leverage ratio of 6.6 per cent is only slightly more than the losses they experienced during the crisis.[33] It also drew attention to the benefits of higher equity ratio and better capitalized banks – a 0.6 to 1.69 percentage point increase in bank lending growth, a significant impact at a time when bank lending is already weak. Clearly the lessons of just a decade ago are already a faint memory. It is one thing for banks to be myopic. After all, compensation models for bank executives incentivize short-termism. But it is painful to see the regulator acquiesce to their demands. Even though such behaviour vindicates the arguments that this book makes and the purpose of the book, we take no pleasure from it. Instead, we view it with alarm.

However, a full discussion of banking regulatory reforms is outside the scope of this book. In any case, people who are vastly more competent have weighed in with their proposals to better regulate the international banking system.[34]

---

[31] Sheila Bair and Ricardo R. Delfin, 'How Efforts to Avoid Past Mistakes Created New Ones: Some Lessons from the Causes and Consequences of the Recent Financial Crisis', in *Across the Great Divide: New Perspectives on the Financial Crisis*, edited by Martin Neil Baily and John B. Taylor (Stanford, CA: Hoover Press, 2014); Thomas M. Hoenig, 'Back to Basics: A Better Alternative to Basel Capital Rules', speech delivered to the American Banker Regulatory Symposium, 14 September 2012, available at https://www.fdic.gov/news/news/speeches/chairman/spsep1412_2.html (accessed on 2 June 2017).

[32] Anat R. Admati, 'The Missed Opportunity and the Challenge of Capital Regulation', Graduate School of Business, Stanford University, December 2015, available at https://www.gsb.stanford.edu/sites/gsb/files/missed-opportunity-dec-2015_1.pdf (accessed on 2 June 2017).

[33] 'The Fed's Capital Mistake', *WSJ*, 19 April 2018, available at https://www.wsj.com/articles/the-feds-capital-mistake-1524180265 (accessed on 8 June 2018).

[34] 'Fundamentals of Central Banking: Lessons from the Crisis', G-30, October 2015; Statement of the Systemic Risk Council to G20 Leaders, February 2017, available at http://www.systemicriskcouncil.org/wp-content/uploads/2017/02/Systemic-Risk-Council-Policy-Statement-to-G20-Leaders.pdf (accessed on 2 June 2017); Andrew Large, 'Financial Stability Governance Today: A Job Half Done', Occasional Paper no. 92, G-30.

## 6.4  Do banks fund real investments?

In theory, the financial sector – banks and capital markets, broadly – exists to fund the investment needs of the commercial sector. The question is if they do that job at all, let alone do it well. Governments and banking regulators have no tools to persuade banks to lend mainly for real investment activity. At the same time, there is no evidence that banks do so of their own volition. In fact, evidence points to the opposite.

In a widely cited paper, Taylor, Schularick and Jordá[35] show that banks in advanced nations have significantly increased their mortgage lending (Figure 6.1). This is true of most advanced nations with very few exceptions. The phenomenon has been more pronounced since the mid-1980s.

**Figure 6.1  Share of real estate lending in total bank lending**

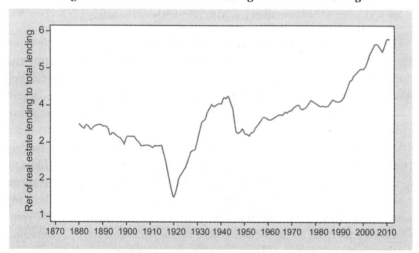

Source: Òscar Jordá, Moritz Schularick and Alan M. Taylor, 'The Great Mortgaging: Housing Finance, Crises, and Business Cycles', Working Paper no. 2014-23, September 2014, available at http://www.frbsf.org/economic-research/publications/working-papers/wp2014-23.pdf (accessed on 8 June 2018).

They attribute it to the risk-adjusted capital requirements that the Basel Committee on Bank Supervision introduced in 1988:

---

[35] Òscar Jordá, Moritz Schularick and Alan M. Taylor, 'The Great Mortgaging: Housing Finance, Crises, and Business Cycles', Working Paper no. 2014-23, September 2014, available at http://www.frbsf.org/economic-research/publications/working-papers/ wp2014-23.pdf (accessed on 8 June 2018).

Loans secured by mortgages on residential properties only carried half the risk weight of loans to companies.

Perhaps, purely unintentionally, the risk-weighted capital adequacy ratios might have played a very big role in distorting the flow of credit to different sectors and thus contributing to increasing financial fragility in the last three decades. It is a good rule of thumb that when policymakers complicate simplicity, unintended consequences result.

Thomas Hoenig spells out the requirements of an effective capital rule well:

> To be useful, a capital rule must be simple, understandable and enforceable. It should reflect the firm's ability to absorb loss in good times and in crisis. It should be one that the public and shareholders can understand, that directors can monitor, that management cannot easily game and that bank supervisors can enforce. An effective capital rule should result in a bank having capital that approximates what the market would require without the safety net in place.[36]

This is why the proposal made by Sheila Bair for a high but simple capital ratio backed by a loosely regulated environment should work better than complex regulations and capital ratios. The latter pays lip service to financial stability. The former has a better chance of working. After three decades of none-too-satisfactory experience with complex regulations, capital ratio formulas, the latter deserves a chance.

Another former regulator who favours higher capital ratios for banks is Andrew Sheng. He regulated banks at Bank Negara Malaysia. Then, he was the deputy chief executive at Hong Kong Monetary Authority and later, he also became the chairman of the Hong Kong Securities and Exchange Commission. In a speech delivered on the seventieth anniversary of Bretton Woods, he spoke out about the dangers of financialization and the consequent misallocation of resources. He spoke in favour of higher capital ratios and tax on financial transactions.[37] We are in favour of the adoption of a simple but higher capital ratio for banks.

---

[36] Thomas M. Hoenig, 'Back to Basics: A Better Alternative to Basel Capital Rules' speech delivered to The American Banker Regulatory Symposium, 14 September 2012, available at https://www.fdic.gov/news/news/speeches/chairman/spsep1412_2. html (accessed on 2 June 2017).

[37] Andrew Sheng, 'International Monetary System and Sustainability', Roundtable Meeting to commemorate 70th Anniversary of the Bretton Woods Conference, Shanghai, 17–18 June 2014, available at https://www.global-economic-symposium.org/ knowledgebase/the-new-global-financial-architecture/virtual-library/international-monetary-system-and-sustainability (accessed on 16 July 2018).

This can be coupled with macroprudential regulations to limit resource misallocation into the real estate sector, the main target for such capital flows. An IMF study of macroprudential and CFM policies from 46 countries in the 2000–13 period (353 cases of policy tightening and 129 of loosening) found that the former has been effective in stabilizing housing markets, especially in Asia.[38] It finds that macroprudential policies like loan-to-value ratio caps and housing tax measures have reduced housing credit growth by 2.6 percentage points annually.

In the context of cross-border CFM, another study of 60 countries in the 2009–11 period found that 'macroprudential measures related to international exposures can significantly improve measures linked to financial fragility, such as bank leverage, inflation expectations, bank credit growth, and exposure to portfolio liabilities'.[39]

We have discussed in Section 4.5 the limitations of macroprudential regulations. However, given the evidence available, we support the use of such instruments as complements, and not a substitute, to monetary policy.

Another area of reform relates to changing the incentives faced by executives and companies. Around the same time as the Basel capital adequacy norms were being developed and imposed on banks, a stock market revolution too was taking shape, which was to have a profound impact on the behaviour of publicly listed companies. In the 1980s, the phenomenon of mutual funds exploded. Stock market investing was no longer the preserve of specialists but households could grab a bite of the cherry through exposure to mutual funds. Brokerage commissions were slashed. The Agency Theory of aligning managers' interests with that of shareholders caught on. Managers were given stocks and then later, stock options that would allegedly make them choose to prioritize the interests of shareholders. We should note here that the prevailing version of shareholder capitalism itself was a relatively new concept. Companies were expected to reconcile the interests of many different stakeholders of which

---

[38] Longmeir Zhang and Edda Zoli, 'Leaning against the Wind: Macroprudential Policy in Asia', IMF Working Paper no. 14/22, February 2014, available at https://www.imf.org/external/pubs/ft/wp/2014/wp1422.pdf (accessed on 16 July 2018).

[39] Kristin Forbes, Marcel Fratzscher and Ronald Straub, 'Capital Flow Management Measures: What Are They Good for?' NBER Working Paper no. 20860, January 2015, available at http://www.nber.org/papers/w20860.pdf (accessed on 2 June 2017).

shareholders were one.[40] There were workers, bondholders, the government and the community.

Not only did managers begin to ignore the larger ecosystem under this new framework but they also began to make a distinction between short-run share price performance and long-run share price performance. The latter is a function of the companies investing in projects with positive net present value. The former involves, largely, ensuring that stock prices climb in the short run. Companies treating labour as a mere factor of production like land and capital rather than see them as partners in the pursuit of enhancing corporate performance also helped. Loyalties faded and withered. It was mutual. As worker insecurity arose, wages dropped. Globalization – offshoring and outsourcing – further deepened worker insecurity and kept a solid lid on wage growth. Executives who ensured that successfully were rewarded with more stocks and stock grants and the stock market too rewarded shareholders with rise in stock prices.

As we have seen in Section 3.1, the ratio of executive compensation to median worker wages rose rapidly and even alarmingly, from a social perspective. After all, whatever does not accrue to labour must accrue to capital. That further reinforced the conviction that only the short-run stock price performance mattered.

Just as the Basel Committee norms unveiled in 1988 encouraged mortgage lending by banks at the expense of corporate lending, the reaction of central bankers to the stock market crash of 1987 cemented the faith of American executives in stock markets. As the stock markets around the world crashed for two days in October 1987, central banks flooded the economies with more money and slashed interest rates. That created housing bubbles in many European nations resulting in banking crises (for example, Scandinavian countries) and played a role in the Savings & Loans crisis of the late 1980s in

---

[40] We must note here that it was the path-breaking work of Michael C. Jensen and William Meckling in 1976 ('The Theory of the Firm: Managerial Behaviour, Agency Costs and Ownership structure', *Journal of Financial Economics* 3 [1976]: 305–360) that paved the way for shareholder value maximization as the key objective of a corporation. In later years, Jensen, though never fully regretting the unintended consequences of his seminal work, wrote the following: 'While remuneration can be a solution to agency problems, it can also be a source of agency problems' ('Remuneration: Where We've Been, How We Got to Here, What Are the Problems, and How to Fix Them', European Corporate Governance Institute [ECGI], Finance Working Paper no. 44/2004, July 2004).

the United States. However, more than that, it convinced many in America that the Federal Reserve had the back of the stock market. That was a game changer. Mr Greenspan's moments of self-doubt about irrational exuberance in stock markets in 1996 were fleeting. He quickly erased such doubts and became the champion of the new era of 'once in a lifetime' lasting gains in American productivity that stock prices reflected.

What happened as a result was that America's publicly listed companies were investing far less than private companies, that is, unlisted companies, were. John Asker and his co-authors[41] came up with some startling conclusions that raise fundamentals questions on the role and purpose of capital markets. Their findings, *in their own words*, are as follows:

- Private firms invest substantially more than public ones on average, holding firm size, industry and investment opportunities constant. This pattern is surprising in light of the fact that a stock market listing gives firms access to cheaper investment capital.
- Second, private firms' investment decisions are around four times more responsive to changes in investment opportunities than are those of public firms.
- IPO firms invest more and are more sensitive to investment opportunities in the five years before they go public than after. Indeed, once they have gone public, their investment sensitivity becomes indistinguishable from that of observably similar, already-public firms.
- Investment sensitivity is especially low among public firms with high levels of transient (that is, short-term focused) institutional ownership and those with a propensity to 'meet or beat' analysts' earnings forecasts. These cross-chapteral patterns are consistent with the notion that short-termist pressures induce public firms to invest myopically.
- Remarkably, our findings hold even during the recent financial crisis, when private firms presumably became (even) more financially constrained compared to public firms.

---

[41] John Asker, Joan Farre-Mensa and Alexander Ljungqvist, 'Corporate Investment and Stock Market Listing: A Puzzle?' October 2014.

Recent work[42] by Philippon and Gutiérrez suggests a potential explanation for the under-investment by publicly listed firms. Ownership by passive investors (index investors) leaves companies vulnerable to the pressures of activist investors. They respond to that pressure by cutting back on investment and diverting profits for stock repurchases, something we discussed in Section 5.3. Another explanation that they offer is increasing concentration in industries, a topic we discuss in Section 6.7.

We believe that the myopia of financial markets and that of publicly listed firms reinforce each other. Take the case of government and corporate debt. In the last several decades, government debt in advanced nations has gone up and yet interest rates have come down. If financial market theories were right, sophisticated and rational investors discounting all future outcomes with an appropriately risk-adjusted discount rate should have been able to offset the perilous effects of low and ever-declining policy rates. Instead, financial markets (investors) priced debt too low even as debt – both private and public sectors were on a borrowing binge – was exploding. Government bond yields have been on a falling trend since the 1980s. Investors priced in the secular decline in inflation and the decline in policy rates (short-term) more than they priced in the risk of the rapid rise in debt. In fact, they ignored it.

Investors were willing to lend more and more to governments at cheaper and cheaper rates even as governments (and corporations and households) became more and more indebted. It does not make sense at all. The BIS called out the bond market for its myopia in its Annual Report 2015–16:[43]

> It might be imprudent to rely heavily on market signals as the basis for judgments about equilibrium and sustainability. There is no guarantee that over any period of time the joint behaviour of central banks, governments and market participants will result in market interest rates that are set at the right level, i.e., that are consistent with sustainable good economic performance.... After all, given the huge uncertainty involved, how confident can we be that the long-term outcome will be the desirable one? Might not interest rates, just like any other asset price, be misaligned for very long periods?

---

[42] Germán Gutiérrez and Thomas Philippon, 'Investment-Less Growth: An Empirical Investigation', National Bureau of Economic Research, Working Paper no. 22897, December 2016, available at http://www.nber.org/papers/w22897.pdf (accessed on 5 June 2017).

[43] 'When the Future Becomes Today,' Bank for International Settlements, 86th Annual Report (Chapter 1), June 2016, http://www.bis.org/publ/arpdf/ar2016e1.htm (accessed 1 June 2017).

That is startling. If financial market prices can be misaligned for long periods, their signals are unreliable for capital allocation. Unless they are drastically reformed, financial markets will keep doing what they are doing – making short-term and incestuous gains just for insiders at the expense of the long-term and societal good. Over time, financial markets have become a public bad.[44]

It is clear that the primacy-accorded stock markets in corporate decision-making have to be addressed. One way to break the vicious circle of incentive misalignment is to eliminate the link between stock market performance and executive compensation.

Several proposals have been mooted to reform executive compensation and make it more aligned with long-term health of the company. We do not propose to examine their relative merits. But we believe some principles should underpin executive compensation – linking them to long-term performance of the company and shareholder control over such decisions. Indeed, managerial compensation is one area that can unite labour (non-executive workers) and capital stakeholders. Find below (Box 6.2) a letter to *Financial Times* that one of us wrote several months before the peak of the financial crisis of 2008, on the issue of executive compensation and the identity of interests between workers and shareholders.

In the immediate aftermath of the financial crisis, Lucian Bebchuk and Jesse Fried made a comprehensive proposal that links executive pay to building long-term firm value creation.[45] It included cash-out restrictions, exclusion of retirement-based holding requirements, grant-based and aggregate limitations on unwinding, prevention of back-end or front-end gaming of equity options and prohibition on hedging and derivative transactions that undermine the beneficial effects of long-term equity plans.

As regards shareholder control, in one of the proposals, Roger Lowenstein suggested that CEO compensation above USD 500,000 per annum should be voted upon by shareholders and that their resolution would be binding.[46]

---

[44] V. Anantha Nageswaran, 'Do We Need Financial Markets?' *Livemint*, 7 June 2016, available at http://www.livemint.com/Opinion/cXUq1qqZGTx3mKmj7qwlmM/Do-we-need-financial-markets.html (accessed on 1 June 2017).

[45] Lucian Bebchuk and Jesse Fried, 'Paying for Long Term Performance', *Pennsylvania Law Review*, Discussion Paper no. 658, 158(2010): 1915–1959.

[46] The article begins with the story that Walt Disney Co. deducted the cost of uniforms for its 16,000 workers from their wages. It cost USD 3.8 million, about a month's salary of its CEO.

## Box 6.2    Letter to *Financial Times*

### FINANCIAL TIMES

| Home | World | Companies | Markets | Global Economy | Lex | Comment | Management | Life & Arts |

| Columnists || Analysis || Opinion || The A-List || Editorial || Blogs || Letters || Corrections || Obituaries |    | Tools |

January 11, 2008 2:00 am

## It is not just bankers' pay that is deeply flawed

F *rom Dr V. Anantha Nageswaran.*

Sir, Zeroing in on the deeply flawed compensation system in US banks, as Raghuram Rajan does ("Bankers' pay is deeply flawed", January 9), is the right way to start to fix the problem. But, the issues he writes about – tail risk, fake alpha – are all applicable to the non-financial corporate sector in the US and in many other countries. Perhaps they are creeping into the corporate sector in emerging economies too.

The problems go to the heart of joint-stock companies with their dispersed shareholding structure where no one really owns the company.

Stock options have not solved the agency problem. They seem to have exacerbated it since most managers treat them as fixed pay by backdating them and by revising down the exercise price. Golden parachutes complete the insult for shareholders.

We know that promoters have enriched themselves at the expense of other shareholders and now, so do managers. The question is: when do shareholders and workers realise that their interests converge and that they have to be in alliance? It was the ingenuity of the intelligentsia to have insulated managers (the educated collude) by pitting shareholders against workers.

Institutional shareholders should think hard about the usefulness of independent labour unions in keeping egregious managerial compensation at bay. If the unfolding global financial meltdown sets in motion such thought processes, it will have done some good.

**V. Anantha Nageswaran,**
**Head of Investment Research**
**(Asia-Pacific and Middle East),**
**Bank Julius Baer, Singapore 049145**

RELATED TOPICS   United States of America

Printed from: http://www.ft.com/cms/s/0/2b2d47c2-bffa-11dc-8052-0000779fd2ac.html

Print a single copy of this article for personal use. Contact us if you wish to print more to distribute to others.
© THE FINANCIAL TIMES LTD 2014 FT and 'Financial Times' are trademarks of The Financial Times Ltd.

The practical implementation of both proposals is the challenge. Who would bell the cat and which company's board would tweak the rules to make compensation long-term value creation incentive compatible and allow for binding shareholder resolutions? With few exceptions, most boards operate under the 'You scratch my back; I scratch yours' principle. It is an oligopoly. The issue must be tackled at the philosophical level. In a recent shareholder meeting, when a shareholder questioned executive pay, Jamie Dimon, the CEO of JP Morgan said, 'You guys are starting to hurt my feelings'.[47] It is a long road or, may be, it is a dead end.

---

[47] Michael Skapinker, 'Theresa May, Jamie Dimon and How to Answer Tough Questions', *Financial Times*, 23 May 2017, available at https://www.ft.com/content/ade5b342-3eef-11e7-82b6-896b95f30f58 (accessed on 31 May 2017).

In a speech[48] to the Occupy Economics on the subject of 'Socially Useful Banking' he made in October 2012, Andrew Haldane, then the executive director in charge of financial stability at the Bank of England (now, its chief economist), called for changes in five Cs – culture, capital, compensation, credit and competition – for banks to become socially useful. This section dealt with two of those five Cs – capital and compensation. In the next section, we would like to touch upon the culture in American corporations and the Federal Reserve – the obsession with stock market prices or asset prices, more generally, for the latter. It is that we explore next.

In the final analysis, how do we make banks or even capital markets fund real investments? No, we are not thinking about mandated lending or credit allocations. It could be a matter of changing the expectation and the possibility of high returns at short horizons. After all, even as the phrase, 'secular stagnation' is freely bandied about, it has only been boom times for corporate profits and in stock markets. The answer may be found in lengthening horizons by reducing the returns available from stock markets in shorter horizons. It is possible. It is up to the Federal Reserve and we point the way in Section 6.5.

## 6.5 The Fed must stop underwriting stock prices

At this stage, things look bleak indeed. Banks do not lend for real investment purposes. Listed companies do not invest. Executives are hurt by questions on their pay. Stock market performance considerations dominate firms' borrowing and investment decisions (stock buyback). Where and how do we start to fix things? The interesting and the tricky part is that when things begin to change in one direction, they do so slowly and gradually over time. However, when we want to turn the clock back, incrementalism will not cut it. One needs a big bang because incrementalism will be too meek and mild for the forces of status quo.[49] They will throttle reforms. That is why crises help. They help to

---

48 Andrew G. Haldane, 'A Leaf Being Turned', speech to Occupy Economics, 'Socially Useful Banking', 29 October 2012, available at https://www.bis.org/review/r121031f. pdf (accessed on 31 May 2017).

49 We were somewhat pleased to note that we were echoing, unknowingly, Thomas Kuhn. He wrote in *The Structure of the Scientific Revolution*, '["anomalies and crises" that show up within the current paradigm] are terminated, not by deliberation and interpretation, but by a relatively sudden and unstructured event like the gestalt switch. Scientists then often speak of the … "lightning flash" that "inundates" a previously obscure puzzle, enabling its components to be seen in a new way … No ordinary sense of the term

push through massive changes in a short time. Think of what happened after the Great Depression, for example. We think that a change in the Federal Reserve Board's economic model and monetary policy framework can bring about many desirable changes in the financial system, enhancing its safety and stability, and in the big socio-economic question of the day: inequality.

On 2 May 2018, when the Federal Reserve Open Market Committee concluded its two-day meeting, the Dow Jones Industrial Average was around 24,100 points. Some five weeks later, it was up 4 per cent. In the meeting, the FOMC emphasized the symmetric nature of its inflation target. Indeed, the minutes of the FOMC meeting had the word 'symmetric' in 11 places. In plain English, the FOMC reassured the market that it would overlook an overshoot of the inflation rate above 2 per cent for some time. How much of an overshoot would be overlooked and for how long were left undefined.

This was their reassurance to bubble investors and speculators even as their research staff warned off elevated vulnerabilities in two areas: asset prices and non-financial sector leverage. Indeed, in recent times, the staff research prepared for the benefit of the FOMC participants had not categorized two risks to financial stability as 'elevated'. Yet, the FOMC was anxious that financial markets did not become unduly anxious about the pace of the tightening of monetary policy.

As long as the Federal Reserve is obsessed with asset prices when they are on their way down and indifferent to them when they are rising, long booms and short but severe busts will be the feature of financial capitalism. Peering long into the future, it may well be the death knell of modern capitalism. This may sound over the top or too prescient or too late. Take your pick.

We think that the FOMC members would do well to familiarize themselves with two research papers by Anna Cieslak and Annette Vissing-Jorgensen.[50] The important message from their 2017 paper sets the stage for our recommendation. Their main conclusions were:

- Reaction of actual economic output (GDP growth) to excess stock market returns is small and is symmetric for stock market gains and losses.

---

"interpretation" fits these flashes of intuition through which a new paradigm is born'. Werner Erhard and Michael C. Jensen, 'Putting Integrity into Finance: A Purely Positive Approach,' *Capitalism and Society* 12, no.1 (2017): Article 1.

[50] Cieslak, Morse and Vissing-Jorgensen, 'Stock Returns over the FOMC Cycle'; Cieslak and Vissing-Jorgensen, 'The Economics of the Fed Put'.

- Reaction of unemployment to excess stock market returns is asymmetric. That is, unemployment rises more when stock market records losses than it falls when the stock market posts gains. However, the Federal Reserve expectations for unemployment change much more than actual unemployment changes themselves!
- Sensitivity of actual private consumption to negative stock market outcomes is small, especially between 1994 and 2016. But the focus of the Federal Reserve on the stock market is driven a lot by its concern over stock market declines on consumption.
- Before 1994, going back to September 1982, there is no significant relationship between the stock market and updates to Federal Reserve growth expectations.
- The Fed updates its macroeconomic expectations (about growth and unemployment) in a way that is highly sensitive to stock market outcomes during the inter-meeting period. This relationship is pervasive starting from the mid-1990s, but is largely absent before that.

It is interesting that Cieslak and Vissing-Jorgensen date the inflection point in the behaviour of the Federal Reserve in the mid-1990s. In an unrelated work,[51] Dong Lee, Han Shin and René M. Stulz found that after the mid-1990s, capital no longer flew more to the industries with the best growth opportunities. From then until 2014, industries with the lowest funding rates had better growth opportunities than industries with the highest funding rates – funding rate being defined as the ratio of new capital provided by the capital markets to assets. They showed that this change was entirely due to high Tobin's Q firms that invested less after the mid-1990s and used the resulting excess cash flow to repurchase shares. The authors concluded consequently that before the mid-1990s, capital markets appeared to be functionally efficient. After the mid-1990s, it was no longer true that capital markets appeared to be functionally efficient if functional efficiency meant that capital flew more to industries with a higher Tobin's Q.

---

[51] Dong Lee, Han Shin and René M. Stulz, 'Why Does Capital No Longer Flow to the Industries with the Best Growth Opportunities?' Working Paper no. 22924, National Bureau of Economic Research, December 2016, available at http://www.nber.org/papers/w22924 (accessed on 5 June 2017).

The structural break occurring in the mid-1990s should not surprise us. The more a central bank signals its willingness to underwrite the stock market, the more is the cash diverted to the stock market than to real investment.

These conclusions lead to the simple but probably the most important financial reform of the last 40 years. The Federal Reserve should publicly forswear the central role of asset prices in its macroeconomic modelling and forecasts. On the face of it, this may seem inconsistent with our berating the Federal Reserve in Section 4.3 for failing to take into account asset price inflation in its policy calculus. Let us explain.

Our suggestion has two parts. The real issue is that the Federal Reserve ignores asset price inflation but takes asset price deflation too seriously. Therefore, what we are calling for is the abandonment of its implicit mandate of underwriting asset prices, particularly stock prices. Simply put, in the first part, it must publicly abandon the Federal Reserve monetary policy Put on stock prices.

In the second part, the Federal Reserve must factor in asset price inflation into its policy calculus. The mere signal or recognition that it is doing so would bring about a transformation in investors' behaviour and attitudes to risk. We recognize, as did Borio and White in 2004 (see footnote 9 of Chapter 4 for details), that intervening in asset price booms is least likely to be popular: 'Its action would probably be seen as aborting a sustainable expansion and fully justified increases in wealth.' More importantly, it would be hard to prove that it was worth it for crises averted and losses avoided would remain invisible.

However, the Federal Reserve must try because the crisis of 2008 has conclusively established that the costs of ignoring asset price inflation are considerable. Second, the costs are not just economic but social and political. Third, just as important, they are still unfolding. As Borio and White wrote, the objections to intervening to rein in asset price inflation will be less formidable if the interventions are couched in terms of addressing financial imbalances rather than stopping a boom on its tracks.

Proving them right is the current asset price boom cycle that began in 2009 which has increasingly featured financial imbalances. In preparation for the FOMC meeting of May 2018, Federal Reserve staff classified asset price risks and leverage risks in the economy as 'elevated' – one of the very few times (or probably the first time they did) they had labelled the twin risks 'elevated'. For instance, the amount of leveraged loans outstanding (loans issued by below-investment grade companies that feature an already high debt–equity ratio in their balance sheets) that are covenant-lite ('covenants' are conditions attached to bonds and loans that protect bondholders or lenders' interests) reached a new record in May 2018, thirteenth new high in as many months. According to 'Leveraged Commentary and Data' (LCD for short – an offering of S&P Global Market Intelligence), in numbers, 'As of May 31, 77.4% of U.S. leveraged loan outstanding was cov-lite. The leveraged loan asset class recently became a $1 trillion market, meaning there is upwards of $800 billion of cov-lite loans outstanding.'[52] In comparison, covenant-lite bonds constituted 29 per cent of leveraged loans in 2007.[53] Never do two crises feature the same risk. It is always different. That is why most 'early warning indicators' are often 'rear-view' indicators. We digress. The case for the Fed to forswear its support for asset prices and to factor in financial imbalances makes itself, thus.

But what would it achieve?

It would solve many problems in one stroke. With its monetary policy, the Fed writes both CALL and PUT options on the stock market. It underwrites the downside risk and enhances the upside opportunities from investing.

The opportunity to make good returns on stocks with the central bank guaranteeing it virtually is too good to pass up. Therefore, executive compensation is linked to stock market performance. Second, investments in real assets are too cumbersome and uncertain. Stock buybacks are far better use of corporate liquidity and leverage.

If the Federal Reserve were to let go of its obsession with asset prices, it would bring stock market returns down and volatility up. Investors would learn to appreciate risk and uncertainty and behave accordingly. They would leverage less. If asset prices rise far less than before because the implicit Fed guarantee is withdrawn, they would also be less prone to busts. Indeed, business cycles and asset price cycles will have shorter peaks but also shorter valleys.

Economies would be far more normal than they have been after the 1980s, driven, in the main, by asset prices and debt. Macroeconomic volatility may indeed rise and cycles might get shorter. But 'The Great Moderation' is a myth. It just stored up very fat tails that show up from time to time. Inequality would

---

[52] See 'Leveraged Loans: Cov-Lite Volume Reaches Yet Another Record High,' 22 June 2018, available at http://www.leveragedloan.com/leveraged-loans-cov-lite-volume-reaches-yet-another-record-high/ (accessed 30 July 2018).

[53] See 'Covenant-lite Leveraged Loans: After Default, Whither Recoveries?' 23 July 2018, available at http://www.leveragedloan.com/covenant-lite-leveraged-loans-default-whither-recoveries/ (accessed 30 July 2018).

reduce as income from wealth and assets has contributed to the rising share of income for the top 1 per cent in the United States.

Once the Federal Reserve abandons its concern for asset markets, its monetary policy would become more symmetric. This would reverse the prevailing belief among stock market investors that while the Fed would pursue monetary accommodation for extended periods it would refrain from raising rates to deflate bubbles. There should be reduced focus on forward guidance and excessive transparency in the monetary policy framework of advanced countries. This will exert a moderating influence on risk assumption in financial markets, which in a globally integrated market ripples across economies. To the extent they are restrained in the United States, the restraint will also spill over to capital markets around the world.

If the Federal Reserve were to signal, categorically and unambiguously, the withdrawal of the Federal Reserve PUT on stock markets, much of the problems associated with financial capitalism – poor returns to labour, excessive absolute and relative executive compensations, short-term investment horizons, preference to financial over real investments, investor indifference to market risk, build-up of public and private debt and systemic risk – will begin to sort themselves out. There will be a virtuous spillover.

Monetary policy allowing credit to be priced correctly is one part of the equation of reining in debt creation. The other part is to eliminate the fiscal incentive that encourages debt over equity. That is the subject of Section 6.6.

## 6.6   End the inducement to pile up debt

Any talk of cross-border capital flows cannot be done without a discussion on the role of debt. It is no hyperbole to claim that the last two decades have been an 'Age of Debt'. It is, therefore, only appropriate that it climax with the coronation of the 'King of Debt' as the president of the country, which has been the undisputed leader of this trend.[54]

The US Federal Reserve has led the way with extraordinary monetary accommodation that, in no small measure, contributed to the attractions of debt. The cheap capital environment has exposed several distortions, most worryingly on the capital structure of firms. The low borrowing cost coupled with its tax advantage has made debt extremely attractive. The result has

---

[54] Matt Egan, 'Donald Trump: "I'm the King of Debt"' *CNN Money*, 7 May 2016, available at http://money.cnn.com/2016/05/05/investing/trump-king-of-debt-fire-janet-yellen/.

been the extraordinary use of debt to finance share buybacks and mergers and acquisitions (M&A). The incentive to leverage up excessively has left a legacy of massively indebted corporates, a fact underlined repeatedly by IMF in its recent quarterly *Fiscal Monitors*.[55]

Low interest rates have provided an undisputed boost to debt. The global stock of debt – households, non-financial corporates and governments – has surged from about USD 105 trillion to USD 145 trillion in the 2008–15 period. As a share of global nominal GDP, it has risen from 180 per cent to about 215 per cent in the same period, with the largest increase from corporates and governments in that order. But as we have seen earlier, this trend of loading up leverage predates the financial crisis. In fact, in the 1990s, corporate equity increased USD 131 billion while debt soared an astonishing USD 1.8 trillion.[56]

One contributor to the attractiveness of debt has been the role of the tax deduction on corporate interest payments. This contrasts with treatment of dividend payouts to shareholders, which are taxed twice, as the company's corporate tax and the shareholder's income tax.

The differential treatment of debt and equity generates two major distortions – the debt bias and debt shifting.[57] The former encourages firms to leverage up while the latter makes them indulge in tax arbitrage.

The tax deduction on interest payments and the attendant preference for debt mean that firm's capital structure is an important determinant of its valuation. The fact that debt helps retain ownership pattern is an added attraction. Since larger firms find it easier to access credit and leverage up, this interest deduction benefits them at the expense of smaller enterprises.

One estimate has found that this deduction is worth around 11 per cent of the value of all US corporate assets.[58] Another estimate found that a

---

[55] 'Achieving More with Less,' *IMF Fiscal Monitor*, April 2017, available at https://www.imf.org/en/Publications/FM/Issues/2017/04/06/fiscal-monitor-april-2017 (accessed on 31 May 2017).

[56] 'Noted Economist Sees Tectonic Shifts in Business Landscape', *Businesswire*, 24 September 2015, available at http://www.businesswire.com/news/home/20150924006015/en/Noted-Economist-Sees-"Tectonic-Shifts"-EconomicFinancial-Landscape (accessed on 31 May 2017).

[57] 'Corporate Funding Structures and Incentives,' Financial Stability Board Report, available at https://www.oecd.org/g20/topics/financial-sector-reform/Corporate-funding-structures-and-incentives-FSB-Report.pdf (accessed on 31 May 2017).

[58] 'What If Interest Expenses Were No Longer Tax Deductible,' The Economist, 4 February 2017, available at http://www.economist.com/news/finance-and-

percentage-point increase in the corporate tax rate increased debt-to-assets ratio by 0.27 percentage points.[59] Yet another estimate of the debt bias for six large EU economies found that its elimination would increase tax revenues by 25–55 per cent of GDP. Economist Luigi Zingales estimates that elimination of the deductibility of interest from the definition of taxable corporate income could lower the corporate tax rate to 10 per cent without reducing tax revenues.[60]

Nowhere are the distortions from the preferential tax treatment for debt more evident than in the financial markets. Leverage ratios touched 30 times the Tier I equity for the largest financial institutions as the sub-prime mortgage bubble inflated.[61] An IMF study found that 'greater tax bias is associated with significantly higher aggregate bank leverage and that this in turn is associated with a significantly greater chance of crisis'.[62] They find that the lower likelihood of financial crisis from the elimination of debt bias could result in potential GDP gains of 0.5 per cent to 11.9 per cent. Another study of six large EU countries estimated that the elimination of the debt bias would reduce the potential public finance losses from failing banks by 25 per cent to 55 per cent.[63]

The other distortion involves debt shifting. One of the negative externalities of globalization has been the trend of corporates indulging in tax arbitrage. It has been estimated that while tax havens contribute just 15 per cent of the value addition of US majority-owned corporations, they form

---

economics/21716050-would-be-risky-time-fiddle-tax-code-what-if-interest-expenses (accessed on 31 May 2017).

[59] Sven Langedijk et al., 'Corporate Debt Bias and the Cost of Banking Crisis, *VoxEU*, 4 July 2015, available at http://voxeu.org/article/corporate-debt-bias-and-cost-banking-crises (accessed on 21 June 2018).

[60] Luigi Zingales, *A Capitalism for the People: Recapturing the Lost Genius of American Prosperity* (New York, NY: Basic Books, 2012), available at https://read.amazon.in/kp/kshare?asin=B00G1SD5XO&id=y2zJPJQkRSCBhxvTWLx8lA&reshareId=4G GR99A8PK79DHNV87HP&reshareChannel=system (accessed on 21 June 2018).

[61] Basel Committee on Banking Supervision, Basel III Monitoring Report, March 2015, available at http://www.bis.org/bcbs/publ/d312.pdf (accessed on 21 June 2018).

[62] Ruud De Mooij, Michael Keen and Masanori Orihara, 'Taxation, Bank Leverage, and Financial Crisis', IMF Working Paper, February 2013, available at https://www.imf.org/external/pubs/ft/wp/2013/wp1348.pdf (accessed on 21 June 2018).

[63] Langedijk et al., 'Corporate Debt Bias and the Cost of Banking Crisis'.

42 per cent of the net income.[64] The two main tax arbitrage strategies involve profit shifting through transfer of IP to subsidiary in a low-tax country and intra-company loans.[65]

A subsidiary established in a low-tax country functions as an internal financing entity, providing high-cost loans to affiliates in higher tax countries. The tax deduction on interest payments enables affiliates to minimize their tax liability in the higher tax country. Tax deduction on corporate incomes is widely exploited by multinational corporations to limit their tax liabilities. It has been estimated that 'taxation induced intra-company loans to reduce tax payments in high-tax locations', with the effects being larger for affiliates located in developing countries.[66]

Apart from the reflexive opposition to any effort to expand the tax base, any attempt to eliminate the preferential treatment on debt is likely to face stiff opposition. Then there is the challenge of global coordination. No country will volunteer to eliminate this distortion since it would lower the competitiveness of their firms and only end up encouraging firms to borrow elsewhere.

The issue of tax shifting has acquired increasing salience in recent years. In 2013, the countries of G-20 and the OECD launched the Base Erosion and Profit Shifting (BEPS) project to modernize international tax rules. Among its objectives was the 'design of rules to prevent base erosion through the use of interest expense'. One of the recommendations submitted in 2015 is to cap interest expense deductions at a net interest/ earnings before interest, taxes, depreciation and amortization (EBITDA) ratio in the range of 10–30 per cent, at the discretion of national governments. However, it allows for actual deductions in cases where the entire group's ratio is higher than the fixed ratio, thereby acknowledging the supremacy of the principle of tax deduction on interest expenses.[67] Still the fixed ratio presents significant progress in addressing tax arbitraging.

---

[64] 'Spill-Overs in International Corporate Taxation', IMF Policy Paper, 9 May 2014, available at http://www.imf.org/external/np/pp/eng/2014/050914.pdf (accessed on 21 June 2018).

[65] Michael C Durst, 'Limitations on Interest Deductions', ICTD Working Paper, June 2015, available at https://assets.publishing.service.gov.uk/media/57aa008d40f0b608 ab000064/41_Limitations_on_Interest_Deductions.pdf (accessed on 21 June 2018).

[66] 'Spill-overs in International Corporate Taxation', IMF Policy Paper.

[67] OECD/G-20 BEPS Project – 2015 Final Reports, available at https://www.oecd.org/ ctp/beps-reports-2015-executive-summaries.pdf (accessed on 21 June 2018).

Accordingly, from 1 April 2017, the United Kingdom led the way by promulgating a *Fixed Ratio Rule* as part of its tax rules.[68]

> The Fixed Ratio Rule will limit the amount of net interest expense that a worldwide group can deduct against its taxable profits to 30% of its taxable earnings before interest, taxes, depreciation, and amortisation (EBITDA). A modified debt cap within the new rules will ensure the net interest deduction does not exceed the total net interest expense of the worldwide group. The Group Ratio Rule allows a 'group ratio' to be substituted for the 30% figure. The group ratio is based on the net interest expense to EBITDA ratio for the worldwide group based on its consolidated accounts.

The best shot at reforming this distortion may be in combination with a lowering of corporate tax rates. In this context, the corporate tax reform plan approved by the US Congress in December 2017, Tax Cuts and Jobs Act, assumes great significance. Among its several elements is the introduction of a limit on the tax deduction on interest expense. The rules state that the deduction shall not exceed the sum of the tax payer's business interest income and 30 per cent of the adjusted EBITDA.[69] The provision becomes tighter by 2021 by making it 30 per cent of EBIT. However, it allows for 'carry forward of disallowed interest', which allows corporates to deduct the remaining interest expense in the following years, up to the fifth year after the expense is incurred.

One is to dispense with the preferential treatment to debt and the other is to offset the loss by lowering corporate tax rates. If successful, this would be among the most radical corporate tax reform undertaken in any major country for decades. An alternative approach would be, like the BEPS Project, to cap tax deductibility on interest expenditure at a certain ratio. This could be combined with a reduction in corporate tax rates.

Eliminating the corporate tax deduction on interest payments has the potential to be a double win. Apart from increasing government revenues, it

---

[68] 'Corporation Tax: Tax Deductibility of Corporate Interest Expense', HM Revenue & Customs, 5 December 2016, available at https://www.gov.uk/government/publications/corporation-tax-tax-deductibility-of-corporate-interest-expense/corporation-tax-tax-deductibility-of-corporate-interest-expense (accessed on 21 June 2018).

[69] Bob Pisani, 'Wall Street Has a Problem with This Part of the New Tax Plan', *CNBC*, 2 November 2017, available at https://www.cnbc.com/2017/11/02/the-new-tax-plan-has-a-catch.html (accessed on 21 June 2018).

would also be an institutional mechanism to discourage the accumulation of excessive debt.

It is, therefore, imperative that the tax advantage be eliminated in a phased manner, to allow firms to maximize their value independent of the capital structure, in accordance with the Modigliani Miller Theorem. 'Debt has been acting as a political and social substitute for income growth for far too long'.[70] Truer words have not been written.

## 6.7 The return of the oligopolist and the need for anti-trust actions

Another consequence of financialization, one that is increasingly evident, has been the alarming rise in firm concentration in both the financial and non-financial sectors. This is reflected in several different measures of business activity. Urgent anti-trust action is essential. There are several signatures of the US economy having a 'market power' problem.[71] Numerous studies, including by the White House, have found significant increase in the concentration of economic activity in many industries in recent decades, a consequence of record levels of M&A.[72]

David Autor and colleagues have found evidence of superstar effect, arising from technology or market conditions, concentrating sales among a few firms, increasing their profits and decreasing labour income shares, across each of the six major sectors covered by US economic census for the 1982–2012 period.[73] Lending credence, research by two economists, Jan de Loecker and Jan Eckhout, shows that markups, the amounts charged by companies over and above their costs, have risen sharply from just 18 per cent above costs to 67 per cent in the 1980–2014 period.[74] Worse still, German Gutierrez and

---

[70] 'When the Future Becomes Today,' Bank for International Settlements.

[71] Jonathan Baker, 'Market Power in the US Economy Today', Washington Centre for Equitable Growth, March 2017.

[72] Council of Economic Advisors, Competition Brief, April 2016, available at https://www.whitehouse.gov/sites/default/files/page/files/20160414_cea_competition_issue_brief.pdf (accessed on 21 June 2018).

[73] David Autor et al., 'Concentrating on the Fall of the Labour Share', *American Economic Review: Papers & Proceedings* 107, no.5 (2017): 180–185, available at https://economics.mit.edu/files/12544 (accessed on 21 June 2018).

[74] Jan de Loecker and Jan Eckhout, 'The Rise of Market Power and the Macroeconomic Implications', 24 August 2017, available at http://www.janeeckhout.com/wp-content/uploads/RMP.pdf (accessed on 21 June 2018).

Thomas Philippon have found that declining competition has been responsible for under-investment by US firms over the past 30 years.[75]

Profits, free-cash flows and returns on capital are at historic highs in the United States. In contrast, labour income share of GDP is at multi-decade lows. At the turn of the millennium, pre-tax cash compensation to workers amounted to 66 per cent of net domestic income. In 2016, it had dropped to 63.4 per cent. The pre-tax corporate profit share was 7.2 per cent in 2000. It had improved to 10.5 per cent in 2016. In the new millennium, American labour has lost to capital with a relative swing of 5.9 per cent in favour of capitalists. But the return to capital is not just about corporate profits. The return to capital share of gross domestic income – profits, proprietors' income and rental income – has increased from 22.3 per cent in 4Q2000 to 24.5 per cent in 1Q2017. In the same period, labour share has gone down from 56.7 per cent to 53.7 per cent for a swing of 5.2 per cent in favour of capitalists. Of course, the erosion of labour share of income was not confined to America alone (Figure 6.2).

**Figure 6.2   Changes in compensation to GDP ratio in select advanced economies**

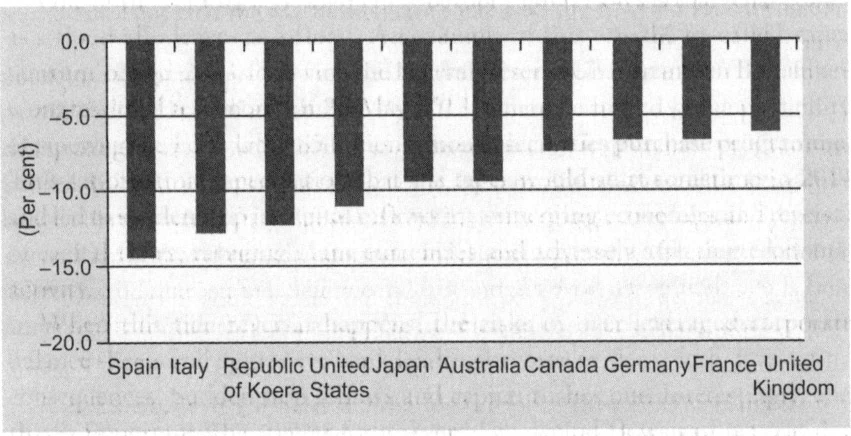

*Source*: Labour share in G-20 economies, report prepared for the G20 Employment Working Group, Antalya, Turkey, February 26–27, 2015, by the International Labour Organization and the Organisation for Economic Co-operation and Development with contributions from International Monetary Fund and World Bank Group.

*Note*: Figures reflect the changes in the adjusted labour share of GDP. Unadjusted compensation/GDP is increased by adjusting for the self-employed.

---

[75] German Gutierrez and Thomas Philippon, 'Investment-Less Growth: An Empirical Investigation,' November 2016, available at http://pages.stern.nyu.edu/~tphilipp/papers/QNIK.pdf (accessed on 21 June 2018).

Up to the mid-1980s, profit share of GDP was on a downtrend for the most part. After that, it has been on an uptrend. For labour share of GDP, it peaked in the 1970s and had a mild revival in the mid-to-late 1990s as the American economy began to pay its technology and banking executives rather sumptuously with stocks and stock options. The bubble in technology stocks explains the pickup in labour compensation share of GDP in the 1990s. It has been downhill since then as the rise in compensation for the top 1 per cent is inadequate to compensate for the stagnation-to- decline in the compensation of the rest of the 99 per cent. Whereas profit share of GDP has only had temporary setbacks.

Although the main purpose of this book is to focus on the toxic impact of financialization on economies and societies, we have to note here that elites have not yet grasped the dangers inherent in Figure 6.2. Normally, technology and international trade are held out as responsible for the dwindling share of labour income in advanced nations. Elites dismiss trade as an explanation and attribute it all to technology. Their aim is not to disrupt global trade since it is beneficial in the aggregate. Then, they argue that technological progress is unstoppable. We are back to square one. This will not work. Eventually, there will be social upheavals.

It has been well documented by Pierce and Schott in the case of the United States that workers and communities had been badly affected wherever manufacturing was outsourced to China. Justin Pierce (Federal Reserve Board) and Peter Schott (Yale School of Management) have come up with research that shows that US manufacturing employment declined after the United States conferred permanent normal trade relations (PNTR) status on China at the turn of the millennium. They account for other factors. The same thing did not happen in Europe. Europe had conferred PNTR in the 1980s itself.[76]

Their research also led them to analyse the impact of trade on mortality:[77]

We find that exposure to PNTR is associated with an increase in mortality due to suicide and related causes, particularly among whites. These results are consistent with that group's relatively high employment in manufacturing, the sector most affected by the change in trade policy. We find that these results are robust to various extensions, including an alternate empirical specification

---

[76] Justin R. Pierce and Peter K. Schott, 'The Surprisingly Swift Decline of U.S. Manufacturing Employment', *American Economic Review* 106, no. 7 (2016): 1632–1662.

[77] Justin R. Pierce and Peter K. Schott, 'Trade Liberalization and Mortality: Evidence from U.S. Counties', November 2016, available at http://www.justinrpierce.com/index_files/mortality_164.pdf (accessed on 1 June 2017).

that places no restrictions on the timing of the effects of the policy change as well including controls for changes in state health care policy and exposure of other counties in the surrounding labour market.

While the results in this book do not provide an assessment of the overall welfare impact of PNTR, they do offer a broader understanding of the distributional implications of trade liberalization.

It is worth noting here that two other researchers have found similar results in the case of Brexit.[78] They found that globalization in the form of the 'Chinese import shock' was a key driver of regional support for Brexit.

The banking, financial and economic crisis of 2008 could have been the watershed moment that arrested and reversed the trend of neoliberalism. But central bankers, particularly in the United States and Europe, ensured that it would not be the case. Now, the advent of robotics and artificial intelligence further threatens to jeopardize jobs and incomes. These are still early days and evidence is slow in coming. But without restoring the balance between capital and labour, between profits and worker compensation, nations cannot hope to continue to hold together.[79]

Entrepreneurship activity, job creation and destruction, and economic dynamism have all been on the decline.[80] Further, workers' internal mobility

---

[78] Italo Colantone and Piero Stanig, 'Globalisation and Brexit', 23 November 2016, available at http://voxeu.org/article/globalisation-and-brexit (accessed on 1 June 2017).

[79] See, for example, Yuval Harari's 'Are We about to Witness the Most Unequal Societies' in History?' *The Guardian*, 24 May 2017, available at https://www.theguardian.com/inequality/2017/may/24/are-we-about-to-witness-the-most-unequal-societies-in-history-yuval-noah-harari (accessed on 1 June 2017); Tyler Cowen, 'Industrial Revolution Comparisons Aren't Comforting', *Bloomberg Opinion*, 16 February 2017, available at https://www.bloomberg.com/view/articles/2017-02-16/industrial-revolution-comparisons-aren-t-comforting (accessed on 1 June 2017); Mira Rojanasakul and Peter Coy's 'More Robots, Fewer Jobs', *Bloomberg*, 8 May 2017, available at https://www.bloomberg.com/graphics/2017-more-robots-fewer-jobs/ (accessed on 1 June 2017); Daron Acemoglu and Pascual Restrepo, 'Robots and Jobs: Evidence from US Labour Markets', NBER Working Paper no. 23285, March 2017, available at http://www.nber.org/papers/w23285 (accessed on 1 June 2017); Steve Levine, 'No One Is Prepared to Stop the Robot Onslaught: So What Will We Do When It Arrives?' *Quartz*, available at https://qz.com/940977/no-one-is-prepared-to-stop-the-robot-onslaught-so-what-will-we-do-when-it-arrives/ (accessed on 1 June 2017).

[80] Ryan Decker et al., 'The Role of Entrepreneurship in US Job Creation and Economic Dynamism', *Journal of Economic Perspectives* 28, no. 3 (2014), 3–24, available at http://pubs.aeaweb.org/doi/pdfplus/10.1257/jep.28.3.3 (accessed on 7 March 2018).

across occupational categories too has been falling.[81] The share of US workers requiring some form of state occupational licensing grew fivefold over the last half of the twentieth century to about a quarter of all US workers in 2008.[82] The consequence of all of these is that only half the children born since the 1980s can hope to be better off than their parents (Figure 6.3).

**Figure 6.3 Baseline estimates of absolute mobility by birth cohort**

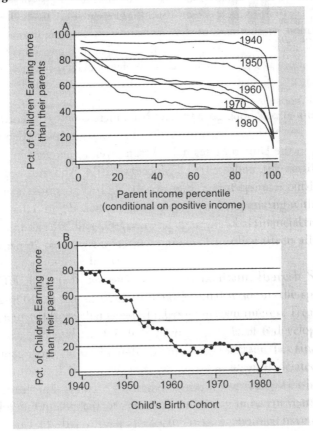

*Source*: Raj Chetty et al., 'The Fading American Dream: Trends in Absolute Income Mobility Since 1940,' *Science*, 24 April 2017.

---

[81] Council of Economic Advisors, Competition Brief, April 2016.

[82] 'Too Much of a Good Thing', *The Economist*, 26 March 2016, available at http://www. economist.com/news/briefing/21695385-profits-are-too-high-america-needs-giant-dose-competition-too-much-good-thing (accessed on 7 March 2018).

Raj Chetty et al. write:

We measure absolute mobility by comparing children's household incomes at age 30 (adjusted for inflation using the Consumer Price Index) with their parents' household incomes at age 30. We find that rates of absolute mobility have fallen from approximately 90% for children born in 1940 to 50% for children born in the 1980s. Absolute income mobility has fallen across the entire income distribution, with the largest declines for families in the middle class. These findings are unaffected by using alternative price indices to adjust for inflation, accounting for taxes and transfers, measuring income at later ages, and adjusting for changes in household size.... If one wants to revive the 'American Dream' of high rates of absolute mobility, one must have an interest in growth that is shared more broadly across the income distribution.

The fruits of economic growth have been increasingly concentrated. That is a cause of low business dynamism. The share of start-ups, or firms less than a year old, in the United States halved from over 16 per cent in 1977 (since when such data were collected) to 8 per cent by 2014. And this secular decline has pervasive across industries (Figure 6.4).[83] 'The Economist' examined US firms in 893 industries, grouped into broad sectors, and found that two-thirds of them became more concentrated between 1997 and 2012 and the weighted average share of the top four firms in each sector rose from 26 per cent to 32 per cent.[84]

Finance, expectedly, leads the way. The number of FDIC-insured institutions fell from more than 15,000 in 1990 to just 6,300 in 2015, and the five largest US financial institutions control half of all financial assets in the country.[85] Their share is up by more than 3 percentage points since 2008! India is better off at 40 per cent, slightly down from 41.2 per cent in 2008. Data are available only up to 2014.

There are also self-reinforcing dynamics at play. The leaders in the technology industry benefit from network effects. Technology-intensive nature of modern manufacturing means companies have to spend less on plant and equipment. The increased reallocation of jobs towards the more productive and

---

[83] 'Dynamism in Retreat – Consequences for Regions, Markets, and Workers', Economic Innovation Group, February 2017, available at https://eig.org/wp-content/uploads/2017/02/Dynamism-in-Retreat.pdf (accessed on 7 March 2018).

[84] 'Too Much of a Good Thing', *The Economist*.

[85] 'Noted Economist Sees Tectonic Shifts in Business Landscape', *Businesswire*.

profitable sectors, which being technology intensive, requires ever declining share of workers.

Figure 6.4  Start-up rate by sector – secular decline

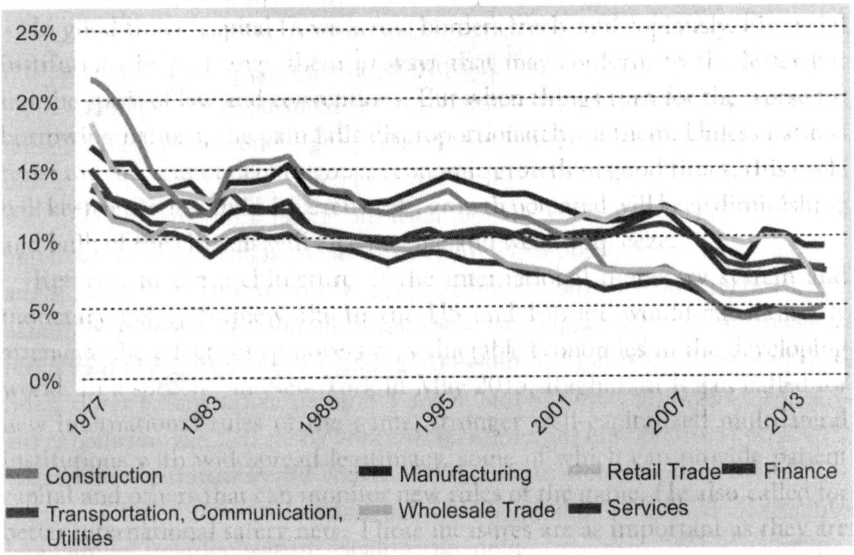

*Source*: Economic Innovation Group, 'Dynamism in Retreat – Consequences for Regions, Markets, and Workers', February 2017, available at https://eig.org/wp-content/uploads/2017/02/Dynamism-in-Retreat.pdf (accessed on 7 March 2018), p. 11.

The implications are clear. Capitalism needs to be saved from capitalists. Encouragingly, the folks at the University of Chicago's Stigler Centre, led by Luigi Zingales, have marshalled impressive research and advocacy platform to fight 'the subversion of competition by special interests'.[86] The irony of the intellectual fathers of rational expectations and market efficiency, which paved the way for financialization, leading the fight to reverse its consequences cannot be missed. Though much more needs to be done to take the fight to policy making tables, this ideological reawakening is a great start.

The time has arrived for aggressive anti-trust action to break up these oligopolies and monopolies and restore the competitive juices of American (and global) capitalism.

---

[86] ProMarket Blog, Stigler Centre, University of Chicago Booth School of Business, available at https://promarket.org/about-this-blog/ (accessed on 7 March 2018).

## 6.8  Tackling spillovers from advanced countries' policies

At the Annual Conference of the Asian Bureau of Financial and Economic Research, 2017, Professor Andrew Rose presented a paper on the (lack of) evidence for a global financial cycle.[87] He denied the existence of a global financial cycle and, in effect, called the spillover complaint a scapegoat. The very fact that 'CARRY TRADE' exists is repudiation of his conclusion that there is no spillover effect. Witness the surge in domestic currency non-financial private sector credit growth in emerging economies post-2008. That is nothing but CARRY TRADE. It was very noticeable between 2002 and 2007 and it resumed after 2009 too, until the 'Taper Tantrum' of 2013.

Second, as long as countries follow a de facto stable or fixed exchange rate arrangement with the US dollar, there will be an internalization of the monetary policy of the United States by these economies. They will synchronize their policies with American monetary policy. Evidence suggests they have. It follows naturally from the role of the US dollar as the global reserve and transaction currency and the unofficial Bretton Woods that has prevailed in the world since 1973 and more so since 2001 – after China joined the World Trade Organization (WTO). Therefore, it is inevitable that there is spillover from American monetary policy to monetary policies in developing economies and to their asset markets and other real economy variables. That is why American technology and telecom stock bubble had its global echoes, as did its housing market boom between 2002 and 2007.

Conversely, the Mexico crisis of 1994, the Asian crisis of 1997–98 and the Brazilian crisis of 1999 are all traceable to US monetary policy tightening episodes. Clearly, in all these episodes, it is not the case that the spillover is the main culprit. Domestic fundamentals and vulnerabilities played a big role. However, to emphasize the role of one is not to deny the role of the other.

Finally, spillovers happen indirectly too. It is accepted that asset markets are correlated and cointegrated. The Federal Reserve is very concerned about asset prices, presumably because of their effect on private consumption and economic growth. It is a different matter that their impact on the real economy

---

[87] Eugenio Cerutti, Stijn Claessens and Andrew K. Rose, 'How Important Is the Global Financial Cycle? Evidence from Capital Flows', preliminary version, updated: 9 May 2017, available at http://faculty.haas.berkeley.edu/arose/CapFlows.pdf (accessed on 31 May 2017).

is far lower than what the Federal Reserve assumes or fears.[88] Therefore, if there is spillover from US stock market trends to global stock markets, then, ergo, there is spillover from US monetary policy to global asset prices because US monetary policy implicitly targets US asset prices.

Denying spillovers or the global financial cycle is not going to advance the cause of global financial, economic and social stability. It is a call for the perpetuation of status quo. It is far better to argue that, notwithstanding the monetary policy decisions made by the centre- countries' central banks – QE or negative nominal interest rates, spillovers are an inevitable consequence of the exchange rate regimes that emerging economies have chosen to adopt – officially or unofficially. They could have always chosen a freely floating exchange rate regime and taken steps to boost domestic household incomes and domestic consumption share of GDP. That would also mean a more open political and democratic regime than what prevails. They do not want to pay that price and hence they had chosen a quasi or fully fixed exchange rate regime. Therefore, they must bear the consequences. That is a better argument to make rather than denying spillovers.

Emerging economies can only partially mitigate spillovers through domestic monetary policy, capital controls and moral suasion to regulate credit growth. Not that there is guarantee of success but they can and must try.

At the same time, we would like to point out that America enjoys the international seigniorage that comes with its role as the global reserve and global transactions currency. Indeed, it wanted it that way. It enjoys the benefits of low cost of capital because its two roles – reserve currency and transaction currency – create a natural demand for dollars globally. Given that it enjoys the privileges that come with it, it must also shoulder the responsibilities. What we had proposed in Section 6.8 is a start.

Unfortunately, no concrete suggestion for handling spillovers has emerged. It is not easy to propose solutions for cross-national policy coordination matters. Institutions of global governance with power to enforce rules are not so much an outcome of economic reasoning as they are of balance of global political power. In his Per Jacobsson Memorial Lecture in 2012, Dr Y. V. Reddy, former

---

[88] Anna Cieslak, Adair Morse and Annette Vissing-Jorgensen, 'Stock Returns over the FOMC Cycle', NBER Working Paper, June 2016, available at https://papers.ssrn.com/sol3/papers.cfm?abstract_id=2687614 (accessed on 15 April 2017). Anna Cieslak and Annette Vissing-Jorgensen, 'The Economics of the Fed Put', April 2017, available at https://papers.ssrn.com/sol3/papers.cfm?abstract_id=2951402 (accessed on 15 April 2017).

governor of the RBI, recognized the difficulty of managing spillovers but did not offer solutions:[89]

> Public policy is conducted at the national level, but at the same time, globalization of economies, often driven by technology, is a reality, and the global macroeconomic environment is an outcome of national policies in a framework of nebulous global governance arrangements. The challenge for national central banks is to find space for the conduct of their own policies in an increasingly inter-dependent global economy.
>
> Too much global policy coordination might lead to the universalization of risks of policy mistakes. The main contention is that good finance is essentially a function of good economic policies, and such good policies are primarily national, though significantly impacted by the global macroeconomic environment – which, as already mentioned, is not a product of design.

Given that addressing spillovers is not even part of the mandate of central banks, and often conflicts with their explicit domestic mandates, Prachi Mishra and Raghuram Rajan argue in favour of a gradual creation of global consensus on the issue, first informally and then formally.[90] Accordingly, they suggest the categorization of monetary policy actions as green, orange and red based on their potential spillover effects. Those with generally positive or domestic effects would be rated green, those to be used temporarily and with care be rated orange and those to be avoided at all times be rated red. Over a period of time, some of these could be codified into an international agreement.

They want a group of eminent economists with reasonable reputation across the globe to be given the responsibility of assessing spillovers and grading policies. Yet, they are realistic about the chances of unanimity among nations on what policies have benign or no (green) spillover effects on the rest of the world, which have ambiguous effects (amber) and which are clearly adverse (red) for other nations.

They reckon – and they are right – that discussion of the spillover of domestic monetary policies and their colour coding would be a start of the process of

---

[89] Dr Y.V. Reddy 'Society, Economic Policies and the Financial Sector', The Per Jacobsson Foundation Lecture 2012, Basel, Switzerland, 24 June 2012, available at http://www.perjacobsson.org/lectures/062412.pdf. (accessed on 17 March 2017).

[90] Prachi Mishra and Raghuram Rajan, 'Rules of the Monetary Game', RBI Working Paper Series, 04/2016, March 2016, available at https://rbidocs.rbi.org.in/rdocs/Publications/PDFs/WPSN40395AE03EE364C8EA2474DFE24E28FD4.PDF (accessed on 23 October 2017).

recognition and acceptance that spillovers are a reality and that they need to be reckoned with in domestic monetary policies. They believe that, over time, analysis and experience would allow for a sharper rating of policies. Their fond hope is that, in due course, after much knowledge and experience have been gained on the appropriate policy behaviour of nations that minimize spillover, there would be greater and better policy coordination and eventually an international conference on new monetary rules of the game.

The conference at Bretton Woods in 1945 had paved the way for nearly a quarter century of exchange rate stability before the system unravelled from the time America began to pursue a war in Vietnam and beggar-thy-neighbour exchange rate policies out of fear of lost competitiveness to Germany and Japan. Since then, the world has lurched from one non-system to another punctuated by crisis in emerging economies singly and collectively. A second conference is long overdue. The crisis of 2008 should have resulted in one. China pressed for it, for a time, in 2009 but soon gave up as it realized that it had to get its economic house in order before it gains any enhanced role, influence and stature out of such a conference. Recent developments in the world – Brexit and the election of President Trump in the United States on a de-globalizing policy platform – have further diminished the prospect of such a conference. However, given the policies pursued since the end of the last crisis, another crisis might well be both inevitable and necessary for such a conference to be convened to begin to end the current international monetary non-regime.

In the meantime, what can developing countries do? Given integrated capital markets and the unipolar importance of the US dollar to the international payment system, commodities and capital markets, spillovers from policies pursued in developed countries to developing countries are inevitable. Developing countries lack instruments and coercive power to dissuade advanced nations from pursuing domestic policies that have negative spillover effects for them. Since the world has no alternative to the US dollar presently, the only option left to avoid spillovers is to reverse integration of capital markets and free capital flows.

In the absence of restrictions on capital flows, both the impossible trinity and the financial market trilemma have been reduced to the impossible duality and financial market dilemma, respectively. Therefore, capital controls cannot be the policy of last resort to be deployed in the event of financial instability. It is central to ensuring financial stability. Developing countries must be cautious in liberalizing external commercial borrowings for their domestic borrowers and in inviting foreigners to invest in domestic debt.

These precautions will come, undoubtedly, with short-term economic growth costs. Developing economies run current account deficits and they need foreign capital. The question is figuring out what sort of capital is compatible with their long-term economic goals and financial stability, then invite such capital to invest in their economy while discouraging other forms of capital with regulatory and explicit costs. Profitable long-term investment opportunities for international capital are shrinking and hence it will seek out those jurisdictions that have long-term growth potential, promise and delivery. If the temptation to offer short-term incentives for footloose capital can be resisted, the game will become progressively easier and the playing field will tilt in favour of countries that are capital seekers away from capital providers.

However, let us not harbour illusions. Even with prudent capital flow and external debt management, the path to sustained financial and economic stability is strewn with other minefields. Even if the Federal Reserve sees light and even if emerging economies erect safety barriers and focus on domestic consumption, it will be a mistake to think that the neoliberal agenda would be reversed, especially things like executive compensation and the 'winner take all' mindset. There is much in the neoliberal agenda that needs to be jettisoned. That is the focus of the next section and more. Much of the normative language that finance has embraced has made it difficult for critics to question them without running the risk of appearing unschooled and ignorant. 'Innovation', 'transparency' and 'liberalization' come to mind. But they must be challenged. The narratives that need changing are that finance is good and hence, more finance is better; that capital account liberalization is an unalloyed good; that technocrats are superhuman; that economic policy has to keep its objectives simple because, finally, most relationships in economics are asymmetric and non-linear.

## 6.9  The narratives that need change

We propose to end with a series of alternative narratives. Narratives define the boundaries of our imagination and world views. Any meaningful attempt to address the problems we described as well as the specific solutions we propose has to start with unsettling such settled wisdoms.

For a start, the excessive financialization of the economy has to be reversed. Stuff gets made, large-scale job creation happens and productive transformations materialize in the real economy. Financial markets should be enablers rather than drivers, with the primary objective of effectively intermediating between savers and borrowers.

The conventional wisdom on financial markets is that it intermediates capital from savers to borrowers by managing risk, generating price signals and alleviating information asymmetry. Resource misallocation into financial markets – the best and the brightest opting for finance and the share of money used for share buybacks exceed the amount spent on investments – does not augur well for capitalism. We should go back to the roots of finance, and that may mean more boring bankers and banking!

Two, there is an urgent need for a nuanced case for external and internal liberalization and deregulation. Markets matter, but since people matter even more, financial market failures, which are pervasive, need to be addressed. Such failures exist inside financial market segments and across national and global financial markets.

Even as the grip of the blind ideological belief that markets know best has come under attack in the real economy, it continues to hold sway in the financial markets. Supporters claim that financial markets are largely competitive by pointing to the breadth and depth of the global financial markets. Accordingly, the prevailing philosophy on regulation is largely premised by the belief that markets know best and market failures are marginal.

This runs contrary to overwhelming evidence across time, regions and market segments. Market failures, especially in financial markets, are pervasive. The need for regulation, therefore, assumes first-order importance. What's more, behavioural economists like Robert Shiller have pointed to the pervasive cognitive blindspots among market participants that engenders recurrent bouts of irrational exuberance. Financial market failures are pervasive and, whether we like it or not, need regulation.

Three, the failure of central bankers to learn the right policy lessons from the crisis of 2008 stems from the failure to learn the cognitive errors committed in the run-up to the crisis. Nobody needs to embrace this narrative more than the central bankers.

In a paper[91] published in 2014, three professors from the Department of Sociology at the University of California at Berkeley teased out the cognitive

---

[91] Neil Fligstein, Jonah Stuart Brundage, and Michael Schultz, 'Why the Federal Reserve Failed to See the Financial Crisis of 2008: The Role of "Macroeconomics" as a Sense Making and Cultural Frame,' Institute for Research on Labour and Employment Working Paper (IRLE Working Paper #111-14), September 2014, available at http://www.irle.berkeley.edu/workingpapers/111-14.pdf.

failures that were behind the Federal Reserve failing to see the financial crisis of 2008. What follows are verbatim quotes from the paper:

> Their conversations focus on standard macro-level indicators like the inflation rate, the unemployment rate, and growth in GDP.... They rarely see the connection between sectors.... By contrast, Committee members rarely devote sustained attention to the 'financial economy.'

> ... they grossly underestimated the extent to which the downturn in housing prices would affect the entire economy. It was not until the summer of 2007 that the Federal Reserve even began to notice the connections between the mortgage market and the functioning of financial markets,... and even then, no one expected the problems generated by bad mortgages to cascade into a full-blown financial collapse.

> Not only was there no one in the room who took an extreme position, but speakers were constantly prefacing their remarks by downplaying the significance of even what they themselves considered to be the worst-case scenario.... One could argue that these group dynamics guaranteed a tendency towards a 'wait and see attitude' as well as a collective attempt to balance opinions.

Four, macroeconomic policies should as far as possible seek to directly target their objective and refrain from targeting second- and latter-order objectives. Consider the example of the theory of change associated with extended monetary accommodation – use interest rate channel to move the GDP lever through the balance sheet repair pathway. It is presumed that it would buy the time required for firms and households to deleverage gradually by keeping their real debt burdens low, thereby preventing consumption and investment from tanking. However, as we have seen from the ongoing economic cycle, low rates, far from backstopping, leave alone restoring, consumption and investment, have only encouraged further indebtedness. Change is harder when sticking to old bad habits is made easier. Further, the economy is far complex an entity, with several moving parts and unknown unknowns, for such latter-order forces to play out as planned. Law of unintended consequences is always in force and it paves the road to hell, good intentions or not. To be mindful of this is to recognize the intrinsic asymmetry of economics.

Five, life is nothing if not asymmetric (see Box 6.3). Consequently, asymmetry marks the relationship between policy decisions and their impacts. In other words, policy may be effective in one direction and impotent in another direction or even counterproductive. Further, real life has too many moving parts. Therefore, 'ceteris' is seldom 'paribus' and counterfactuals are impossible. Failure to recognize the fact of asymmetry and these factors that cause asymmetry leads to unintended destinations even if the road is paved with good intentions.

### Box 6.3   Asymmetry is a feature of economics

**We value what we covet or miss more than what we possess**
'The grass on the other side is always green'. Most of us will be familiar with this wise saying. There are variants of it in many other languages. What it reveals is the intrinsic asymmetry of human behaviour and human interaction. We covet what we miss and we take for granted for what we have. Once what we miss becomes what we own, it meets with the same fate as everything else that we own. In other words, the happiness derived upon possession is not proportional to the sadness felt while we were coveting it. This attitude is evident in the way we react to good health and sickness. The former does not lift us as much and as often as the latter weighs us down. That is an asymmetric response of the human mind. That characterizes human behaviour. Since economics is about human behaviour, it is no surprise that our (human) responses to economic variables are asymmetric too.

**Positive factors and hygiene factors in human motivation**
Before we get there, let us also note that behavioural science discusses positive factors and hygiene factors with respect to employee motivation. Positive factors motivate and when they are withdrawn, they are demotivating. Hygiene factors are asymmetric. Their existence or availability or presence may not be motivating but their absence will be annoying and demotivating. A vending machine or a water cooler or free coffee in the office pantry might not mean much when they are available. When they are withdrawn, employees will feel let down and short-changed. Somewhat more seriously, salary increases cease to be motivating. Employees tend to expect that. It becomes an entitlement. So, unless it is far higher than expected, it ceases to make a difference to our moods or happiness. But if the firm denies salary or wage increases, it results in substantial unhappiness.

**Loss aversion**
The endowment effect is one of the most well-known cognitive biases. In a famous experiment, Daniel Kahneman, Jack Knetsch and Richard Thaler gave participants coffee mugs and offered them the opportunity to trade it. They found that the participants' willingness to accept a compensation to give up their mugs was twice as high as their willingness to pay to acquire the same mug. In other words, once people own a thing (becomes part of one's endowment), they value it much more than when purchasing the same thing.

They attributed this 'endowment effect' to 'loss aversion' – people are more averse to losing something than are interested in an equivalent gain. In other words, people attach a much greater weight to losing (or foregoing) a thing than gaining (or buying) the same thing.

From the literature on attitudes to risk, we know that humans have intense loss aversion. They feel more pain at losing something they possessed than if they did not realize an anticipated gain. That is why it has been documented that it is relatively easier to negotiate and share profits between partners than to negotiate and place demands for additional monies from them to meet losses. This is an asymmetric reaction. Our reactions to losses and profits are not the same. This attitude is a substantial part of the explanation behind why investors do not cut losses easily but take profits all too easily.

That brings us to the ultimate asymmetry: policymakers may not be able to help but they can hurt with their actions.

**Policy can hurt more than it can help**
That makes sense for two reasons. One reason arises out of the concept of 'necessary and sufficient' conditions in economics. If something is both 'necessary and sufficient' for something else, then the relationship between the two is bound to be symmetric. However, if 'A implies B' is true but if it is also true that 'A implies C', then B is a necessary condition but not sufficient condition for A. The relationship between A and B is bound to be asymmetric. For example, if capital spending requires lower rates but also risk appetite, then lower rates can only be a necessary condition at best but never enough to trigger capital spending without improved appetite for risk.

There is a second reason as to why governments can hurt but not help. That stems from an understanding of governments' peripheral role in economic activity and economic development which, for the most part, was spontaneous. In economic terms, development happened not because a bunch of aging (mostly) men sat around the table and set interest rates or planned outputs in various sectors. Yes, both are the same. Central banking is central planning especially when it comes to monetary policy. Countries did not prosper not because of policy actions but because of spontaneous decisions made by several people reacting to the circumstances they found themselves and the opportunities that such circumstances threw up.

Governments came into the picture when people became conscious of ownership and property rights. Laws, rules and regulations were required and so were courts. Once ownership got established, the desire to own more came into the picture. That required armies and national budgets to maintain the army. Wars had to be financed, and hence, taxation and government borrowing.

Hence, the central bank came into being. Then, inflation was required to avoid paying back government loans in full. As one can see, the need for the government was not for facilitating economic activity but for other purposes. In other words, policymakers need to accept that they were not created to influence economic activity and that they cannot.

The failure to grasp this truth lies both at the heart of government's policy actions and in the criticisms of their failure. Governments take decisions thinking that their actions are 'necessary and sufficient'. But they are more often in the realm of 'necessary' but not 'sufficient'. Put differently, by not doing the necessary things, governments can harm the economy or society. But doing them does not guarantee economic and social benefits. Other economic agents – the private sector – may have to do their bit and governments may only have limited influence, if at all, on their decisions and choices.

This logic applies to central bank actions too. In resisting a higher inflation rate or overheating in general, its monetary policy tightening may be both necessary and sufficient, but with respect to helping an economy grow or triggering a higher inflation, its actions may be 'necessary' at best and harmful at worst.

This explains why William White said that central banks might be able to lean but not clean.

Reflecting on the above should lead intellectually honest central bankers to the conclusion that their effectiveness is rather specific and circumscribed. It should induce humility.

Six, for a world facing the headwinds from structural shifts arising due to demographic transitions, skill-biased technologies, growing automation, stagnant productivity and numerous environmental challenges, growth expectations should be moderated and obsession with restoring the Goldilocks age of 1980s and 1990s abandoned. Macroeconomic policymaking has not been fraught with such challenges for more than a generation. A better understanding of history helps. As Churchill said, the longer you can look back, the further you can look forward. The post–World War II boom was a reconstruction boom and the post-1980s 'Great moderation' was largely debt induced. The time has come to return to growth rates that were normal for the major part of modern history.

Seven, not only do we have to grapple with dimmer economic prospects, but also, again like most of modern history, with more uncertain times in general. Uncertainty is the new normal. As Gillian Tett pointed out in a column,[92] economic and political uncertainties, the characteristic features of developing countries, have now been embraced by their counterparts in the developed world. If the GFC shattered the comfort that accompanied the Great Moderation, political events and trends on both sides of the Atlantic have demolished the much-vaunted political stability associated with developed societies. This realization and the attendant humility would help in a big way in dealing with the big challenges that lie ahead.

Finally and more importantly, we should be both humble about and wary of unleashing forces whose effects we are incapable of fathoming: smartphones, genetic modification, fracking, 3-D printing, artificial intelligence and robotics.

In a thoughtful piece for *Project Syndicate*, Lord Adair Turner wrote as follows:

> In short, ICT (Information and Communication Technology) creates an economy that is both 'hi-tech' and 'hi-touch' – a world of robots and apps, but also of fashion, design, land, and face-to-face services. This economy is the result of our remarkable ability to solve the problem of production and automate away the need for continual labour.
>
> But, it is an economy that is likely to suffer two adverse side effects. First, it may be inherently unstable, because the more that wealth resides in real estate, the more the financial system will provide leverage to support real-estate speculation, which has been at the heart of all of the world's worst financial crises. *Major changes in financial and monetary policy, going far beyond those introduced in response to the 2008 crisis, are required to contain this danger.* (Emphasis ours)[93]

---

[92] Gillian Tett, 'Political Risk Means All 2017 Investment Bets Are Off,' *Financial Times*, 30 December 2016, available at http://www.ft.com/cms/s/0/4cc59f38-c6cb-11e6-8f29-9445cac8966f.html#axzz4V5suO5fg (accessed 1 June 2017).

[93] Lord Adair Turner, 'The High-Tech, High-Touch Economy,' *Project Syndicate*, 16 April 2014, available at http://www.project-syndicate.org/print/adair-turner-explains-how-a-fresh-wave-of-automation-is-transforming-employment-and-much-else.

# 7 | Finance in India

## 7.1 Introduction

The earlier chapters focused on the rise of finance mostly in the context of advanced economies. This chapter examines its relevance for India. It goes further than that – it evaluates the state of the financial sector in India. As with many things, India's finance sector too is a phenomenon of many parts. Some are rudimentary and some are sophisticated. Unlike the advanced economies, India's challenges are different. On the one hand, a significant share of its citizens is financially excluded and its credit markets suffer from several deficiencies. On the other hand, pockets of the economy as well as certain economic activities are experiencing an increasing trend of financialization. India needs to walk this trade-off going forward.

As a large continent-sized economy with many states of the sizes of countries in Europe and Africa folded in it, India is always in a state of churn. But India's financial sector seems to be in a particular state of heightened churn. Fortunately, crises and churns always provide opportunities for charting a new path, a better road map for the future. Indeed, a lot has been achieved. One way to gauge that is to look back at the agenda that was deemed essential for India sometime in the past and see how much of it has been achieved.

In 2008, Raghuram Rajan had delivered a speech at the Institute for Economic Growth in Delhi on the topic of financial sector reforms in India and the global crisis.[1] In the speech, he had recommended that India implement a bankruptcy code, make it easy for foreigners to invest in Indian bond market, enable no-frills accounts for the vast majority of the population and establish credit bureaus and allow foreign direct investment in asset reconstruction companies. In the decade since, all of these have been accomplished. Yes, many

---

[1] Raghuram Rajan, 'The Global Crisis and Financial Sector Reforms in India', speech to the Institute for Economic Growth, Delhi, March 2008, available at https://faculty. chicagobooth.edu/raghuram.rajan/research/papers/global%20crisis.pdf (accessed 24 June 2018).

things remain to be done but much has been done too. This is the state of affairs in Indian public policy, in general. Given its continental size and huge population, issues will keep surfacing even as some are settled.

For analytical comfort, we can distinguish between finance and financialization for a developing country. Developing countries need access to finance, especially for their low-income citizens and small and medium enterprises (SMEs). That is also referred to as financial inclusion and bulk of the financial inclusion is provided by the banking sector. Then, there is financialization. In the context of this book, it involves asset prices, the leverage that feeds into asset prices and cross-border capital flows.

In an earlier work, we had examined India's long-term economic growth challenges and had identified constraints on production, consumption and financing.[2] As regards financing, we found concerns on the credit origination (savings rates and tax base), intermediation (banks and capital markets) and deployment (consumption and investment) sides.

The issue of financialization, the subject of this book, intersects with the origination (partially) and intermediation sides. On the origination side, we had written:

> India's savings rate and capital formation rate have both been in decline, a trend that started even from a level below the one reached by the East Asian economies during their high-growth phases.... India is constrained by its low savings rate and narrow capital base, both of which constrain it from generating the capital required to sustain a high economic growth rate for a sufficiently long period.

Greater financial inclusion, or enabling access to formal banking sector and other financial market instruments, can help partially address this through at least two channels. One, it would provide appropriate and attractive instruments to save and also make those savings available for efficient financial intermediation. Two, by enabling access to formal finance, it would facilitate entrepreneurship and business growth and thereby increase capital accumulation and broaden the tax base.

On the intermediation side, as share of the GDP, the banking sector and capital market are smaller than their peers elsewhere, even in the developing

---

[2] V. Anantha Nageswaran and Gulzar Natarajan, 'Can India Grow,' Carnegie Endowment for Peace, October 2016, available at https://carnegieendowment.org/files/CEIP_CanIndiaGrow_Final_.pdf.

world. We made the case for the promotion of more efficient financial intermediation channels:

India, it appears, is trapped in a low-level equilibrium. Problems of access, volatility in equity markets, limited liquid fixed income savings instruments, and a grossly underdeveloped insurance market have kept investors out of the financial markets. Furthermore, the inflation tax has been a big disincentive to investing in financial assets. In contrast, thanks to recurrent booms, and for historical reasons, land and gold have appeared to be relatively attractive investment options. Their allure is amplified by the attraction of their being safe conduits to stash away black, or ill-gotten, money as well as avoid taxes. In turn, this self-reinforcing savings-investment channel is a formidable deterrent to the emergence of a deep and broad financial market.

The case for greater financial inclusion and increasing the efficiency of financial intermediation is compelling. Given deficient financial inclusion and intermediation, India may actually be suffering from too little finance for financialization to become a problem.

This special chapter on India and its financial sector will examine the various financial inclusion initiatives and the challenges facing the country's credit markets and propose some measures to reform the banking sector and the capital markets and enhance the efficiency of financial intermediation.

India's banking system is dominated by government-owned banks. They hold around 70 per cent of the total banking system assets, household deposits, etc. In recent years, India has been buffeted by a banking crisis of severe proportions. Government-owned banks had run up huge bad debts and they show, as yet, no sign of stabilizing. As recently as in February 2018, the premier banking institution in the country, the State Bank of India (SBI), had to restate the amount of bad loans it was carrying in its books. The total amount of stressed loans in the banking system amounts to around 8 per cent of GDP. On top of this, in February 2018, the country's second largest public sector bank, Punjab National Bank, disclosed that it had been defrauded of nearly USD 2.0 billion by some diamond merchants.

What is a satisfactory resolution to the problems faced by Indian banks? Should India use the bad loans crisis to move away from five decades of public sector banking to banking owned by private capital predominantly? What should be the balance between banking, non-banking and capital market sources of finance? What are the pros and cons of each?

On financial intermediation, widening and deepening of capital markets has been a longstanding policy goal. While certain segments of the market like derivatives trading have matured, more important segments like corporate bond issuances have been slow to develop. Only a very small proportion of the population deploys savings through the capital market. Then there is the problem posed by financial repression – the government pre-empts most of the household savings that go into bank deposits through the statutory liquidity ratio and directed bank lending forms a significant share.

It is clear that India has a long way to go before experiencing both the opportunities and threats that financial globalization represents. However, it is important that India prepares itself for the inevitable and increasing financialization of the economy. Monetary policy and banking regulation have to be geared up to handle higher credit volumes. Further, monetary policy goals may have to be modified to accommodate feedback effect from financial markets to the real economy. Asset prices may become more important influences on monetary policy than they are now. Though shadow banking serves those that banks do not cater to, its growth has to be monitored. Similarly, the development of the bond market and consumer credit have to be managed such that the economy does not become vulnerable to excessive leverage. All these raise important questions about financial intermediation in India.

What can India learn from international and Asian experience in this regard? What should be India's attitude towards capital flows – both capital outflows and inflows? Should it continue with the current caution or should it open the doors wider and if so, for what type of capital flows? What should be India's attitude towards financial innovations? Should it shun them totally or embrace them? Is there a middle ground? Is there a criterion that makes this decision easier?

If the relationship between finance and growth is an inverted U-shaped curve, is India still in the ascending part of the curve?

This chapter will attempt to answer the above questions in the light of the international evidence and experience presented in the earlier chapters.

## 7.2  Indian banking system – where to from here?

### 7.2.1  *Nationalization of banks and financial inclusion*

Any discussion of India's financial sector, in these times, must start with the predominantly government owned banking system. It has been in the news for the last few years and mostly for the wrong reasons. In 1969, the government led by Prime Minister Indira Gandhi nationalized India's banking sector in one stroke.[3] There may have been political compulsions and rationale behind the action but apart from those, the economic reasons were that banks under private ownership were not discharging the role of intermediating savings and credit dissemination efficiently. They were acting mostly as creditors to the promoters and their industries. Indeed, credit became a barrier to hold back competition. Thus, there was also siphoning off of funds to promoters of banks and numerous bank failures. In a poor country, the lack of broad-based availability of credit for industrial growth was a big handicap. Then, there was a need to finance agriculture – the largest sector in terms of number of people dependent on it for livelihood – and the government's development and anti-poverty programmes.

It cannot be denied that public-sector-dominated banking system has had significant successes. Robin Burgess, Rohini Pande and Grace Wong used state and household data for the 1961–2000 period across Indian states and certain abrupt policy shifts to demonstrate that India's 'social banking' programme 'significantly lowered rural poverty'.[4] They attribute this to the expansion of rural branch network and directed lending towards weaker sections in the society. Despite the recurrent bouts of banking sector stress from rise in non-performing loans, India's banking system has not experienced the credibility crisis among both depositors and other market participants, which has been not uncommon among other developing countries. But there have been costs too.

In a recent speech,[5] Y. V. Reddy, one of the most illustrious governors of the RBI and a distinguished civil servant of the country, said that nationalization of the banking system achieved financing of government priorities without parliamentary oversight:

> The nationalisation of banks changed balances in a fundamental manner. Union Government had till then no official functionaries in the States for

---

[3] In his book *Accidental India: A History of the Nation's Passage through Crisis and Change* (Aleph Book Company, 2012), Shankkar Aiyar points out that the Congress Party had passed two resolutions in the year 1948 advocating nationalization of banks and financial institutions including insurance.

[4] Robin Burgess, Rohini Pande and Grace Wong, 'Banking for the Poor: Evidence from India,' 22 September 2004, available at http://econ.lse.ac.uk/staff/rburgess/eea/jeeabankindia.pdf.

[5] Y. V. Reddy, 'State of Banking in India,' K. L. N. Prasad Memorial Lecture, Administrative Staff College of India, Hyderabad, 1 February 2018, available at http://www.yvreddy.com/asci-kln-prasad-memorial-lecture-2018/.

initiating or implementing its programmes. The Union Government acquired a country wide presence of its functionaries, albeit indirect. Second, the private sector had to depend on the Union Government owned banks for funding of their activities since financial intermediation in formal sector was mostly confined to banks. Third, the Reserve Bank of India's command over monetary policy, especially transmission and regulation of bank was diluted. Fourth, large financial resources became available for the Government, which could be used without Parliamentary oversight. The banking system in India, thus, became a useful means to launch many Prime Minister's country-wide programmes, even though they were in the jurisdiction of states.

In *Accidental India*, Shankkar Aiyar documents the progress made under government ownership of the banking system in terms of reaching finance and credit to the sectors that needed them the most. He writes, 'Till the beginning of the 1960s, banking was concentrated in cities and major towns. In 1960 India's population touched 420 million of which 340 million people lived in rural India'.[6] The web of controls through inter-connected holdings and directorships in companies and banks meant that banks were both ill-equipped to and disinterested in catering to the development needs of a relatively poor nation:

> 188 persons who served as directors in twenty leading banks held 1,452 directorships of other companies besides controlling 1,100 companies. A more detailed study of five leading banks revealed the intricate web of influence that ruled the banking sector. Through common directors these five banks were connected with thirty-three insurance companies, six financial institutions, twenty-five investment centres, 584 manufacturing companies, twenty-six trading companies and fifteen not-for-profit organizations.... As many as 617 towns out of the 2,700 in the country had not been covered by commercial banks. Of these, 444 did not have cooperative banking facilities either. And, worse still, of about 600,000 villages, hardly 500 had banks.[7]

Although the then Congress government led by Mrs Indira Gandhi promulgated an ordinance to nationalize banks in 1969, the Supreme Court struck it down and the Indian parliament passed the final legislation on nationalization in March 1970.[8] Shankkar again notes:

---

[6] Aiyar, *Accidental India*.
[7] Ibid.
[8] Ibid.

In 1969, after twenty-two years of independence, the Indian banking system had barely 6,900 bank branches. By 1979 India boasted 30,202 branches and by 1989 the number had increased to 57,699 branches. Between 1969 and 1989 the number of branches in rural India, in villages, shot up from 1,833 to 33,014.... Between 1969 and 1990, branches were set up in 30,000 rural locations and this led to rural savings rising from 3 per cent to 15 per cent and the share of credit to rural areas from 1.5 per cent to 15 per cent.[9]

In short, again as Shankkar points out with evidence in his book, it is likely that left to themselves, private sector banks would not have achieved anything remotely comparable.

For the period from 1991 to 2011, following the liberalization of the economy and the advent of private banks, only 30,000 bank branches were added. Contrast this with the twenty years between 1969 and 1989 when banks added over 50,000 branches across India. Between 1969 and 1989, banks added 31,181 branches in rural India while between 1991 and 2011 less than 1,000 branches have been added in rural India.[10]

In spite of these impressive achievements, easy access to credit was still not the norm but the exception especially for micro, SMEs. Charan Singh and Poornima Wasadani note that, historically, the bulk of the funding for the SMEs came from informal sources and self-finance.[11] The Government of India had to set up the Small Industries Development Bank of India in 1990 to cater exclusively to the SME sector. Even then, credit to this sector has been somewhat slow to pick up. Of course, there are many reasons and not all of them are because of banks' reluctance to lend to smaller enterprises which are inherently deemed riskier than larger ones. For one, they have less or no collateral to offer. Two, most of them operate on an informal basis and audited financial accounts for a consecutive period of few years might be difficult to obtain. More than financial assistance for capital investment purposes, what SME lacked the most was timely access to working capital. They were more often at the mercy of their large buyers who paid up, more often than not, at their will and pleasure. Informal lenders, though expensive, were accessible and convenient, and therefore remain their dominant funding source.

---

[9] Ibid.

[10] Ibid.

[11] Charan Singh and Kishinchand Poornima Wasdani, 'Finance for Micro, Small, and Medium-Sized Enterprises in India: Sources and Challenges,' ADBI Working Paper Series, July 2016.

The Raghuram Rajan-led Committee on the road map for financial sector reforms in India appointed in 2008 focused attention on financial inclusion, including for the SMEs. The report recommended that receivables due to small businesses typically from large buyers be securitized and traded. Then, RBI appointed a working group which submitted its report in November 2009. RBI then issued a concept paper in 2014. Then, the draft guidelines were issued followed by final guidelines. Receivables Exchange of India, India's first Trade Receivables Discounting System (TReDS), started operating only in January 2017. The time taken underscores the glacial pace at which crucial reforms that would lift the economy on to a higher growth path are pursued. Even now, companies are not enthusiastic about this as it would mean that they have to pay up on the due date to the financial institution that has discounted the amount due and paid the supplier. The Government of India in October 2017 had announced that it would require central public sector enterprises to compulsorily participate in TReDS. It is expected that, after the initial resistance, the corporate sector would participate widely making working capital availability less of a barrier for the SME sector.

As for financial inclusion for individuals, the current Indian government, taking up from where the previous governments had left off, launched a programme called 'Pradhan Mantri Jan Dhan Yojana' aimed at massive enrolment of Indians without a banking account into the banking system. It was a mega financial inclusion project. It was also aimed at helping the government transfer its subsidies and welfare benefits directly to the beneficiaries ('Direct Benefit Transfer'). This national financial inclusion was a big success. Over 320 million new bank accounts have been opened till date.[12] A vast majority of the population has now bank accounts. It mirrors the mobile phone penetration that India achieved for its citizens in the first decade of the millennium.

An empirical study[13] has shown that PMJDY accounts are increasingly actively used over time:

> 70% of the accounts migrate out of dormancy into active use. Second, activity levels in PMJDY accounts increase over time, a pattern not necessarily seen in non-PMJDY accounts. In many specifications, activity increases in PMJDY accounts relative to non-PMJDY accounts. These findings are especially stark

---

[12] PMJDY website https://pmjdy.gov.in.

[13] Yakshup Chopra, Nagpurnanand Prabhala and Prasanna Tantri, 'Bank Accounts for the Unbanked: Evidence from a Big Bang Experiment, 11 March 2017, available at https://www.bentley.edu/files/2017/04/04/pmjdy_final.pdf.

given that non-PMJDY accountholders in our sample appear to be much poorer and have transaction sizes that are one order of magnitude smaller. Finally, we find that the active accounts experience significant increases in cash balances. Government direct benefits transfer aids but does not fully explain usage. Overall, the data indicate that the unbanked learn by doing, and increase usage of accounts for transactions, liquidity management, and increasingly, balance accumulation.

More good news is possible out of the successful financial inclusion initiative. Another paper[14] suggests that 'financial development facilitates economic growth by moving workers out of less productive, informal entrepreneurial activity into formal jobs in more productive firms'. If this were to happen, India could reasonably aspire to resemble in due course the prosperous high growth economies of the West.

While government ownership of the banking system has undoubtedly helped significantly deepen financial inclusion, it has not been without its costs.

### 7.2.2 *Has the medicine expired? Government ownership of banking*

If financial inclusion was one of the key pillars of the bank nationalization first carried out in 1969, it appears that nearly five decades later, the government seems to have a grip on the issue and might have achieved critical mass, even though it may be a while before it ceases to be an issue. That begs the question of whether the banking sector in India should continue to be predominantly government owned.

As mentioned in the introduction to this chapter, in India, the public sector banks face an existential crisis. Their burden of non-performing assets (NPAs or debts that are unlikely to be serviced and repaid at all or only partially) remains high and is showing no signs of coming down. In fact, in February 2018, the RBI, the banking regulator, issued a notification on the classification of loans as performing and non-performing. Those guidelines that end all forms of regulatory forbearance are expected to lead to the declaration of a higher pile of NPAs.

---

[14] Rajeev H. Dehejia and Nandini Gupta, 'Who Wants to Be an Entrepreneur? Financial Development and Occupational Choice,' 16 May 2016, NYU Wagner Research Paper No. 2494551, available at https://ssrn.com/abstract=2494551 or http://dx.doi.org/10.2139/ssrn.2494551.

In October 2017, the Government of India announced a massive recapitalization exercise for government-owned banks. The recapitalization came without any major conditions attached to it for better performance or improved governance. The amount was ₹2.1 trillion[15] or approximately USD 32.0 billion. It appeared enough. In its report on the Financial System Stability Assessment for India, the IMF[16] had calculated that, under an adverse scenario, capital requirements in Indian banks would not exceed 1.5 per cent of GDP. The government had provided recapitalization funds to banks amounting to 1.4 per cent of GDP (USD 32.0 billion out of nominal GDP of USD 2.267 trillion as of March 2017). Notwithstanding the above, more capital might still be needed, for a few reasons.

One is that, as mentioned earlier, a big bank fraud was unearthed in Punjab National Bank, India's second largest public sector bank, in February 2018. It had gone undetected for 7 years. Following the news, frauds in other banks were also detected and reported. In its wake, as discussed earlier, the RBI signalled the end of regulatory forbearance and tightened norms for disclosure of NPAs by banks. This is expected to result in greater disclosure of NPAs. Third, according to recent research[17] by Nomura, 'the power sector now poses another significant concern. It has become apparent that almost half of the banking sector's exposure to the power sector (~INR 1.25 trillion, or 0.7 per cent of GDP) has the potential to become NPAs, and the majority of this is not yet recognized as such. This means provisioning requirements are likely to rise, and the public sector banks will again need additional capital'. When public sector banks need capital, the government has to come up with the funds. Hence, the banking sector will be hostage to the government's budget constraint. A similar stress cannot be ruled out in the telecommunications sector, and perhaps even solar renewable energy.

The banking crisis is not without precedents. In the last three decades, this is the third time that the public sector banks are facing a bad debt crisis. This is the longest and the biggest. As of May 2018, we are unable to say that the problem has peaked. As Y. V. Reddy said in his lecture on 1 February, the

---

[15] See Alekh Archana, 'Govt. Announces Rs 2.11 Trillion PSU Bank Recapitalisation Plan,' *Livemint*, 24 October 2017, available at https://www.livemint.com/Industry/xje0dmj5lYHZkSZnqVRjwJ/Cabinet-approves-Rs21-trillion-PSU-bank-recapitalisation-pl.html (accessed 29 July 2018).

[16] 'Financial System Stability Assessment for India,' December 2017.

[17] 'Asia Insights: Postcard from India,' International Monetary Fund, Nomura Global Markets Research, 4 May 2018.

seeds of NPA are sown the moment a loan is made. But with respect to India's current NPA problem, the seeds were probably sown during the credit boom of the 2003–08 period. As a McKinsey report[18] noted, in the first decade of the new millennium, India missed economic growth forecast only once. In all the other years, actual growth exceeded expectations. Hence, optimism was rife and that informed both borrowing and lending decisions.

Based on the BIS data on credit gap (actual growth in the ratio of credit/GDP versus trend growth in the ratio), one can also see that the credit gap was both positive and steeply rising before the crisis of 2008. Figure 7.1 shows that historically, credit gap had never been as positive as it was during the boom years of 2004–09. The decline since the crisis has been precipitous. Hence, it is possible that the bulk of the NPAs was seeded then.

**Figure 7.1 India: credit gap: credit/GDP actual–trend**

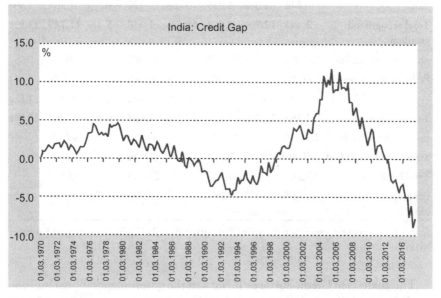

*Source*: Bank for International Settlements. Data up to the quarter ending September 2017 (accessed 6 May 2018).

---

[18] 'Private Equity in India: Once Overestimated, Now Underserved', February 2015, cited in V. Anantha Nageswaran, 'Incremental Policy Progress, One Fraud at a Time,' *Mint*, 27 February 2018, available at https://www.livemint.com/Opinion/kHQL1puGMRNYrQ6elkAk9J/Incremental-policy-progress-one-fraud-at-a-time.html.

As of December 2017, gross NPAs stood at 10.5 per cent (of all loans) for the Indian banking system (Table 7.1). It is much higher for public sector banks in general. More so, if one excluded the SBI.

**Table 7.1  India banking NPA problem (December 2017)**

| Dec-17 | SBI | | PSU (Ex-SBI) | | Pvt Banks | | Total | |
|---|---|---|---|---|---|---|---|---|
| | Rs bn | % | Rs bn | % | Rs bn | % | Rs bn | % |
| **Gross NPA** | **1,991** | **10.4%** | **5,781** | **14.3%** | **1,047** | **4.3%** | **8,820** | **10.5%** |
| Provision Coverage (%) | 48.6% | | 45.8% | | 50.3% | | 47.0% | |
| **Net NPA** | **1,024** | **5.6%** | **3,133** | **8.3%** | **520** | **2.2%** | **4,677** | **5.8%** |
| Restructed loans | 209 | 1.1% | 974 | 2.4% | 162 | 0.7% | 1,345 | 1.6% |
| SDR, 5:25, S4A | 248 | 1.3% | 1,215 | 3.0% | 120 | 0.5% | 1,584 | 1.9% |
| **Total recognized problem** | **2,449** | **12.7%** | **7,971** | **19.7%** | **1,330** | **5.4%** | **11,749** | **13.9%** |
| -as % of bank capita | *132.1%* | | *260.2%* | | *32.6%* | | *130.7%* | |
| Problem asset cover (%) | *43.2%* | | *34.6%* | | *40.4%* | | *37.0%* | |
| Watch list / SMA-II | 103 | 0.5% | 1,102 | 2.7% | 332 | 1.3% | 1,537 | 1.8% |
| Total stress loans | **2,552** | **13.3%** | **9,072** | **22.5%** | **1,662** | **6.7%** | **13,287** | **15.8%** |
| -as % of bank capital | *137.7%* | | *296.2%* | | *40.8%* | | *147.8%* | |
| **Stress asset cover (%)** | *41.4%* | | *30.4%* | | *32.3%* | | *32.7%* | |
| Total bank loans | 18,262 | | 37,737 | | 24,120 | | 80,119 | |
| Banking system capital | 1,854 | | 3,063 | | 4,076 | | 8,993 | |

*Source*: India financial sector, Credit Suisse Asia-Pacific/India Equity Research, 19 February 2018.

The analysts in Credit Suisse estimate that the government's capital infusion of USD 32.0 billion might prove to be adequate, under certain assumptions about the quantum of NPAs that would default and loss given default. But they concede that not much would be left for 'growth capital', that is, for banks to start lending again and expand their balance sheet. That is what we had meant when we said that continued majority government ownership would make banks hostage to government's budget constraint. Nationalization of banks was an intervention needed then for India to emerge out of poverty. Today the sector has to prepare to cater to a more prosperous India.

### 7.2.3 The future for Indian banking

Y. V. Reddy concedes[19] that the time has come for India to rethink the architecture of the Indian banking system:

> 2017 is vastly different from 1969. The balance between Union and States has been changing. The balance between State and market is different now. Private Sector is more nimble than ever before. Private sector is used even for a sovereign function like issue of Passports. People are demanding more choices than before. India is an integral and important component of global economy and, indeed, global finance. Finance is more complex now, and goes beyond banking.

> The context of banking in India is also different now. We are already in a mix of public and private sector banks. We are in a world of public sector banks having a mix of public and private ownership. We are in a world where empirical evidence for comparing their performance is available – though subject to multiple interpretations. More important, we are in a new world where foreign investors have strong presence both in private sector banks and in public sector banks. So, for policy makers, the choice is more difficult and, processes more complex than in 1969. The degrees of freedom available for arbitrary decisions by Government are circumscribed by dynamics of financial markets.

> In brief, the future of public sector banks is unclear to them; and this itself undermines their efficiency, and also efficiency in the banking system, as a whole.

> A White paper on the future of Public Sector banking may be placed before the Parliament at the earliest in view of their criticality for efficiency in financial sector as a whole, to be able to serve a globally competitive economy.

Elsewhere in the same speech, Y. V. Reddy stresses that ownership of the banking system should be mostly in Indian hands. 'Banking is too important to allow foreign presence freely and WTO commitments of all countries are a testimony to this'. He calls for a thorough review of the current policy of ownership and governance in Indian banking before it is irrevocably passed on to foreign hands.

But that raises questions on the eligibility of Indian owners. Most of the NPAs in the Indian banking system have arisen out of loans made to private

---

[19] Reddy, 'State of Banking in India'.

non-financial corporations. Quite a sizeable chunk of the NPAs could be attributed to fraud and malfeasance arising from collusive lending practices. Therefore, it is fair to ask whether Indian ownership of the banks will take the country back to the pre-1969 days when banks were incestuous financial entities that protected the promoters' business interests. Not much appears to have changed since. The numerous recent controversies over questionable practices, including among some of the country's largest and most reputed companies, show that India's corporate governance standards remain weak. This has to be kept in mind when India contemplates jettisoning the dominant government-owned banking system model to opt for a privately owned banking system in Indian hands.

Also, the experience of the West before and after the financial crisis of 2008 suggests caution in embracing the fully privately owned model of banking. As Raghuram Rajan observed in his famous speech in August 2005[20] on the lessons of the Greenspan era for the future, when he presciently warned of the consequences of the culture of excessive risk-taking, 'even though there should theoretically be a diversity of opinion and actions by market participants, and a greater capacity to absorb risk, competition and compensation may induce more correlation in behaviour than is desirable.... Competition forces them to flirt continuously with the limits of liquidity'. Almost 15 years since he uttered these prophetic words, the situation has not changed much, if at all. As we discussed in Chapter 3, competitive banking system with executive compensation practices as they are could well be an important contributor to systemic instability.

Therefore, we strongly believe that India should continue to have a mixed banking model. Further, in the absence of a comfortably large eligible pool of private sector promoters either to set up new private sector banks or to buy the government's stake in public sector banks, privatization, even of select institutions, has to be a slow and careful process. In the meantime, as recommended by multiple banking sector reform committees including by the latest P. J. Nayak Committee, the government should initiate steps to strengthen management and governance in public sector banks. Foremost, separation of ownership from management is a long overdue imperative.

---

[20] Raghuram G. Rajan, 'The Greenspan Era: Lessons for the Future,' speech, August 2005, available at https://www.imf.org/en/News/Articles/2015/09/28/04/53/sp082705.

We propose that the government may consider the following reforms for the banks under majority state ownership:[21]

(i) To start with, reduce the government ownership to below 26 per cent in two majority government-owned banks. Then, in the second stage, the remaining 25 per cent too will be sold as and when more favourable market conditions emerge.

(ii) The government shall form a Bank Holding Company that will hold all the shares that the government is currently holding in public sector banks. The government shall hold the majority stake in the holding company.

(iii) All public sector banks formed under special acts of parliament shall be converted to joint-stock companies so that they are governed by the Companies Law. This levels the playing field for government-owned banks with respect to private sector banks. The RBI will, of course, remain the banking regulator.

(iv) Banks where non-government entities and individuals hold majority stake shall continue to be subject to priority sector banking requirements. If they choose to comply with the requirement by subscribing to bonds issued by designated banking institutions, those bonds will carry a lower coupon and there will be an annual service charge too on banks not directly discharging their priority sector obligations.

(v) In order to improve the performance of public sector banks, the government should accept the suggestion made by the fourteenth Finance Commission to evolve criteria for the future fiscal support from budgetary resources for majority government-owned financial institutions and, in the process, go into the multiplicity of enterprises in each financial activity.

---

[21] The proposals presented here are drawn from an article that one of us wrote for *Swarajya* (V. Anantha Nageswaran, 'A Speech That Prime Minister Modi Could Make on Banking Reforms', available at https://swarajyamag.com/economy/a-speech-that-prime-minister-modi-could-make-on-banking-reforms, 27 March 2018). In turn, that article had drawn inspiration and ideas from several speeches of Dr Y. V. Reddy, former governor of the Reserve Bank of India, and the recommendations of the P. J. Nayak Committee (https://rbidocs.rbi.org.in/rdocs/PublicationReport/Pdfs/BCF090514FR.pdf). It also draws from our earlier joint work, 'Can India Grow?'

(vi) Government should refrain from burdening public sector banks with fiscal losses from the implementation of welfare programmes. Such activities should be ring-fenced and the true cost of their implementation reimbursed.

(vii) Government's role in the appointments of the top management of banks should be drastically curtailed. The Bank Board Bureau should be given greater autonomy and become responsible for all such appointments. The government can retain some form of oversight and veto rights over such appointments, though to be exercised under exceptional circumstances.

(viii) The government, through the Department of Financial Services, should reduce its engagement with the regular administration of public sector banks. Once the various policies are broadly defined, the respective banks and their boards should have complete autonomy over operations and should have to rely on the government only under rare circumstances for major deviations.

Bank reforms constitute only one part of the sector reforms. We turn next to financial repression, which directly impinges on credit intermediation through the banks.

### 7.2.4 *Financial repression and monetary policy transmission*

As the *Economic Survey 2014–15* highlighted, India suffers from a double financial repression that penalizes savers. On the asset side of the bank balance sheets, reflecting fiscal dominance, the statutory liquidity ratio (SLR) mandates that banks should keep 19.5 per cent of their assets in low interest-bearing government securities. This provides the government with a captive source of cheap financing. In addition, the priority sector lending responsibility means that 40 per cent of loan advances have to be made to specified sectors with a view to ensuring all-round economic development. On the liabilities side, the persistence of high inflation has forced down real interest rates, thereby penalizing savers. Adding to these are the policy distortions – the administered interest rates on savings channels like employee's provident fund and small savings, the plethora of interest subvention subsidies on everything from housing to agricultural loans and the recurrent loan waivers.

Amartya Lahiri and Urjit Patel have shown that the biggest forms of fiscal repression may be the binding SLR requirement and the fiscal dominance from government deficits.[22] They have the effect of hindering monetary policy transmission. Consider the former. A cut in the policy rate reduces the demand for bank deposits by savers while the binding SLR prevents the banks from reallocating scarce deposits away from government bonds towards higher returns that private loans offer. The net result is a fall in the loans, which in turn depresses output and aggregate demand. In other words, a binding SLR constraint makes a lower interest rate on government bonds act as a higher tax on the banking sector, with contractionary effects on the real economy. They write:

> Intuitively, the government budget dictates a unique deposit spread in order to finance the fiscal spending which, through the SLR constraint, renders the lending spread invariant to changes in the policy rate as well. Effectively, the imposition of an exogenous fiscal spending on top of the binding SLR constraint removes all degrees of freedom from the banking sector.

Further, contrary to theory which suggests that a rise in policy rate depresses demand and thereby lowers inflation rate, in this environment, a hike in policy rate, through the cost-push channel, raises inflation. In other words, the combined effect of SLR constraint and fiscal dominance is to scramble the effect of monetary policy on inflation.

In addition to this, the limited depth and breadth of India's financial markets as well as distortionary regulations too hamper the effective transmission of monetary policy.

There are several reasons for the trouble with monetary policy transmission. For a start, their deeply stressed balance sheets naturally encourage banks to immediately pass on the cuts into deposit rates and limit the pass-through into lending rates, so as to increase their net interest margins. A more fundamental reason is the nature of the bank liabilities itself. Unlike in the advanced economies and even the larger emerging economies, Indian banks are heavily dependent on bank deposits to finance their asset purchases. As a comparison, the client deposits as a share of total bank liabilities have been the highest for Indian banks, at 80–90 per cent since the turn of the millennium, compared to the 55–70 per cent range for other similar emerging economies.[23]

---

[22] Amartya Lahiri and Urjit R. Patel, 'Challenges of Effective Monetary Policy in Emerging Economies,' RBI Working Paper Series – 01/2016, available at https://rbidocs.rbi.org.in/rdocs/Publications/PDFs/MPWPCB7E6836912E4F64B28548319C780FEC.PDF.

[23] BMI Research Database

Clearly, deposits as a share of total liabilities are easily the highest in India among all large emerging economies. Since a significant share of deposits have interest rates locked-in, a bank's ability to immediately reduce their cost of capital in response to the reduction in policy rate is constrained. In contrast, in the advanced economies, deposits make up just half of total liabilities, with the remaining coming from various types of borrowings, including inter-bank lending, which can be immediately swapped for lower cost borrowing once the central bank lowers the benchmark rate. To put this in perspective, just 1 per cent of SBI's borrowing came from the open market making it very difficult to meaningfully take advantage of the repo rate cuts and reduce the bank's overall cost of funds.[24]

Amplifying the problem is the nature of the deposits itself. For example, as on 31 March 2015, the outstanding demand and time deposits were ₹7940 lakh crores and ₹77,393 lakh crores, respectively, a tenfold difference. This too constrains the bank's ability to respond quickly to transmit repo rate changes.

This also contributes to a wedge between the bank lending rate on the one hand and long-term bond yields and the money market rates on the other, which in turn gets transmitted across the fixed-income markets in general.

As can be seen from Figure 7.2, the wedge between the lending rate (here, taken as the SBI base lending rate) and the money market rate and 10-year government bond yields is considerable. Encouragingly, the wedge has been on a decreasing trend. It is, therefore, no surprise that short-term commercial paper and similar instruments become more attractive for short-term borrowers following a central bank repo rate reduction.

Financial repression has another important consequence – the high cost of financial intermediation through India's banking system. The difference between what the borrower pays for the loan and the savers get for their deposits is very high. Or as a former RBI Governor Dr Y. V. Reddy has said, the 'the bank depositors are subsidizing the government's borrowing program through SLR, the building of forex reserves through CRR; and the Government's developmental objectives through priority sector program'.[25] In fact, he goes as far as to say that 'there is no crisis in banking but banks are over-burdened with policy induced obligations'.

---

[24] David Keohane and James Crabtree, 'RBI's Rate Cuts Evade India's Real Economy', *Financial Times*, 21 April 2015, available at https://www.ft.com/content/54cce06c-e4d0-11e4-bb4b-00144feab7de.

[25] Reddy, 'State of Banking in India'.

**Figure 7.2 Monetary policy response in India**

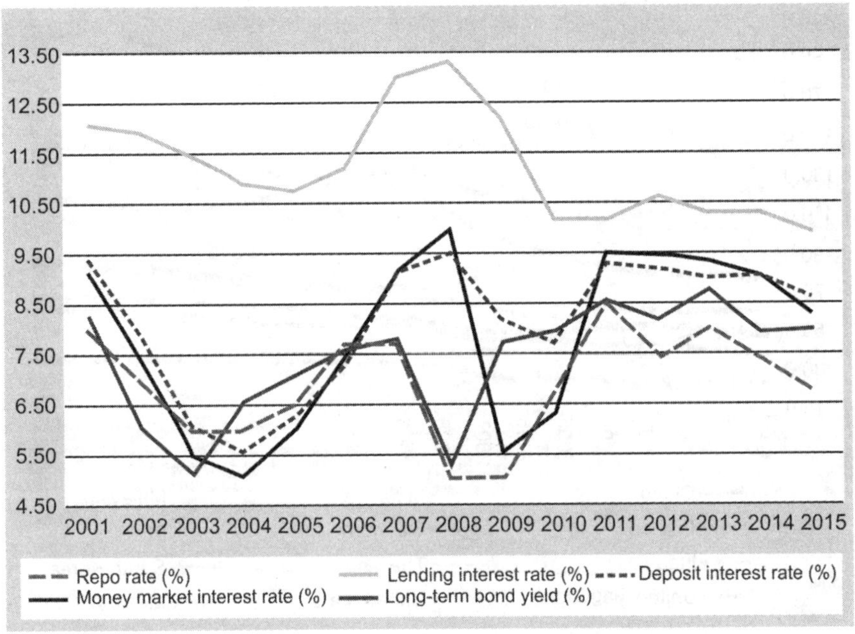

*Source*: RBI database (https://dbie.rbi.org.in/DBIE/dbie.rbi?site=statistics, accessed on 15 September 2016).

## 7.3 Credit market

India's non-banking sources of finance are not fully developed to pick up the credit intermediation from the predominantly government-owned banking system that is hobbled by bad debts. The overall credit market size is modest. The most comprehensive measure of the small size of India's credit markets is reflected in the M2 money supply, which is easily the lowest among all major developed and developing countries (Figure 7.3).

The total stock of credit to non-financial sectors from all sources as a share of GDP is very low, compared to the aggregate for EMs or other major economies.[26] If we confine this analysis to just the private non-financial sector, the situation gets worse (Figure 7.4).

---

[26] Federal Reserve Bank of St. Louis FRED Database, https://fred.stlouisfed.org/series/QINPAM770A#0 and https://fred.stlouisfed.org/series/QINPBM770A#0 (accessed on 10 March 2018).

**Figure 7.3  M2 money supply (as % of GDP)**

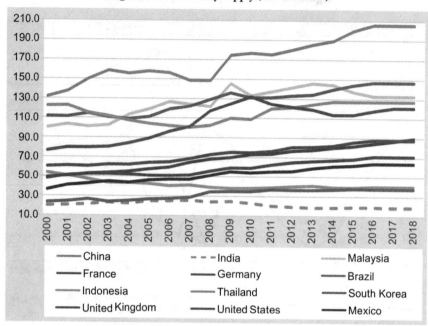

*Source*: Economic Research, Federal Reserve Bank of St. Louis, FRED (https://fred.stlouisfed. org/categories/32264, accessed on 29 October 2017).

India's external exposure presents interesting features in several dimensions. In terms of capital market borrowings, the Indian government has never issued global debt securities. In fact, even combining all other borrowers, India has the lowest exposure to foreign currency debt securities among all major economies (Figure 7.5). It dwarfs even those of Africa and Middle East.

And the trends have remained very stable over time, even as it has risen for most others.[27] In fact, India's stock of cross-border and local currency USD borrowing, including both loans and debt securities, has been declining continuously since 2008.[28] Since the beginning of 2015, the total stock has been contracting in successive quarters. It is, therefore, no surprise that the debt-service ratio of the private non-financial sector is among the lowest.[29]

---

[27] BIS Statistics Warehouse, https://stats.bis.org/#ppq=SEC_OUTST_IDS_BY_ CUR;pv=15~8~0,0,0~both (accessed on 21 March 2018).

[28] BIS Statistics Warehouse.

[29] BIS Statistics Warehouse.

### Figure 7.4 Total credit to private non-financial sector

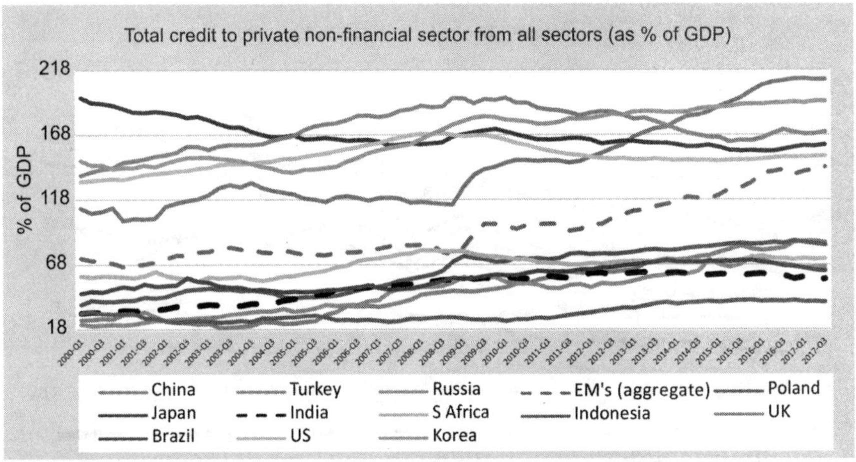

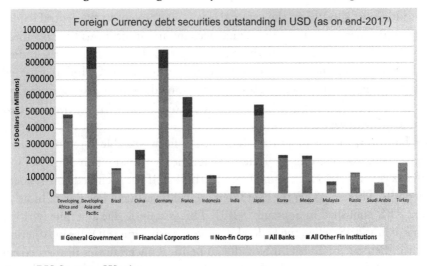

*Source*: BIS Statistics Warehouse, available at https://stats.bis.org/#ppq=CRE_BILLIONK_TO_PRIV_NF;pv=1~7~1,0,0~both (accessed on 10 March 2018).

### Figure 7.5 Foreign currency debt securities outstanding

*Source*: BIS Statistics Warehouse.

Even the more desirable form of foreign capital exposure, foreign direct investment (FDI), is very low. While recent flows have been high and rising, the total stock of FDI is among the lowest. Interestingly, as a share of GDP, it is comparable to that of China (Figure 7.6).

**Figure 7.6 Inward FDI stock**

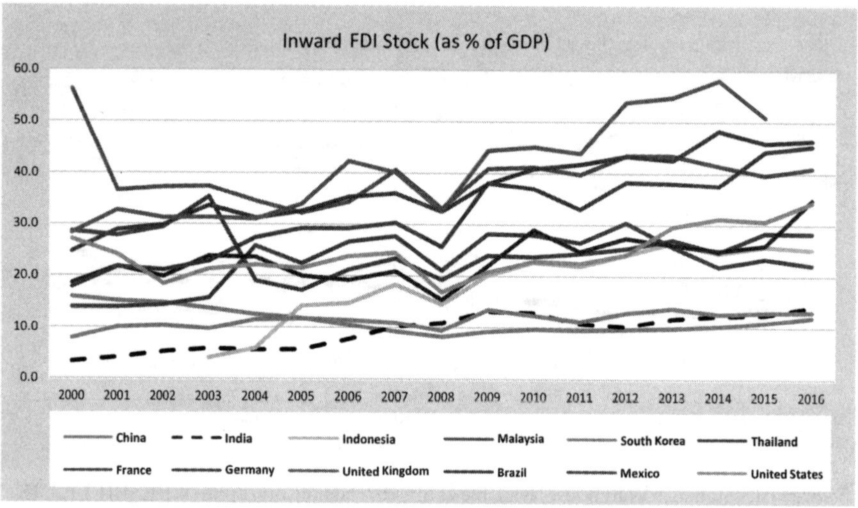
Inward FDI Stock (as % of GDP)
60.0
50.0
40.0
30.0
20.0
10.0
0.0
2000 2001 2002 2003 2004 2005 2006 2007 2008 2009 2010 2011 2012 2013 2014 2015 2016
China
India
Indonesia
Malaysia
South Korea
Thailand
France
Germany
United Kingdom
Brazil
Mexico
United States

*Source*: OECD iLibrary (https://www.oecd-ilibrary.org/finance-and-investment/fdi-stocks/indicator/english_80eca1f9-en, accessed on 29 October 2017).

This low exposure on the external side is a testament to the central bank's very tight management of the capital account and its cautious liberalization. It has had its undoubted benefits. Primarily, it has helped insulate the Indian economy from some of the worst consequences of the GFC. India's external vulnerability is, therefore, confined to the immediate risks arising from flow problems – rising current account deficits coinciding with a period of EM capital flow reversal.

However, in the short run, India has a fairly sizeable foreign currency repayment dues coming up. External liabilities with residual maturity of less than a year for 2018 are around USD 120 billion, if one excluded non-resident deposits. This was as per the 'Net International Investment Position of India' as per RBI, published in September 2017. This is coming due at a time (writing this in July 2018) when the Federal Reserve is raising interest rates in America, when the price of oil is climbing due to political uncertainties in the Persian Gulf and due to the length of the global expansion that is defying the law of averages and when many other emerging economies are coming under pressure due to political troubles and weak macroeconomic fundamentals.

Then, again, this needs to be seen in the backdrop of the country's growing credit needs. The declining savings rate only compounds the problem further. The national savings rate has declined nearly 7 percentage points and the household savings rate has declined 9 percentage points from their peaks.[30] Between April and May 2018, RBI issued a few circulars relaxing the limits on foreign portfolio investors' (FPI) holdings of Indian government and Indian corporate securities. On 6 April 2018, it announced that the limit for FPI investment in central government securities (G-secs) would be increased by 0.5 per cent each year this financial year and next to 5.5 per cent of outstanding stock of securities in 2018–19 and 6 per cent of outstanding stock of securities in 2019–20. The limit for FPI investment in state development loans (SDLs) would remain unchanged at 2 per cent of outstanding stock of securities. The overall limit for FPI investment in corporate bonds was fixed at 9 per cent of outstanding stock of corporate bonds. All the existing sub-categories under the category of corporate bonds were discontinued and there would be a single limit for FPI investment in all types of corporate bonds.[31]

On 27 April 2018, RBI announced that the minimum residual maturity requirement for G-sec and SDL categories stood withdrawn, subject to the condition that investment in securities with residual maturity below 1 year by an FPI under either category shall not exceed, at any point of time, 20 per cent of the total investment of that FPI in that category. FPIs were required to invest in corporate bonds with a minimum residual maturity of 3 years. Henceforth, FPIs are permitted to invest in corporate bonds with minimum residual maturity of above 1 year. The cap on aggregate FPI investments in any G-sec was revised to 30 per cent of the outstanding stock of that security, from 20 per cent earlier.[32]

Then, on 1 May, RBI further clarified that FPI investment in securities with residual maturity of less than 1 year shall not exceed 20 per cent of that FPI's investment in that category. The categories are Government of India bonds, SDLs and corporate bonds. Some of these stipulations could be deemed

---

[30] The peak national savings rate was 36.9 per cent in 2007–08 and it was 30.0 per cent in 2016–17. The household savings rate peak was 25.2 per cent in 2009–10 and it had dropped to 16.3 per cent in 2016–17. These are all percentages of GDP. Strictly speaking, the savings rates since 2011–12 are not comparable to the savings rates before that since the Central Statistical Organisation revised the base year for national income statistics from 2004–05 to 2011–12.

[31] See https://www.rbi.org.in/Scripts/NotificationUser.aspx?Id=11241 (accessed on 18 May 2018).

[32] See https://rbi.org.in/Scripts/NotificationUser.aspx?Id=11266 (accessed on 18 May 2018).

excessive with dubious benefits.[33] After all, FPI can invest in securities with longer maturities but hold them for a very short horizon. Hot money flows are a consequence of short investment horizons and not a function of the residual maturities of the securities.

Be that as it may, the higher limits would increase the external exposure of Indian financial markets and could potentially make the economy that much more vulnerable to the recurrent episodes of cross-border capital flow reversals. However, this can also be a disciplining force on state and central governments to be fiscally responsible. These are inevitable trade-offs that India will have to consider and decide on in the immediate future itself.

The relatively small credit market, with the narrow banking and capital market base and its limited penetration, coupled with the low external exposure, should also draw attention to the opportunities available as well as the possibilities as the country develops. Unlike with the developed economies, India's financialization challenge may be to manage its inevitable credit market deepening and broadening as well as capital account liberalization without engendering some of the egregious features of financialization that are seen in the former.

### 7.3.1 *Bond market in India – stillborn*

Enough has been written on why India does not have a well-developed bond market. India's sovereign bond market size was INR 46.5 trillion (USD 717 billion) as of March 2017. Its corporate bond market size was INR 22.5 trillion (USD 347 billion).[34] It compares rather poorly with even much smaller countries in the region. 'In Asia, India's Corporate Debt to GDP number compares well with China (~20%) but is substantially lower than that of South Korea (77%), Malaysia (44%) and Singapore (32%)'.[35] Not having a bond market is not such a big problem for the economy. Countries in Europe warmed up to the bond market rather slowly and only in recent decades. Germany and Japan became developed nations on the back of bank financing and not bond

---

[33] See https://rbi.org.in/Scripts/NotificationUser.aspx?Id=11268 (accessed on 18 May 2018).

[34] See Shadab Rizvi, 'Sizing the Indian Government and Corporate Debt Capital Markets,' May 2017, available at https://www.linkedin.com/pulse/sizing-indian-government-corporate-debt-capital-markets-shadab-rizvi/ (accessed on 20 June 2018).

[35] Ibid.

financing. All the same, it will be useful to a well-developed bond market alongside a well-capitalized banking sector.

Several reasons have been advanced for the slow development of a thriving bond market in India. Domestic financial repression is one of the principal causative factors. Financial repression is the absence of choices for savers and restrictions on the deployment and disposal of their savings in investments of their choice. Until the 1990s, Indians were largely restricted to bank deposits, small savings deposits, national savings schemes and post-office savings accounts. Stock markets existed but they were narrow and shallow and were deemed highly speculative for ordinary households to trust them with their savings.

As discussed in Section 7.2.4, by imposing SLRs on banks that required them to hold a certain share of their deposits in government securities, the government had a 'sequestration right' on household savings for its spending priorities.

This was necessary because, in India, the combined fiscal deficit of the union and state governments was always on the high side. Even now, it is of the order of 7 per cent of GDP. But the high fiscal deficit keeps the inflation and default risk premium components of the cost of funds to the government high. Then, to the extent that the government borrowing cost serves as the benchmark, it raises the cost of funds for private sector borrowers too. Creditworthy borrowers might be able to negotiate better terms with banks with whom they have a long-standing relationship than having to borrow from the arms-length bond market that might demand a higher risk premium.

A thriving bond market requires credit-rating agencies. It can be safely said that India has them. But credit-rating agencies, in turn, will need financial information and disclosure standards that are of a very high standard to be able to assess credit risk reliably and reasonably accurately. Barring some companies, the overall disclosure standards in India are still evolving and fall short of the desired level of transparency.

Unfortunately, it is also true that Indian corporations prefer the relationship banking model in which projects of doubtful financial viability can be deemed eligible for loans. Indeed, quite a good chunk of the bad loans in the Indian banking system could be traced to loans sanctioned for projects of questionable viability whose risk the bank could not assess properly.

In August 2016, the RBI announced a package of measures for the development of fixed income and currency markets, including the permitting of the issuance of 'Masala' bonds by Indian banks and for financing infrastructure and affordable housing.[36] 'Masala' bonds are bonds denominated in Indian rupees. They are 'rupee bonds overseas' as the RBI. About a year earlier, the framework was put in place for the issuance of masala bonds by Indian corporations. Masala bonds are an interesting and welcome development. At its core, it reflects confidence that India's debt denominated in Indian currency will find willing buyers among foreigners. It is a small step in the long road towards internationalization of the Indian rupee.

Some high-quality issuers have tapped the masala bond route to raise funds. The amount raised through masala bonds is modest at little under USD 4.0 billion.[37] One important thing to keep in mind as and when masala bonds become popular is that the exchange rate risk at the macro level is borne by India. If foreign investors, for some reason, decide to sell their holdings in a herd-like manner, then the Indian rupee will weaken as they take the proceeds back home in their respective currencies. As long as the currency of the investor is not the Indian rupee, exchange rate risk is not eliminated. That said, it is the step in the right direction for financing India's huge investment needs for the next decade or two. The regulator will keep iterating the framework for the issuance of these bonds as it has done already in the course of last year.[38]

Again, in August 2016, RBI announced steps to enable credit supply to large borrowers through the market mechanism rather than through banks. The guidelines placed limits on the quantum of exposure of banks to specified borrowers and stipulated both higher provisioning and higher risk weights for exposure beyond the 'normally permitted lending limit'.[39] That was an indirect way to wean both borrowers and the banks off each other. The crisis that India's government-owned banks are facing with respect to non-performing loans is likely to have a silver lining. Most of the government-owned banks are receiving the 'prompt corrective action' treatment from the regulator. PCA simply means

---

[36] See https://www.rbi.org.in/scripts/bs_pressreleasedisplay.aspx?prid=37875.

[37] A factsheet on masala bonds issued by the London Stock Exchange in August 2017 can be found here: https://www.lseg.com/sites/default/files/content/documents/20170822%20 -%20Masala%20Bonds%20Factsheet.pdf (accessed on 20 June 2018).

[38] For example, in September, Reserve Bank of India announced that 'in consultation with the Government of India, excluded issuances of Rupee Denominated Bonds (RDBs) from the limit for investments by Foreign Portfolio Investors (FPI) in corporate bonds with effect from October 3, 2017'. See https://rbi.org.in/scripts/PublicationsView. aspx?Id=18033#IR.

[39] Reserve Bank of India, 'Guidelines on Enhancing Credit Supply for Large Borrowers through Market Mechanism,' 25 August 2016, available at https://rbi.org.in/Scripts/ NotificationUser.aspx?Id=10574 (accessed on 20 June 2018).

that banks have to get their balance sheet in shape and until then their lending and borrowing (accepting deposits) activities are circumscribed. Private sector banks have not been as enthusiastic about lending for commercial purposes as they are in growing the retail and personal loan books. Therefore, most creditworthy borrowers with a good financial performance, over the years, will increasingly turn to the capital market to fund themselves. So, India's bond market will grow in size and may even become a dominant provider of finance compared to the banking sector.

But the banking sector must be there as well. Japan and Germany did not become developed nations drawing on funds provided by the bond market. Their banks did. Second, there is mounting evidence – from both the developed and the developing world – that bond markets are not good at pricing risk. Bond markets are just as bad as equity markets in mispricing risk. They overdo it both ways – rewarding some borrowers too much for too long (think European sovereigns) and punishing some too much for long (think emerging borrowers) in bad times while encouraging them to borrow recklessly by underpricing risk in good times. Capital markets, in practice, have been very poor at enforcing discipline on debt and equity issuers quite simply because investors have become undisciplined themselves, seeking speculative and short-term returns. Of course, central banks were there to encourage them amply in this endeavour. In short, India cannot and should not rely exclusively on capital markets and must continue to nourish its banking sector well.

Even in the United States, community banks play a vital role in supporting SMEs. They know the borrowers and their business strengths, potential and risks well. They offer advice and can hold hands when the borrower is negotiating difficult times, instead of pulling the plug. When loans are made by 'shadow banks' such as private equity and venture capital funds and hedge funds, they do not play the role of a partner, counsellor and mentor to the business besides being financiers. They are there for short-term profits and exit. 'Arms-length' capitalism can also be aloof, unfriendly and unhelpful capitalism.[40]

In sum, to finance its growth needs, India needs a healthy and sizeable banking sector with some banks being owned by governments and a bond market. It is not a question of choosing one over the other. In fact, for several years now, non-bank entities have almost matched banks in the supply of incremental credit (Figure 7.7).

---

[40] See V. Anantha Nageswaran, 'Unelected Policymakers Brew Another Debt Cocktail,' *Livemint*, 29 May 2018, available at https://www.livemint.com/Opinion/84RUhbR9HX buqAINcQZaYO/Unelected-policymakers-brew-another-debt-cocktail.html.

## Figure 7.7  Incremental credit flow to commercial sector

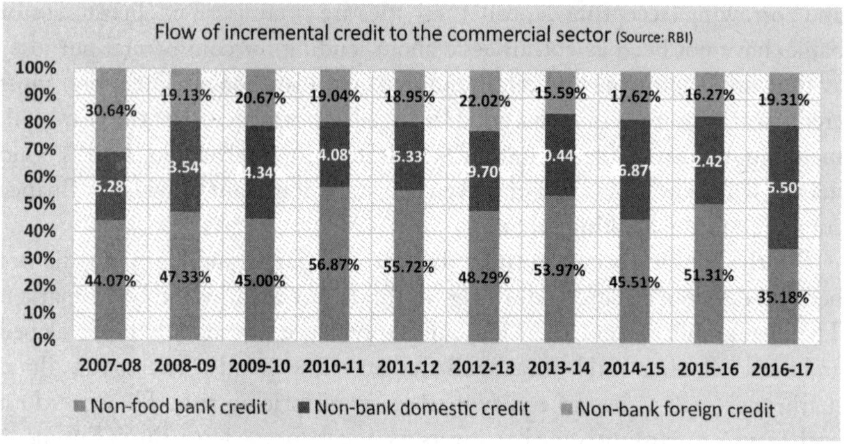

Flow of incremental credit to the commercial sector (Source: RBI)

*Source*: Rakesh Mohan and Partha Ray, 'Indian Financial Sector: Structure, Trends, and Turns,' IMF Working Paper WP/ 17/7, 20 January 2017, p. 21, Table 6, and RBI Annual Report 2016–17.

Underlining the increasing importance of non-bank financing channels for credit disintermediation, in the 2011–17 period, while the share of bank loans in new credit advances to the commercial sector has declined from 56.3 per cent to 38.4 per cent, that of non-bank sources (commercial paper, corporate bonds and external commercial borrowings) has risen from 43.7 per cent to 61.6 per cent.[41] In the aftermath of demonetization, inflows into mutual funds, especially debt-oriented funds, have risen significantly. As of end-July 2017, mutual funds' share of corporate bond investments was 45.98 per cent of debt assets under management, compared to 37.31 per cent a year earlier.[42]

This has been part of the slow shift away from the excessive reliance on banks for corporate financing. In fact, banks formed just over a fifth of the incremental credit accessed by non-financial companies in 2016–17, down from

---

[41] R. Ayyappan Nair, M. V. Moghe and Yashwant Bitra, 'Credit Disintermediation from Banks: Has the Corporate Bond Market Come of Age?,' Mint Street Memo No. 9, 3 January 2018, available at https://www.rbi.org.in/Scripts/MSM_Mintstreetmemos9. aspx.

[42] Suvashree Choudhury and Krishna Merchant, 'Indian Corporates Find Saviour in Bonds as Loans Dry Up, *Livemint*, 16 November 2017, available at http://www.livemint. com/Money/fXTztFG7JX4fvH5Ptzk9vI/Indian-corporates-find-saviour-in-bonds-as-loans-dry-up.html.

above 45 per cent in 2013–14. Corporate bond and short-term commercial paper issuances have risen sharply to compensate.[43] The sharp increase in mutual fund investments in resources raised through bond markets has exceeded that raised from banks sources for the last 2 years (Figure 7.8).

**Figure 7.8 Capital sources of Indian companies**

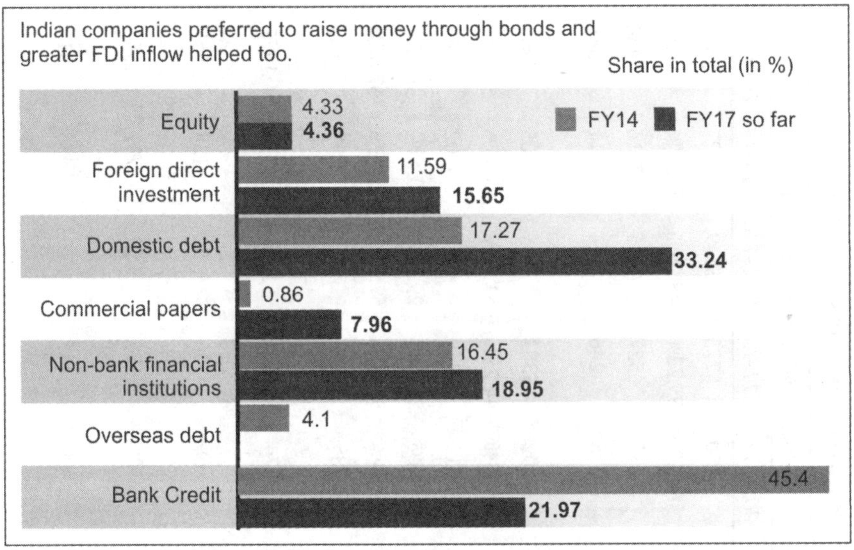

Indian companies preferred to raise money through bonds and greater FDI inflow helped too.

Share in total (in %)

FY14  FY17 so far

| | FY14 | FY17 so far |
|---|---|---|
| Equity | 4.33 | 4.36 |
| Foreign direct investment | 11.59 | 15.65 |
| Domestic debt | 17.27 | 33.24 |
| Commercial papers | 0.86 | 7.96 |
| Non-bank financial institutions | 16.45 | 18.95 |
| Overseas debt | 4.1 | |
| Bank Credit | 45.4 | 21.97 |

*Source*: Aparna Iyer, 'The Decline and Fall of Bank Credit', *Livemint*, 24 March 2017, available at http://www.livemint.com/Money/7pV8tTRGhNeXl5pIBeAdqN/The-decline-and-fall-of-bank-credit.html.

On the non-bank side, despite the rise in FDI inflows, domestic sources have been the major source of supply. Public equity and debt issuances contribute only a small share of the total non-bank flows, with the latter being marginal.[44] A significant share comes from private placements. On the corporate debt side, private placements have been a big source, with housing finance companies and non-bank finance companies (NBFCs) being the others major contributors (Table 7.2).

---

[43] Aparna Iyer, 'The Decline and Fall of Bank Credit,' *Livemint*, 24 March 2017, available at http://www.livemint.com/Money/7pV8tTRGhNeXl5pIBeAdqN/The-decline-and-fall-of-bank-credit.html.

[44] Rakesh Mohan and Partha Ray, 'Indian Financial Sector: Structure, Trends, and Turns,' IMF Working Paper WP/ 17/7, 20 January 2017.

## Table 7.2 Financial resource flows to commercial sector

| | Flow of Financial Resources to Commercial Sector (Rs Billion) | | | | | | | | | |
|---|---|---|---|---|---|---|---|---|---|---|
| | 2007-08 | 2008-09 | 2009-10 | 2010-11 | 2011-12 | 2012-13 | 2013-14 | 2014-15 | 2015-16 | 2016-17 |
| A. Adjusted Non-Food Bank Credit | 4448 | 4211 | 4786 | 7110 | 6773 | 6849 | 7627 | 5850 | 7754 | 5025 |
| | 44.07% | 47.33% | 45.00% | 56.87% | 55.72% | 48.29% | 53.97% | 45.51% | 51.31% | 35.18% |
| 1 Non-food credit | 4328 | 4118 | 4670 | 6815 | 6527 | 6335 | 7316 | 5464 | 7024 | 3950 |
| 2. Non-SLR Investment by Commercial Banks | 120 | 93 | 117 | 295 | 246 | 514 | 311 | 386 | 731 | 1075 |
| B. Flow from Non-Banks (B1+B2) | 5646 | 4686 | 5850 | 5392 | 5383 | 7335 | 6505 | 7005 | 7358 | 9257 |
| | 55.93% | 52.67% | 55.00% | 43.13% | 44.28% | 51.71% | 46.03% | 54.49% | 48.69% | 64.82% |
| B1. Domestic Sources | 2552 | 2984 | 3652 | 3011 | 3079 | 4212 | 4302 | 4740 | 4899 | 6499 |
| | 25.28% | 33.54% | 34.34% | 24.08% | 25.33% | 29.70% | 30.44% | 36.87% | 32.42% | 45.50% |
| | 45.20% | 63.68% | 62.43% | 55.84% | 57.20% | 57.42% | 66.13% | 67.67% | 66.58% | 70.21% |
| 1. Public issues by non-financial companies | 515 | 142 | 320 | 285 | 145 | 119 | 199 | 87 | 378 | 155 |
| 2. Gross private placements by non-financial entities | 682 | 779 | 1420 | 674 | 558 | 1038 | 1314 | 1277 | 1135 | 2004 |
| 3. Net issuance of CPs subscribed to by non-banks | 107 | 56 | 261 | 68 | 36 | 52 | 138 | 558 | 517 | 1002 |
| 4. Net credit by housing finance companies | 418 | 266 | 285 | 428 | 539 | 859 | 737 | 954 | 1188 | 1346 |
| 5. Total gross accommodation by RBI regulated FIs | 223 | 314 | 338 | 400 | 469 | 515 | 436 | 417 | 472 | 469 |

*Contd.*

*Contd.*

Flow of Financial Resources to Commercial Sector (Rs Billion)

| | 2007-08 | 2008-09 | 2009-10 | 2010-11 | 2011-12 | 2012-13 | 2013-14 | 2014-15 | 2015-16 | 2016-17 |
|---|---|---|---|---|---|---|---|---|---|---|
| 6. Systemically important non-deposit taking NBFCs (net of bank credit) | 365 | 768 | 607 | 795 | 912 | 1188 | 1124 | 1046 | 840 | 1245 |
| 7. LIC's net investment in corporate debt, infrastructure and social sector | 243 | 658 | 422 | 361 | 419 | 441 | 354 | 401 | 369 | 277 |
| B2. Foreign Sources | 3093 | 1702 | 2198 | 2381 | 2304 | 3123 | 2203 | 2265 | 2459 | 2758 |
| | 30.64% | 19.13% | 20.67% | 19.04% | 18.95% | 22.02% | 15.59% | 17.62% | 16.27% | 19.31% |
| | 54.78% | 36.32% | 37.57% | 44.16% | 42.80% | 42.58% | 33.87% | 32.33% | 33.42% | 29.79% |
| 1. External Commercial Borrowings/FCCB | 912 | 380 | 120 | 539 | 421 | 466 | 661 | 14 | -388 | -509 |
| 2. ADR/GDP Issues excluding banks and FIs | 118 | 48 | 151 | 92 | 27 | 10 | 1 | 96 | 0 | 0 |
| 3. Short-term credit from abroad | 689 | -312 | 349 | 426 | 306 | 1177 | -327 | -4 | -96 | 435 |
| 4. FDI to India | 1374 | 1586 | 1578 | 1324 | 1550 | 1470 | 1868 | 2159 | 2943 | 2833 |
| C. Total Flow of Resources (A+B) | 10094 | 8897 | 10636 | 12503 | 12156 | 14184 | 14132 | 12855 | 15112 | 14282 |

*Source:* Rakesh Mohan and Partha Ray, 'Indian Financial Sector: Structure, Trends, and Turns,' IMF Working Paper WP/ 17/7, 20 January 2017, p. 21, Table 6, and RBI Annual Report 2016–17.

## 7.4 Capital markets

Arjun Jayadev, J. W. Mason and Enno Schroder classify the evolution of India's financial system into three periods based on the level of state control – unregulated finance (1947–69), increasing direct intervention starting with the bank nationalization or the era of nationalization (1969–91) and the movement towards a more privatized market-oriented financial system starting with the financial liberalization of 1991 or the era of financial reform (1991 onwards).[45] The last period is notable for the emergence of India's capital markets.

The growth of capital markets over the past two decades must count as one of the more impressive achievements of the Indian state. In terms of capitalization as a share of GDP, the Indian stock market is comparable to that of developed countries. The progressive deregulation, even if opportunistic and not part of a grand plan, has seen it emerge as one of the better regulated and performing capital markets among developing countries.

### 7.4.1 *Capital market reforms – an Indian success story*

Initially all that India had was the Bombay Stock Exchange (BSE), established in 1875 (and Asia's first stock exchange), which ran under archaic trading and settlement systems. Indeed, till the mid-1990s, India's long stock market history was its disadvantage. It was the world's greatest and the longest paper chase to execute trades and settle stock market transactions. The BSE is now modernized too and, together with the NSE, these two exchanges are in the top five markets in the world in terms of trading volumes.[46]

India's capital market reforms began when the Securities and Exchange Board of India (SEBI) was formed in 1988. It attained autonomous status and became an independent regulator in 1992. Capital market reforms and gradual liberalization in India are a success story, overall. The National Securities Clearing Corporation of India was incorporated in August 1995. It resulted in the elimination of counterparty and settlement risk. Online position monitoring and automatic disablement became feasible. The passing of the

---

[45] Arjun Jayadev, J. W. Mason and Enno Schroder, 'The Political Economy of Financialisation in US, Europe, and India,' 6 September 2017, available at http://jwmason.org/wp-content/uploads/2015/05/Jayadev-Mason-and-Schroeder-The-Political-Economy-of-Financialization.pdf.

[46] V. Anantha Nageswaran and K. N. Vaidyanathan, 'India's Capital Market at 70,' Gateway House, India, 24 August 2017, available at http://www.gatewayhouse.in/indias-equity-market-successes-2022/ (accessed 24 June 2018).

Depositories Act in 1996 enabled the formation of two depositories – National Securities Depository Limited (NSDL) and Central Depository Services (India) Limited (CDSL). The clearing corporation and the depositories institutions did away with physical exchange of securities and dematerialization of securities was initiated.

NSDL pushed paperless trading or dematerialization ('demat') which enabled high volumes in trading, eliminated clearing and settlement risk and ensured good delivery. NSDL was timely as stock market crimes on duplicate stock ownership certificates had begun and could have taken on alarming proportions. Terrorism appeared in the early 1990s as a global curse. A paper-based market would have been vulnerable to considerable and sustained economic terrorism.

The establishment of NSDL is a fine case study for not just the world but for India too. The government restricted itself to being the legislator. It passed the Depository Act. But it did not sit at the table in the implementation. That was the preserve of the stock exchanges, NSDL and the market as a whole. SEBI oversaw the entire programme and ensured coordination.

The goal of demat trading was achieved in a strategic way, with an implementation focus on ensuring early success, firing bullets before cannonballs. NSDL started with eight stocks that were important for institutional investors. These were the most traded and constituted around 80 per cent of the trading volumes. Slowly, all other stocks were converted to the paperless format. In 5 years, over 95 per cent of the 'free float' was in demat form.

As the stock market became more transparent and efficient and open to foreign institutional investors (FII), domestic promoters too began to see their own role in a different light. Stock prices started to reflect faith in the 'owner/manager' by a differential price–earnings (PE) ratio – higher integrity attracted higher PE and lower integrity was cursed with lower PE. The Indian promoter saw that a rupee stolen from the company was just a rupee in his pocket but a rupee left behind in the company was wealth (in terms of market capitalization), which was 10 or 20 times the company's earnings. This singularly changed the promoter attitude to minority shareholders.

The regulator's mission of protecting the small investors was also evident in the aftermath of the crisis of 2008, when many advanced nations banned short selling. India did not – making it one of the only three markets in the world along with Hong Kong and Singapore that did not ban short sales. This proved effective in managing the volatility in the markets. Information flow is critical to market efficiency and functioning. Banning short selling is banning information that is critical to two-way bets in the market. It is not the same as banning speculation since speculation on the long side is encouraged in many ways, including by cutting interest rates to zero and flooding the economy and markets with liquidity (QE or quantitative easing) – which was the response of advanced nations, preaching one thing and practising another.[47]

While these are impressive and while in terms of breadth Indian stock markets are mature enough, more remains to be done about its depth and the liquidity that comes with it. The narrow depth undoubtedly constrains efficient price discovery and makes the market vulnerable to the actions of a few large participants. The number of companies – privately held or public limited companies – with share capital of over 1 billion rupees totals just above 200 in a total of 800,000 corporate entities.[48] In recent years, foreign institutional investors have had an outsized role to play in determining the market direction. This gives rise to vulnerabilities as we had discussed in Chapter 5 on spillovers. Another area of concern with respect to Indian equities market is the rapid growth of derivatives trading in Indian stocks. That is what we turn to next.

### 7.4.2   *The financialization of Indian stock markets*

To reiterate, Indian equity markets have made tremendous strides with respect to settlement, delivery and transaction costs. It ranks among the best in the world. Its settlement cycle (T+2) is one of the fastest in the world. The depth and breadth of the Indian stock markets partly depends on the creation of many publicly listed corporations, reduced role of promoters, etc. Those issues belong to corporate governance and business and social cultures, norms and practices impinge on them. They are not drawbacks of the capital market, per se.

One of the areas where financialization has caught up with India in a big way is in the area of derivatives trading, particularly with respect to equities. Indian bourses, the National Stock Exchange (NSE) in particular, are very proud of the derivatives turnover that goes through their exchanges every year. The NSE regularly features among the top five and top ten exchanges around the world with respect to derivatives turnover. Whether it is healthy or not and whether it adds to economic welfare or not are unsettled questions. We are clear that they add very little value to the economy. It is not even clear that they help to complete the markets as is often claimed.

---

[47] Nageswaran and Vaidyanathan, 'India's Capital Market at 70'.
[48] This is per data available in the website of Ministry of Corporate Affairs of the Government of India for the year 2012–13.

Somanathan and Anantha Nageswaran in their joint-work, *Economics of Derivatives*, had documented that, the world over, derivatives are used for speculative purposes predominantly, notwithstanding their alleged utility as hedging instruments.[49] Speculative instinct is particularly strong among Asians. When the turnover in derivatives instruments far exceeds the turnover in the underlying instruments that they are derived out of, it is safe to assume that derivatives contracts are not used for hedging functions but for speculative purposes. That appears to be the case with equity derivatives in India. The *Handbook of Statistics* published by the Securities and Exchange Board of India (SEBI) provides information on turnover in the cash segment (trading in equities) and in equity derivatives. The latter massively overwhelms the former. Table 7.3 provides the information.

Derivatives turnover includes turnover on index and single stock futures. Options include CALLs and PUTs traded on stock indices and on single stocks. Notional turnover on options is measured as the product of quantity and (strike price + premium):

**Table 7.3  Derivatives trading volumes in India**

| | *Turnover in Cash segment* | *Derivatives Turnover (Rupees Crores)* | *Ratio of Derivatives turnover/Cash turnover* |
|---|---|---|---|
| | *(Rupees Crores)* | | |
| 2010-11 | 4,685,033.6 | 29,248,375.4 | 6.2 |
| 2011-12 | 3.484,381.6 | 32,158,207.9 | 9.2 |
| 2012-13 | 3,261,700.4 | 38,696,522.7 | 11.9 |
| 2013-14 | 3,341,416.0 | 47.430,842.6 | 14.2 |
| 2014-15 | 5,184,500.6 | 75,969,193.9 | 14.7 |
| 2015-16 | 4,977,278.0 | 69,300,842.5 | 13.9 |
| 2016-17 | 6,054,422.0 | 94,377,241.0 | 15.6 |
| Apr 17–Dec 17 | 5,985,941.2 | 115,494,889.2 | 19.3 |

*Source*: Tables 12 and 23 of the *Handbook of Statistics* (vol. 1), Securities and Exchange Board of India.

*Note*: 1 crore = 10 million.

---

[49] T. V. Somanathan and V. Anantha Nageswaran, 'The Economic Functions of Derivatives Markets', in *Economics of Derivatives*, ch. 3 (India: Cambridge University Press, 2015).

The primary purpose of capital market, at least in theory, is resource mobilization for productive investment and provision of attractive savings options for households. Since corporations use debt (leverage), they can generate more returns for savers than typical bank deposits can. Hence, it makes sense for investors, seeking to earn real returns, to allocate a portion of their investments to shares of listed companies. Derivatives do not figure in any of these. They are leveraged instruments and they are short term in nature and are often used for speculative purposes or, in plain English, gambling.

It does not mean that one adopts a moralistic stance and bans derivatives. What is banned does not disappear but goes underground. That makes it more difficult for regulators to watch over them and be able to forestall their adverse effects on systemic stability. Other approaches are needed. Repeated customer education initiatives are one of them. The other is to insist on adequate net worth on the part of financial speculators. The third is to ensure that product providers appraise investors of the risks of such instruments in simple and plain language. Fourth, the regulator does not have to be the promoter of financial products and actively promote the Indian marketplace. Some developments should be allowed to happen on their own with the passage of time and the growth of the economy. That would ensure that both the economy, in the aggregate, and market participants are better able to withstand shocks.

In this regard, the discussion paper that SEBI had released last year[50] raised some important questions on the excessively large turnover of derivatives compared to the cash market turnover (see Table 7.3) and the presence of a fairly high proportion of individual investors in derivatives markets. The Indira Gandhi Institute of Development Research (IGIDR) had provided a detailed response[51] to the SEBI discussion paper, which dismissed many of the implicit and explicit concerns of the regulator in floating the discussion paper.

The high derivatives turnover ratio in relation to the cash market was put down to the low liquidity in the cash market and other countries have equity derivatives traded OTC too. Therefore, their overall derivatives turnover ratio, including OTC derivatives turnover, is not that low, in comparison to

---

[50] 'Discussion Paper on Growth and Development of Equity Derivative Market in India,' Securities and Exchange Board of India, 12 July 2017, available at https://www.sebi.gov.in/reports/reports/jul-2017/discussion-paper-on-growth-and-development-of-equity-derivative-market-in-india_35295.html.

[51] 'Response to SEBI's Discussion Paper on Growth and Development of Equity Derivatives Markets in India,' Finance Research Group, IGIDR, 10 August 2017, https://www.ifrogs.org/PDF/201708SEBI_response.pdf (accessed 16 July 2018).

India's. Even accounting for OTC transactions, India's derivatives turnover is far higher. Second, it may well be the case that there is a liquidity problem in the cash market but that does not answer the question of whether there is excessive growth of trade in derivatives in the country.

One of us wrote a collaborative piece in response to the SEBI discussion paper that the minimum contract size be increased further to rupees 10 lakhs (one million rupees) from rupees 5 lakhs. We recommended that the regulator set up a Financial Products Authority, on the lines recommended by Professor Eric Posner at the University of Chicago, 'to issue guidelines and eligibility criteria for high-risk financial products such as derivatives. This will also mean that SEBI will not be the sole judge of financial innovation but an empowered body with industry participants'.[52]

The discussion on derivatives, their regulation and product representation set the stage for a discussion on India's financial sector regulation.

## 7.5 Financial sector regulation – strengths and gaps

### 7.5.1 *Regulatory philosophy*

Until the SEBI became active in the 1990s, India's financial sector regulation was in the hands of its central bank, the RBI. Most of the governors of the RBI came from the Indian Administrative Service and they were comfortable with a prominent role for government in regulating the financial sector and with government ownership in the banking industry. Philosophically, they were not against the idea. Financial inclusion was an important national priority and the private sector was not viewed as the right agency to translate that priority into reality. This philosophical comfort with a prominent regulatory role for the government actually stood India in good stead. It enabled the governors to navigate the global crises that they encountered and to insulate India from the effects of those crises. For example, Governor Bimal Jalan handled the Asian crisis rather well and India was relatively largely unscathed. More recently and importantly, Dr Y. V. Reddy's handling of the Indian economy and the credit and investment boom that characterized the high growth years of 2003 to 2008 came in for much praise globally.

---

[52] See Praveen Chakravarty and V. Anantha Nageswaran, 'How Can SEBI Moderate India's Derivatives Cholesterol?' *Livemint*, 27 July 2018, available at https://www.livemint.com/Opinion/y16JftNyKPj9VqHrafS7NJ/How-can-Sebi-moderate-Indias-derivatives-cholesterol.html (accessed on 16 July 2018).

Joe Nocera of the *New York Times* flew to India to understand what Dr
Y. V. Reddy did that was different from other central bankers.[53] Joseph
Stiglitz invited him to teach monetary policy at the Columbia University.
Dr Reddy did not take up the offer for personal reasons. Jim Walker,
former chief economist with Credit Lyonnais Securities Asia, wrote that
he was a far better central banker than Greenspan whose monetary policy
and philosophical framework were considered two of the most responsible
factors for the mortgage bubble and the subsequent crisis that followed in
the United States.[54] Quite what did Dr Y. V. Reddy do in the years leading
up to 2008 that earned him much acclaim and respect among the central
banking fraternity and in the academia?

To start with, Dr. Reddy had a very healthy scepticism of the benefits of
financialization. In a speech he delivered in Manchester in July 2008,[55] he
outlined India's approach to financial sector regulation and questioned the
supposed benefits of financialization. Specifically, he said that the focus in
India was on regulatory comfort going beyond regulatory compliance. In other
words, he hinted that India favoured substance over form when it came to the
regulation of the banking sector. 'In a choice between emphasis of regulations
on saving capital and protecting depositors' interests or reinforcing financial
system stability, the latter have always prevailed'. He wondered if liberalization
of trade in goods and services had contributed more to economic growth and
price stability than did financial sector initiatives. He was right. Subsequent
research – which we had cited in Chapter 5 – has vindicated him. Finance
was growth friendly only up to a point and only under certain conditions. He
stated, in his own inimitable style, 'In particular, it may be argued that the
incentive frameworks for financial intermediaries appear to be disproportionate
to their conceivable contribution to the economy. The arguments in favour of
persevering with financial innovation and urging regulators to continue to give
priority to facilitate innovations should be viewed in this context'.

---

[53] Joe Nocera, 'How India Avoided a Crisis?' *New York Times*, 19 December 2018, available
at https://www.nytimes.com/2008/12/20/business/20nocera.html (accessed on 17 July
2018).

[54] In his article 'How India Avoided a Crisis?', Joe Nocera simply called him 'anti-
Greenspan'.

[55] Y. V. Reddy, 'Global Financial Turbulence and Financial Sector in India: A Practitioner's
Perspective,' Address at the Meeting of the Task Force on Financial Markets Regulation
organized by the Initiative for Policy Dialogue at Manchester, United Kingdom, on 1
July 2018, https://rbidocs.rbi.org.in/rdocs/Speeches/PDFs/85529.pdf (accessed on 17
July 2018).

The emphasis on regulatory comfort in contrast to regulatory compliance is not just a matter of semantics. It is fashionable to think that regulation is needed only to address market failures and that, otherwise, markets will take care of themselves. But finance is different (see Box 2.1). In the case of finance, regulation exists to ensure that the market functions. To reiterate, in financial markets, 'more is demanded at higher prices and less at lower prices. This attitude leads to asset prices being chased higher. And credit creation linked to asset prices rises together with asset prices. The whole financial system is pro-cyclical by its sheer nature and it is true to this very date. Hence, regulation is necessary not to address financial market failures, but because financial markets are not well-functioning markets as defined by economic theory'.[56] In other words, regulation of finance is necessary because of the seeds of systemic risk that inhere in finance.

The willingness to go against Western conventional wisdom on the virtues of finance put Dr Y. V. Reddy on guard against its excesses, well before they became manifest in advanced nations. We recall with not-so-inconsiderable satisfaction that one of us wrote rather appreciatively about the stewardship of monetary policy by the RBI under Dr Reddy in April 2007[57] and May 2007.[58] In his article in *New York Times*, Joe Nocera lists some of the steps that the RBI, under Dr Reddy's leadership, had taken to forestall and pre-empt a crisis arising in India.

One, Dr Reddy made lending standards more stringent during the bubble. He banned banks from lending for the purchase of raw land for real estate projects. Bankers could get involved only when the developer was about to commence construction. He banned banks from setting up off-balance sheet vehicles. He increased risk weightings on bank loans for the construction of commercial buildings and shopping malls doubling the amount of capital banks had to hold in reserve against these loans.

---

[56] V. Anantha Nageswaran, 'The Biased Work of FSLRC,' *Livemint*, 1 April 2013, available at https://www.livemint.com/Opinion/zw2TIQKepaoSxDh2uQcOmJ/The-biased-work-of-FSLRC.html (accessed on 18 July 2018).

[57] V. Anantha Nageswaran, 'In Defence of RBI's Position,' *Livemint*, 10 April 2007, available at https://www.livemint.com/Opinion/kFPyr258tL9zZV9K7RawcI/In-defence-of-RBIs-position.html (accessed on 17 July 2018).

[58] V. Anantha Nageswaran, 'The Monetary Policy Lab,' *Livemint*, 1 May 2007, available at https://www.livemint.com/Opinion/qQdhCzKDaUn5euwolWJxjM/The-monetary-policy-lab.html (accessed on 17 July 2018).

Dr Reddy himself listed the following measures that RBI had taken to douse the credit and investment boom:[59]

- Monetary policy prudently focused on consumer price inflation and on monetary and credit aggregates.
- Use of moral suasion (on loans to companies that speculated in foreign exchange, on LTV on home loans), regulation and market instruments.
- Stress testing the financial system for rising interest rates in the world when actually interest rates were falling.
- Asking banks to set aside a higher provision for 'Investment Fluctuation Reserve' on assets Held for Trade when there was no stress in the system.
- Risk weighting higher than 100 per cent for certain classes of loans as early as in 2004 and in 2005 (for example, commercial real estate from 100 per cent to 125 per cent in 2005 to 150 per cent in 2006).
- Securitization profits allowed to be realized only over the life of the securitized asset rather than immediately. This effectively discouraged the 'originate to distribute' practice seen in the United States.

These were macroprudential measures before the term became fashionable in the West and they were accompanied by monetary policy tightening as well. In spite of these various measures, India experienced a credit and investment boom that faltered once the global crisis struck in 2008. One can only speculate on the severity of the impact on India had the above measures not been undertaken. India too had to resort to substantial massive fiscal and monetary stimulus post-2008 to resurrect economic growth. It is a different story that they remained in place too long and paved the way for overheating of the Indian economy with high current account deficit and double-digit inflation that lasted 5 years resulting in the collapse of the Indian currency in 2013.

India experienced investment boom and a speculative boom in the stock market, despite the central bank taking prudent measures because foreign portfolio investment flows into Indian stocks were copious in the years between 2003 and 2008. By then, India had effectively opened its capital account to

[59] Y. V. Reddy, 'Global Financial Turbulence and Financial Sector in India: A Practitioner's Perspective,' Address at the Meeting of the Task Force on Financial Markets Regulation organized by the Initiative for Policy Dialogue at Manchester, United Kingdom, on 1 July 2018, available at https://rbidocs.rbi.org.in/rdocs/Speeches/PDFs/85529.pdf (accessed on 17 July 2018).

foreigners. There was full capital account convertibility for foreigners but not so for domestic residents. This was despite RBI harbouring concerns over the efficacy of unrestricted financial flows across borders. Money is fungible until it is not. Capital remembers its place of origin and retreats to its safety in crises. Dr Reddy recognized that and stated bluntly once that international investors treated emerging economies differently (from advanced nations) and hence he was justified in treating them differently (from domestic investors). Of course, his advice and warnings were not heeded because the political executive succumbed to global fashion and international coercion with respect to free capital flows. You may recall from Section 6.2 that IMF acknowledged the need for managing capital flows only in 2012. One could imagine Dr Reddy smiling triumphantly.

In concluding this section, we will reiterate the regulatory philosophy for finance. It is necessary not to address financial market failures but to address financial market functioning: its inherent cyclicality. In the EM context of which India is a part, spillovers are a reality. We discussed it in detail in Section 5.6. To deal with spillover risks, regulation of capital flows – inward and outward – is necessary. The IMF has come around to this view as well but still views it as temporary and to be deployed as last resort. We think that it is an essential part of the policy arsenal for emerging economies and will likely be so for quite some time to come. Third, regulators must be on the alert for the emergence of the risks of financialization – too much finance. We have highlighted the case of derivatives trading in equities. Derivatives trading in other asset classes – interest rates and foreign exchange – have not become yet. When they do, they may become the tail that wags the dog.

We are also conscious of the risk that the regulatory philosophy with respect to finance might be carried to far. So, we will propose three regulatory axioms to temper or complement the regulatory philosophy propounded above:

(i) *Regulator may be able to hurt but not help* – this is in line with the discussion of asymmetry in economics in Section 6.9. Regulators' quasi-judicial status and enforcement authority means that they have disproportionately large power to hurt than to help market participants. This recognition must temper the application of such power.

(ii) Closely related to that is the second axiom that, once let out, *it is not easy to put the genie back into the bottle.* Either tighter or looser regulation, once implemented, will set off consequences that might not be foreseen. After that, even if the regulator wishes to correct or reverse the decision, it may not be feasible because the context will have changed. For example, one may not be able to attract capital back once they have been scared off by a new regulation because trust and credibility will have been damaged by the regulation and it may be impossible to restore or regain them even if the regulation is retracted.

(iii) *Regulatory priorities must not clash with national priorities.* For example, India needs foreign capital inflows because of its persistent current account deficits. Regulators, on the other hand, wish to discourage and even eliminate money laundering. Both may clash if the right balance is not struck between measures aimed at discouraging money laundering and their effect on foreign investor interest in Indian markets. The international context too must be kept in mind. Regulatory change that induces uncertainty in market participants must be cognizant of the domestic and international market and policy environment. It makes little sense to compound uncertainty when uncertainty is already rising. That would discourage capital inflows just when the country needs them.

## 7.5.2 *The Financial Sector Legislative Reforms Commission*

Given the sound philosophical attitude on the part of the Indian regulator – RBI – towards finance, financialization and capital flows, the recommendations made in the report of the Financial Sector Legislative Reforms Commission (FSLRC) headed by Justice Srikrishna released in 2013 came as a surprise. Its underlying philosophy – unstated – was that unfettered financial markets were a public good. It was almost as though the GFC of 2008 did not happen. Many of the commission's members dissented on one crucial aspect or the other of the report.

The Commission, as constituted by the finance ministry in 2011, had 11 members. One of them, from the ministry, was meant to provide administrative support. Out of the remaining 10, one was member, convenor and the other was a joint secretary from the capital markets division of the ministry. Quite interestingly, he did not sign the report. Out of the remaining eight, two were former judges who had no prior knowledge of the financial sector. In any case, one of them was so seriously ill that he could not sign the report. That left six of them. One of them passed away within the first few months of the appointment of the Commission. Out of the remaining five, Govinda Rao was an expert on tax matters and the other, Jayant Varma, was an expert on capital markets. Three of them – P.J. Nayak, K. J. Udeshi and Y.H. Malegam – were concerned with banking regulation, monetary policy and capital flows. All three appended dissenting notes on several important recommendations of FSLRC. That is 100% dissension on the Commission's recommendations from the domain experts. No finance minister should disregard such an overwhelming consensus on the rejection of the work of a Commission of which they were a part. [60]

The fundamental premise of the FSLRC regulatory paradigm is that *financial markets are inherently efficient and regulation is required to address market failures and not necessary to enable market development*. Further, its specific proposals on realigning the regulatory architecture are equally transformational – *shift from multiple to single capital and money markets regulator*, and the *judicial review of RBI's regulatory actions*. There is no evidence whatsoever, from India or elsewhere, to warrant such a radical departure – by way of either the superiority of the new paradigm or the relative inferiority of the prevailing system – on something like financial market regulation on which there is little global consensus on what is the best approach.

The RBI's banking sector regulatory decisions would come for appeal before the Financial Sector Appellate Tribunal. In fact, this judicial oversight is not just confined to issues like the magnitude of penalties, but also on "'policy decisions' (involving exercise of judgement) like whether to ban a particular financial instrument or the magnitude of leverage caps on trading positions, which are not explicitly laid down as policy but would result from regulators exercising their discretion in response to emergent situations. Such decisions are invariably deeply judgemental in nature, based on a very comprehensive appreciation of trends and the theory and model being used to make the assessment. Further, most such decisions have a compelling enough counter-point, again based on a different judgement arrived at through a different theory and model. In the circumstances, defending the decision before a court of law can become very tricky. It will encourage banking regulators to play safe – delay decision-making on throwing sand into the wheels of a booming asset market till the bubble bursts. It will also embolden financial market participants and their lobbyists to question, for example, emergent policy decisions that address systemic safety.

---

[60] V. Anantha Nageswaran, 'Stop the Task Forces, Mr. Jaitley,' *Livemint*, 6 October 2014, available at https://www.livemint.com/Opinion/J5v0wbIVDdeFpzLLMovFWK/Stop-the-task-forces-Mr-Jaitley.html (accessed on 18 July 2018).

As the then governor of RBI has argued against the move saying that the tribunals would 'simply not have the capability, experience, or information to make, and where precise evidence may be lacking ... a lot of regulatory action stems from the regulator exercising sound judgment based on years of experience. In doing so, it fills in the gaps in laws, contracts, and even regulations'.[61] In this context, it is worth remembering that India's recent experience with the Securities Appellate Tribunal and its judgements on SEBI decisions has not been encouraging.

> On the issue of capital controls, the commission, presumably based on wrong advice, tied itself into knots. It split capital flows into inward and outward and wants to place all inflows under the control of the government and outflows under the control of the central bank. Some of the commission members, as noted above, had expressed themselves rather well against this division of labour, which had little basis either in concept or in convenience.[62]

In fact, equity flows are subject to much the same global financial linkages-induced volatility as debt flows. Also, such separation of responsibilities and the resultant *regulatory arbitrage* opportunities may engender systemic distortions in equity and debt inflows. It, therefore, *goes against the argument that capital flow management measures have to be undertaken in a comprehensive manner.* Further, it increases the moral hazard for governments to keep open the equity market gates in good times and to that extent *restrict the RBI's ability to impose counter-cyclical macroprudential measures* to effectively manage the overall current account balance. We discussed these issues in detail in the context of financialization in Chapter 6.

FSLRC suggested that the central bank be responsible only for microprudential regulation and that too only for some time before handing it over to an independent regulator with the central bank remaining responsible only for monetary policy! On macroprudential measures, FSLRC recommended that macroprudential regulation be vested in a Financial Stability and Development Council headed by the finance minister. To a degree, it is understandable. Some decisions involve distributional consequences and

[61] Raghuram G. Rajan, 'Financial Sector Legislative Reforms Committee (FSLRC) Report: What to Do and When?' Talk at the First State Bank 'Banking and Economic Conclave', 17 June 2014, available at https://rbi.org.in/Scripts/BS_ViewBulletin.aspx?Id=15008.

[62] V. Anantha Nageswaran, 'The Biased Work of FSLRC,' *Livemint*, 1 April 2013, available at https://www.livemint.com/Opinion/zw2TIQKepaoSxDh2uQcOmJ/The-biased-work-of-FSLRC.html (accessed on 18 July 2018).

that call can only be taken by the political executive that has the democratic mandate and democratic accountability to make such decisions. However, not all macroprudential decisions have significant distributional consequences. Some are operational. In fact, even in case of those decisions that involve allocation or withdrawal of credit or the pricing of credit to certain sectors, it might be easier and convenient for the executive to hand over the responsibility to the central bank in order to being pulled and pushed by competing interests.

If the alleged aim was to ensure that decisions that have distributional consequences be taken by the political authority with democratic legitimacy, then even monetary policy should not be in the hands of the central bank but vested in the executive! After all, monetary policy redistributes wealth between borrowers and savers all the time!

### 7.5.2.1 *Bailing in bank depositors*

To a large extent, one of the unintended positive effects of the unfortunate crisis in Indian banks' balance sheets is that the recommendations of FSLRC had not been given much attention. That is a good thing. Indeed, as an offshoot of the recommendations of FSLRC, in 2017, a government-appointed panel recommended that all banks' creditors, including depositors, be bailed in, to ensure that taxpayers were not in the dock for bank failures. In a low-income country such as India where a substantial majority of the households held their financial savings in the form of bank deposits, the proposal caused consternation and panic. The government had gone as far as to put the idea in a draft legislative proposal – Financial Resolution and Deposit Insurance Bill.

It is part of the ongoing reform efforts in G-20 that are aimed at ensuring minimal impact on the taxpayer from having to bail out financial institutions in trouble and at ensuring that economic activity continued uninterrupted while the failed institution is resolved. The bill proposes to bail in bank deposits in the resolution process. In other words, India's bank depositors cannot take for granted that their deposits would be unaffected by bank failures and that the State would be behind them. That has unsettled scores of pensioners, widows, old-age people and the middle class.

That the taxpayer shall not be on the hook to bail out failed financial institutions and the costs, if any, should be first borne by insider-stakeholders is sound, in principle. But, in any resolution, when the market value of the liabilities of the failed institution exceed the market value of its assets, the first hit is to the current equity-holders of the institution. In terms of the hierarchy of claims, they are the most junior. In the case of the Indian banking system, the predominant owner is the government and hence, the taxpayer. Hence, in the Indian context, the taxpayer is the first to be bailed in! In other words, the principle that the resolution mechanism shall protect the taxpayer is a non-starter. Therefore, before bailing in depositors, the government must climb down from its occupation of the commanding heights of the banking system. The idea that one can apply a so-called market-economy solution to a government-owned banking system is risible. The sequencing is wrong.

The second principle is that those who stood to gain from the banks' profitable expansion of assets and operations should be prepared to lose from its failures. That is why equity-holders are first in the list of those to be bailed in. Then come bondholders. To a degree, they participate in the upside. If banks perform well, their bond prices rise and they gain from trading them for higher prices and from the higher coupons they get for accepting junior and subordinated claims compared to secured and senior bondholders. The depositor is already short-changed by the high average inflation rate in the Indian economy. Second, banks are willing to cut deposit rates faster than they cut lending rates when interest rates go down. Finally, bank depositors have no participation in the upside. Hence, to bail them in is against fairness and natural justice.[63]

Even developed countries do not bail in depositors and they had gone out of their way, during the crisis of 2008, to raise deposit insurance limits to protect vast swathes of bank deposits and depositors. Dr Y. V. Reddy said as much in an unusually blunt and direct speech on 1 February 2018:

> This approach has not stood test of time in other countries. In fact, half of G20 countries have not even considered this approach so far. The current proposal is, therefore, trying to find a risky and untried solution where no problem exists and in the process, problem of trust in banking has been created… The current approach of treating Banks as special and bank depositors as special must be continued, and an assurance to this effect may be extended by the Government.[64]

The Financial Resolution and Deposit Insurance Bill was tabled in the parliament and referred to a parliamentary committee. Soon it triggered widespread public concerns about the safety of bank deposits and the

---

[63] V. Anantha Nageswaran, 'The Government Must Bail Out of the Bail-In,' *Livemint*, 12 December 2017, available at https://www.livemint.com/Opinion/SeiuZFjYxc8FvP2acpilzK/The-government-must-bail-out-of-the-bailin.html (accessed on 18 July 2018).

[64] Y. V. Reddy, 'State of Banking in India'.

government protection for the same. Good sense finally prevailed and it has, at least for now, been shelved. However, with the genie out of the bottle and the enabling ideological framework provided by FSLRC, it is more likely to come back when the time is ripe.

### 7.5.2.2 *Inflation-targeting framework*

India moved to an inflation-targeting framework partly as a result of the work of FSLRC. Of course, India's double-digit annual inflation rate from 2009 until 2014 played a big role in influencing the decision of the government to opt for an inflation-targeting framework for its central bank. Further, notwithstanding the crisis of 2008 which exposed the limitations of the inflation-targeting homework, it remains *de rigueur.* Therefore, India opted for the seeming clarity and simplicity of an inflation-targeting framework in 2014. To implement the new monetary policy framework with an explicit inflation target, the government opted for a MPC as is the practice in many developed countries. FSLRC had recommended that government nominees constitute the majority of members of the MPC. That did not happen. Currently, there are three government nominees and three from RBI. The governor of RBI is the ex-officio chairperson of MPC. He has the casting vote in case of a tie.

Earlier, the regime was that RBI followed a multiple-indicator approach which included tracking inflation, monetary and credit aggregates. The 'unofficial' inflation target was 5 per cent then. The governor took the decision and he was advised by a Technical Advisory Committee whose recommendations were not binding on the government. It was working fine until the high-inflation years of 2009 to 2014 raised doubts on the effectiveness of the old approach. Of course, it was not a flaw in the system that led to the high inflation. It was an outcome of classic overheating of the economy caused by simultaneous monetary and fiscal stimuli that were in place for a long time.

India's inflation-targeting regime is relatively young and hence it is too early to pass judgements on it.[65] The shortcomings of such a regime that were evident in the West have not become apparent yet for the simple reason that India has not had a situation of rampant credit growth, asset price inflation and quiescent consumer price inflation. In the last 2 to 3 years, Indian banks have

---

[65] We deliberately have chosen to avoid a discussion on whether the inflation target of 4 per cent with a symmetric band of 2 per cent around it is the most appropriate one or if it could be different for such a discussion does not fit with the overall purpose of this book. We have our views on it but it is a topic for a different book altogether!

been grappling with non-performing loans and have been reluctant to extend credit. Credit growth has been muted at best. The system will be put to test only when India's banks become powerful money creators as has been the case in some advanced countries. The flaw in the inflation-targeting framework is that price stability is not the only sign of economic overheating. Whether India's inflation-targeting framework comes up short or not will be tested only when the central bank fails to withdraw the punch bowl when credit and asset markets party hard even as inflation remains well behaved.

A prominent critique of inflation targeting comes from the view that inflation in India is primarily driven by foodgrain prices, which have a 45.86 per cent weight in the consumer price index. Since conventional monetary policy instruments cannot impact food prices in the short term, they argue that inflation targeting is likely to be blunt.[66]

A recent study by ICRIER and OECD appears to question this view. It calculates producer support estimates – a combination of the globally benchmarked output prices and the various subsidies that farmers receive directly and indirectly – and finds that India is among a tiny minority of countries where farmers receive lower revenues than would have been the case without all types of subsidies.[67] In other words, fiscal policy, by way of various kinds of transfers, is keeping foodgrain prices low.

What this tells us is that India's inflation problem is not a supply or food price problem. India has a fiscal policy problem and a productivity problem. So, 'inflation-targeting' regime cannot be criticized on this score. India's inflation problem seems to be in spite of policy shafting farmers and not because of policy supporting farmers!

Whether inflation targeting is appropriate or necessary at all for any country (let alone developing countries) and whether it really serves the purpose of stabilizing and lowering inflation expectations are important questions. Empirical evidence from around the world does not credit inflation targeting regimes with stabilizing inflation expectations. In India's case, despite more than three years of inflation targeting, RBI surveys indicate that household inflation expectations are stubbornly high.

---

[66] Harish Damodaran, 'The Age of Surplus,' *The Indian Express*, 12 June 2018, available at https://indianexpress.com/article/opinion/columns/agrarian-crisis-farmer-protests-rural-distress-surplus-production-crop-procurement-the-age-of-surplus-5213499/.

[67] Ashok Gulati and Carmel Cahill, 'Resolving the Farmer–Consumer Binary,' *The Indian Express*, 9 July 2018, available at https://indianexpress.com/article/opinion/columns/farmers-india-agrarian-crisis-narendra-modi-government-5251281/.

Inflation targeting in the developed world is a reflection of anti-labour bias and in the developing world, it reflects pro-urban bias in policymaking. Therefore, it might be appropriate to review the necessity for the inflation targeting regime in the Indian context. Nevertheless, the situation that Paul Tucker deals with in his book 'Unelected power' does not apply to India. That is, in India, the RBI is far from becoming the 'only game in town'. In a recent interview, he said, 'There's been a bit of an overshooting by activist judges, central bankers and regulators being the solution to every problem'.[68] India suffers from judicial activism but central bank activism is not a headache for the elected government in India. If anything, the opposite is true. Politicians have felt very comfortable wading into the domain of central bankers rather than respecting institutional boundaries. Therefore, institutional autonomy for the central bank and focus on systemic considerations rather than short-term electoral considerations would not hurt.

In his last speech as RBI governor, Subbarao had to remind the government that, in the end, it would be happy that RBI was there, after the finance minister of the day had publicly criticized the central bank for not cutting rates to lift economic growth.[69] In fact, one can say that Dr Subbarao had anticipated Paul Tucker 5 years earlier. He said, in the same speech, that the central bank should be as zealous about rendering accountability as it is about guarding its autonomy. The context in India differs from the one that Western societies confront now where elites have encroached upon political turf a little too excessively and persistently for over a quarter century. 'Since the 1990s, international organisations have been promoting independent agencies as a "good thing".... The IMF advocates independence for financial regulation. The Organisation for Economic Co-operation and Development promotes delegated governance across a wider terrain.'[70]

---

[68] See Asher Schechter, 'A Former Central Banker Tells Other Central Bankers: "Stay Away From Davos", 3 July 2018, available at https://promarket.org/former-central-banker-tells-central-bankers-stay-away-davos/ (accessed on 18 July 2018).

[69] These were his words: 'I do hope Finance Minister Chidambaram will one day say, "I am often frustrated by the Reserve Bank, so frustrated that I want to go for a walk, even if I have to walk alone. But thank God, the Reserve Bank exists".' See 'Five Years of Leading the Reserve Bank – Looking Ahead by Looking Back', Tenth Nani A. Palkhivala Memorial Lecture delivered by Dr Duvvuri Subbarao, Governor, Reserve Bank of India, in Mumbai on 29 August 2013, available at https://www.rbi.org.in/Scripts/BS_SpeechesView.aspx?Id=833.

[70] Paul Tucker, *Unelected Power: The Quest for Legitimacy in Central Banking and the Regulatory State* (Princeton University Press, 2018).

### 7.5.3 *Regulatory architecture*

Before we began to write this section, we sent emails to market participants in India – a journalist, a former banker and an analyst – to confirm if our understanding of the Indian regulatory architecture was correct. One of them did not reply. The two who replied were not sure of their responses. This may be too small a sample to draw broad conclusions but it was interesting, nonetheless.

This is what we sent them, for confirmation:

| | | |
|---|---|---|
| 1. | Equity and Bond markets and Equity Derivatives (Futures and Options) | SEBI |
| 2. | Mutual Funds and Alternative Investment Funds including Private Equity | SEBI |
| 3. | Interest Rate Futures (including credit default swaps) on G-Sec and Money Market | RBI |
| 4. | Foreign Exchange Market and Foreign Exchange Derivatives | RBI |
| 5. | Banking Sector, Non-Banking Finance Corporation and Microfinance Sector | RBI |
| 6. | Insurance Sector and Insurance Products | IRDA |

This is what we got back:

| | | | |
|---|---|---|---|
| 1. | Equity and Bond markets and Equity Derivatives (Future and Options) | SEBI | Bond markets are regulated by both RBI and SEBI |
| 2. | Mutual Funds and Alternative Investments Funds including Private Equity | SEBI | |
| 3. | Interest Rate Futures (including credit default swaps) on G-Sec and Money Market | RBI | But, futures are under both SEBI and RBI; OTC IRS/CDS/CCS etc. are under RBI |
| 4. | Foreign Exchange Market and Foreign Exchange Derivatives | RBI | OTC with RBI ; Exchange traded insturments: jointly by RBI and SEBI |
| 5. | Banking Sector, Non-Banking Finance Corporations and Microfinance Sector | RBI | |
| 6. | Insurance Sector and Insurance Products | IRDA | |

*Notes to acronyms:*
OTC: Over the counter (not traded through organized exchanges)
IRS: Interest rate swap
CDS: Credit default swap
CCS: Cross-currency swap

It is a bit of a regulatory maze and there is scope for improvement. The FSLRC proposal swings to one extreme. It advocates the creation of a super-regulator Unified Financial Regulation Agency that would subsume

SEBI (securities trading), Insurance Regulatory and Development Agency (insurance), Pension Fund Regulatory Development Authority (pensions), Forward Markets Commission (FMC) (commodities trading) and the RBI's bond trading regulation activities. This is proposed on grounds of synergies from such consolidation. This raises the question as to the need to fix institutions that are at least not broken. India's experience with financial market regulation has been far better than that elsewhere in the world. Its regulators, led by the central bank, have adopted a heterodox mixture of macroprudential measures to limit asset and credit bubbles, keep a leash on the shadow banking system and manage capital flows, with far greater success than in most other economies, developed and emerging. The resilience in the aftermath of the GFC is a resounding testament.

Further, there are no best-practice examples from anywhere in the world. A large variety of practices are the norm. Therefore, the most prudent strategy would be to introduce reforms in a gradual manner as has been happening – crossing the river by feeling the stones. In any case, there is little evidence either way to argue that unified regulatory institutions are superior to fragmented architecture. The example of countries with unified regulators like the United Kingdom – where the Bank of England, through the Financial Policy Committee and the Prudential Regulatory Authority, is the sole regulator – is not encouraging enough to merit a whole-hearted switch to a single regulator regime.

There is some merit in having all instruments that are 'traded' or all instruments that are defined as 'security' to be brought under one regulator, as was proposed by FSLRC. Alternatively, one regulator must be held ultimately responsible for regulating the development, issuance and the trading of such securities and the systemic issues that arise from them. The task may involve and require coordination, sharing and pooling of information with another regulator, and that is normal. But the final accountability has to rest with a single agency so that the 'ball is not dropped'.

In his comments on the proposals of FSLRC, the then RBI governor, Raghuram Rajan, had some comments to make on the regulatory architecture:

> In forward trading where a real commodity is delivered, regulatory oversight over the real markets for the commodity where price is discovered, as well as over warehouses where the commodity is delivered, may be important sources of regulatory synergy. Should the FMC be subsumed under the Unified Financial Agency or would it be better off having stronger links to the ministries overseeing the real commodities? I think the answer needs more investigation.

Similarly, is the regulation of bond trading more synergistic with the regulation of other debt products such as bank loans and with the operation of monetary policy (which requires bond trading) than with other forms of trading? Once again, I am not sure we have a compelling answer in the FSLRC report. My personal view is that moving the regulation of bond trading at this time would severely hamper the development of the government bond market, including the process of making bonds more liquid across the spectrum, a process which the RBI is engaged in.

The FSLRC also seems to be inconsistent in its emphasis on synergies and regulatory uniformity. It proposes all regulation of trading should move under one roof, all regulation of consumer protection should move under another roof, but the regulation of credit should be balkanized – banks should continue to be regulated by the RBI but the regulation of the quasi-bank NBFCs should move to the Unified Financial Agency, a regulatory behemoth that would combine supervision of trading as well as credit. This balkanization would hamper regulatory uniformity, the supervision of credit growth, and the conduct of monetary policy.[71]

Rajan was correct on the balkanization of regulation on credit. It is reasonable to keep the banking regulator responsible for non-banking financial corporations and firms so that the risk of the emergence of a substantially big 'shadow banking' system is hugely minimized. At the same time, it should be stressed that the central bank that is responsible for monetary policy should remain the banking regulator with the authority to deploy micro- and macroprudential regulation. When in doubt as to whether the decision involves distributional consequences or requires democratic legitimacy, they may be taken to the Financial Stability and Development Council which is headed by the Finance Minister, who is part of a democratically elected government. But there is no case for separation of banking supervision from the central bank and monetary policy. Academics are clear on that.

Anil Kashyap said:

One of my friends has a nice analogy. As the lender of last resort, you are never sure who is going to come through the door and ask for a date. When you meet your date on a Friday night and your date is AIG, the question at hand

[71] Raghuram Rajan, 'Financial Sector Legislative Reforms Committee Report (FSLRC): What to Do and When?' Talk at the First State Bank 'Banking and Economic Conclave' held at Mumbai on 17 June 2018, available at https://www.rbi.org.in/Scripts/BS_SpeechesView.aspx?Id=900 (accessed on 18 June 2018).

is whether you'd like to know something about them before you have to pay $85 billion to buy them dinner. If we mandate that the Fed is not involved in supervision then we make hasty, uninformed decisions inevitable when it is called upon as a lender of last resort...

First, having direct information on the condition of the banking system can improve the conduct of monetary policy and the central bank's information on the condition of the economy can improve the supervisory process. A pair of papers by Peek, Rosengren and Tootell (1999, 2009) establishes these two-way synergies. Their first paper shows that confidential bank supervisory information could improve the forecasts of inflation and unemployment that are presented at FOMC meetings and are the starting point for many policy discussions. The more recent paper demonstrates that bank supervisory models based on banking data alone can be improved by including the macroeconomic forecasts that are presented to the FOMC in their monetary policy deliberations.[72]

## Eric S. Rosengren et al. said:

.... Although it may be possible to obtain this information without direct supervisory responsibility, it likely would be costly to separate supervisory and monetary policy responsibilities, unless the central bank continues to be fully apprised of all information obtained through the examination process. While this point is relevant in developed as well as developing countries, it is particularly so in countries with less developed capital markets that have been especially hard hit by the simultaneous occurrence of banking and economic crises (Caprio and Klingebiel 1996). The supervisory information in those countries not only may be useful in forecasting the economy in general, but may be particularly critical to other important functions of the central bank such as maintaining the payments system and crisis management, given the much larger role played by banks in their credit markets. Our results indicate that access to all the information available through bank exams should be important considerations as countries consider the role of their central bank.[73]

---

[72] Anil K. Kashyap, 'Testimony on "Examining the Link Between Fed Bank Supervision and Monetary Policy"', House Financial Services Committee, 17 March 2010, available at http://faculty.chicagobooth.edu/brian.barry/igm/kashyaptestimony.pdf (accessed on 18 June 2018).

[73] Joe Peek, Eric S. Rosengren and Geoffrey M. B. Tootell, 'Is Bank Supervision Central to Central Banking?' mimeo, Federal Reserve Bank of Boston, Research Department Working Papers No. 99-7, July 1997, available at http://www.bos.frb.org/economic/wp/wp1999/wp99_7.htm (accessed on 18 July 2018).

Again Eric S. Rosengren et al. noted:

> First, an important nexus exists among monetary policy responsibilities, bank
> supervision responsibilities, and concerns about financial instability.... it is
> important for the Federal Reserve to understand both the problems being
> experienced by financial intermediaries and the associated risk that banking
> problems could result in contagious failures that might lead to significantly
> more severe outcomes than are generated in most macroeconomic models....
> Second, supervisory policy and programs to promote financial stability are
> likely to be improved when integrated with monetary policy. The stress tests
> conducted on banks earlier this year show the advantage of using scenario
> analysis and macroeconomic assumptions to better understand the risk
> exposures of individual financial institutions and of groups of financial
> institutions.
>
> Whatever regulatory reform is adopted, it should exploit the synergies between
> monetary policy, supervisory policy, and policies to promote financial stability.
> While policy makers are still collecting "lessons learned" from the recent
> crisis, it is clear that the economic outcome would have been much worse had
> the central bank not had the access to the knowledge about, and the hands-
> on experience with, financial institutions and financial markets required to
> take immediate actions to stabilize financial markets and the real economy...
>
> Furthermore, much more research needs to be focused on achieving an
> improved understanding of how future crises can be avoided, and if they do
> occur, how their impacts can be mitigated through the exploitation of the
> symbiosis shown to be present among monetary policy, bank supervisory
> policy, and concerns about financial instability.[74]

While we are convinced of the need for keeping monetary policy and
banking regulation together, we are also conscious of the fact that nothing in
economics (including regulatory structures) is independent of the context and

---

[74] Joe Peek, Eric S. Rosengren and Geoffrey M. B. Tootell, 'Is Financial Stability Central
to Central Banking?' Federal Reserve Bank of Boston, October 2009, available at
https://www.bostonfed.org/-/media/Documents/conference/54/peek-rosengren-
tootell.pdf?la=en (accessed on 18 July 2018). The relevant texts and the references in
footnotes 72–74 have been taken from: V. Anantha Nageswaran, 'Comments on the
Financial Sector Legislative Reforms Commission's Recommendations,' Discussion
document, Takshashila Institution, 16 April 2013, available at http://takshashila.org.
in/wp-content/uploads/2013/04/TDD-FSLRCComment-VAN-1.pdf.

the context can and does change. As Willem Buiter had noted,[75] the risk of a regulatory capture has to be minimized. That might become an important consideration in the regulatory architecture that India chooses when the share of government-owned banks shrinks, as it invariably would, sometime in the future. Right now, the challenge for the Indian banking sector is not resisting and avoiding 'capture' by the private sector. The challenge is that the government is 'constraining'.

Somewhat simplistically, formal government ownership of the banking system constrains monetary policy effectiveness in many ways thanks, in part, to government's social obligations. Informal government interference constrains the central bank's regulatory effectiveness.

At a later stage, this may change. Private sector capture risks might come to the fore. At the time, there may be a case for creating multiple regulators even for the banking system, rotation of personnel, fixed and limited terms for regulatory officials and induction of truly independent outsiders into regulatory roles. The idea of regulatory competition is worth thinking about, with mechanisms for limiting the potential dysfunctionalities such as regulators deliberately undermining each other and working at cross-purposes.

## 7.6  Conclusion: too less and not too much finance

On balance, India has done well with the evolution and regulation of the financial sector, notwithstanding the still-unresolved and ongoing crisis in the banking system which, in the uniquely Indian way, should eventually end in a more robust and stable banking system with less frequent occurrences of bad debts. India has been gradual and deliberate in the liberalization of the financial sector. Sometimes, it might have appeared excruciatingly slow to many in the market. But as described by Joe Nocera, in the aftermath of the 2008 crisis, such an approach has been, on balance, more right than wrong. The Asian crisis of 1997–98 too underscored the perils of excessive and rapid liberalization of the financial sector. India's relative success in seeing off two of the defining global financial market crises of our times is a testament to the application of a practical heterodox policy toolkit.

---

[75] Willem Buiter, 'The Role of Central Banks in Financial Stability: How Has It Changed?' Discussion Paper No. 8780, Centre for Economic Policy Research, January 2012, available at https://voxeu.org/sites/default/files/file/DP8780.pdf (accessed on 30 July 2018).

There is a less charitable view. It attributes the success in resisting 'too much finance' not to conscious policy and regulatory choices but to the fact that many of the asset classes in India are traded informally and not through recognized and organized markets. If they were, then India's prudent record with respect to financialization might look less impressive. That is somewhat extreme and unfair. In recent decades, regulatory policy has consciously and actively resisted economically unproductive and needless financialization.

Another view is that India has avoided the excesses of financialization because it has been a bank-dominated rather than a capital-market-dominated economy. Had the latter been the case, it might have experienced the same costs of financialization as Western societies. Instead, the Indian economy has experienced the costs through periodical occurrence of bad debts in the banking system. To that extent, India has suffered the problems of too much finance except that it happened through the banking channel. Therefore, just as the crises in the West exposed the failures of capital market regulation, India's recurring bad debt problems have exposed its banking regulation failures. That is a thoughtful criticism of India's banking regulation and regulator. However, government ownership of the banking system and government interference in operational decisions make it difficult to fix 'substantial accountability', to quote Willem Buiter, on the RBI, for the problems of bad debts. It is also unfair because RBI is unable to respond to such criticisms in public since that would amount to eroding the authority of the government from which the central bank derives its authority and independence. The responsibility to ensure that an enterprise performs well rests primarily with its promoter and owner and only secondarily with the regulator.

Interestingly and inadvertently, India's recent policy decisions might accelerate financialization. In November 2016, the Government of India demonetized 500- and 1000-rupee notes. Its effects are still unfolding. Digital and banking transactions have picked up as a result. While that is about formalizing economic activity, it may also encourage financialization as cash parked in banks will invariably find its ways to other markets seeking better returns. The second development is the implementation of the Goods and Services Tax (GST) from July 2017. That too has the potential to formalize commercial transactions substantially even as it aims to integrate India into a common market. GST taxpayers will receive credit for the taxes paid on the inputs they buy only if suppliers had paid their taxes. That means formal recording of commercial transactions, recourse to banking systems for payments for transactions, etc., and hence more liquidity with banks too. The third is the implementation of the Insolvency and Bankruptcy Code (IBC) in the country, which enables lenders to recover their dues from defaulting borrowers by seizing and auctioning off their assets. If IBC succeeds in better recovery of defaulting loans or in discouraging wilful defaults, bank credit in the economy will grow faster and bank credit as a share of GDP will rise, over time, to levels seen in other EM peers and in developed countries. That will be a mixed blessing.

All these three were epochal changes in policies. For the most part, the changes they have brought about in the behaviour of households and businesses are welcome and desirable. But, concomitantly, they may also accelerate the financialization of the Indian economy. That needs to be watched.

Ultimately, financial sector growth must be concomitant with the evolution of institutions of economic governance and economic resilience. If it runs ahead, economies cannot keep up and run into trouble. So, 'making haste slowly' and 'crossing the river by feeling the stones' have not only kept in India in good stead but will continue to do so.

In sum, notwithstanding the evidence of excessive speculation (a feature of financialization) seen in derivatives markets related to equities, India suffers from too little rather than too much finance. There is plenty of scope for finance to contribute positively to India's economic growth and development rather than retard them. Whether it is in financial inclusion or infrastructure funding or in the evolution of specialized financial institutions, there is scope for new institutions and innovations to emerge.

Although they do not appear ready and are even resisting it, 'boring banking' is ideal for the West given the costs associated with excessive financialization of their economies. India on the other hand has scope to ride the excitement of increasing financial sophistication and specialization before the law of diminishing returns to finance catches up with India too.

# 8 | Conclusion

It may not be inaccurate to describe the short financial history of recent decades largely in terms of three trends – progressive financial market liberalization, excessive financialization and the emergence of a new paradigm for central banking in which monetary policy had a role in destabilization of the economy and yet was invoked to help stabilize it too!

Our contention is that financial liberalization and financialization drove the monetary policy framework to accord a higher priority to preserve and to further financialization of the global economy. That is, the monetary policy framework that the United States and the rest of the developed world adopted is a consequence of financialization and, later, it worked to reinforce financialization.

While UMPs may have brought things to a head and exposed the depth of the challenge, these trends have been a result of long-term choices, especially those made by authorities and politicians in the United States. As we explained in Chapters 2 and 4, the economic policy preferences of the United States and the evolution of Fed's monetary policy paradigm have been the long-term drivers. Globalization and financial market integration ensured that the ripples were amplified and felt on a global scale.

The economic manifestations of these trends have been the resource misallocations (both human and physical capital) away from the real economy to the financial markets, concentration of market power and oligopolies across sectors, spillovers from monetary policy actions in United States and other developed economies, shorter cycles of asset bubbles and painful clean-ups, surges in cross-border capital flows followed by the inevitable sudden stops that engender fiscal imbalances, exchange rate volatility, egregious executive compensations and tax advantages that favour capital over labour, penalization of savers to benefit debtors and a widening of income inequality and concentration of wealth that matches the Gilded Age.

The inevitable political and social dynamics associated with them have been gradually building up. While widening inequality is intrinsically bad, the more corrosive impact is felt in the capture of political institutions that set the rules of the game. A global plutocracy is entrenched across countries. The populist political backlash in developed countries is only to be expected.

Public policy in general and crisis response in particular have become oriented towards monetary policy actions that prioritize the arrest of 'contagion' effects through bailouts of the 'TBTF' institutions with the hope that its trickle down effects revive the general economy. Central bank policies have enriched a fabulously rich minority who invest actively in global financial markets at the cost of the savings of the overwhelming majority of ordinary citizens leaving a legacy of trillions of dollars in unfunded pension fund liabilities.

Recurrent bouts of overheating followed by pain, with the former benefiting the rich and the latter devastating the poor, largely driven by the dynamics of unfettered internal and external market liberalization, have become commonplace across developing countries. The difficulty of managing effective redistribution of the gains from globalization and trade has only amplified these problems.

We have proposed a revision of the current monetary policy paradigm to correct its excessive focus on equity markets and their 'wealth effect' and to embrace a more symmetric response to the economic cycle, and a mandate to focus on financial stability as much as price stability. That is the cornerstone of our proposals.

Addressing spillovers from monetary policy actions of major economies will require building international safety nets: monetary policy actions to take into account cross-border spillovers as much as domestic factors and use of a wide toolkit of CFM measures and macroprudential regulations, especially to manage inflows.

At the micro-foundations, we propose measures like elimination of the tax deduction accorded to interest payments and vigorous anti-trust actions to reverse the alarming trend of business concentration across sectors, including financial markets.

We make the plea that the only country with the authority and competence to lead this agenda is the United States. Much change is demanded of the Federal Reserve. It is a fact that they have not shown any indication that they are ready, willing and able to change. The charge of 'capture' still resonates. They do not seem cognizant of the fact that 'central banking has drifted into being, or always was, a vehicle serving the interests of a globalized metropolitan elite: policy by and for "Davos Man".... More could also be done to insulate central bankers from the risk of capture by their private sector counterparts in the global financial elite. As well as staying away from cosmopolitan business gatherings that are not open to scrutiny, this might involve reinforcing the soft norms of their service'.[1] Willem Buiter suggests[2] multiple and overlapping regulatory bodies that cooperate and compete and staff that turn over regularly and truly independent members in key decision-making committees. This, he feels, will go some way in minimizing capture and avoiding groupthink.

Indeed, the global backlash against free trade, immigration and inequality is not just about resisting globalization and its side effects. It represents concerns over democratic accountability of 'Independent Agencies' (of which the Federal Reserve is an example) and the delegation of powers to them by the executive class.

As Paul Tucker writes in his book (see footnote 1), world over, there is increasingly governance by unaccountable, technocratic elites. This is not just with respect to the European Union. It is about BIS making rules. It is about Financial Stability Board making macroprudential directives. It is about many such regulatory agencies in the United Kingdom. Since the 1990s, international agencies have actively encouraged technocratic and elitist solutions. It was a tacit charge that the political class cannot be trusted to do the right things and that only technocratic elites could do that. When we have Wall Street, private equity firms and Silicon Valley firms demanding and influencing policies that suit their goals and agendas and benefitting from the low interest rate and lax regulatory policies[3] of the Federal Reserve, we can see that it has nothing to do with elected representatives, government and the people. It has become governance of the elites, for the elites and by the elites. That is what Paul Tucker means by 'policies by and for the Davos man'.

---

[1] Paul Tucker, 'The Only Game in Town: Central Banking as False Hope', 18 May 2018, available at https://promarket.org/game-town-central-banking-false-hope/ (accessed on 17 July 2018). Extracted from his book *Unelected Power: The Question for Legitimacy in Central Banking and the Regulatory State.*

[2] Willem Buiter, 'The Role of Central Banks in Financial Stability: How Has It Changed?' Discussion Paper No. 8780, Centre for Economic Policy Research, January 2012, available at https://voxeu.org/sites/default/files/file/DP8780.pdf (accessed on 30 July 2018).

[3] 'Morgan Stanley, Goldman Got Help from Fed on Stress Tests,' *Wall Street Journal*, 2 July 2018, available at https://www.wsj.com/articles/wall-street-gets-the-friendlier-fed-its-been-waiting-for-1530558419 (accessed on 17 July 2018).

At its core, the problem with UMPs is their democratic deficit. Well before Paul Tucker, Willem Buiter had written[4] about limited 'substantial accountability' for Federal Reserve and none for the ECB. 'Substantial accountability' includes judgement and other unpleasant consequences for the agent. This needs to be rectified or their mandates need to be drastically curtailed because the backlash has begun. We have seen that in the United Kingdom, the United States and across several European nations in the last 2 years. The safety valve that policy decisions made by democratically elected politicians provide is critical. It is time people's preferences are reflected in the conduct of the independent agencies like the Federal Reserve. In other words, the criteria for delegation to independent agencies have to be set clearly and their decisions evaluated against such criteria, rigorously.

'It is time for the technocrats to heed the lessons of recent political upheavals, pull back their power, retreat a bit, engage with the public in a wider debate and leave more space for politics'.[5] Also, the onus shifts to the democratically elected members of the Congress and the president to wrest control of the policy agenda and redefine delegation of powers to the Federal Reserve. In other words, the swamp is very much ready to be drained. But unfortunately, it has not happened yet. If anything, the American president has complained about the Federal Reserve raising interest rates after having complained[6] about low interest rates favouring 'Wall Street' interests. It may need one more and a bigger crisis than the one the world faced in 2008 to bring about these changes. If it comes down to that, it would be one more piece of evidence of the human inability for rational and far-sighted decision-making.

Finally, we have outlined a set of alternative narratives that would have to unsettle the settled wisdoms.

The fundamental shifts required in modern capitalism go beyond policy shifts and demand wholesale behavioural and cultural shifts. Overturning such hegemony requires powerful enough narratives that can build broad-based coalitions and sustain popular movements. They need counter-revolutions to

---

[4] Buiter, 'The Role of Central Banks in Financial Stability'.

[5] Interview with Sir Paul Tucker: 'A Former Central Banker Tells Other Central Bankers: "Stay Away From Davos"', 3 July 2018, available at https://promarket.org/former-central-banker-tells-central-bankers-stay-away-davos/ (accessed 17 July 2018).

[6] See 'Trump Criticizes Federal Reserve Interest Rate Policy despite Strong Economy,' *Reuters*, 20 July 2018, available at https://www.reuters.com/article/us-usa-trump-fed/trump-criticizes-federal-reserve-interest-rate-policy-despite-strong-economy-idUSKBILLION1K92KC (accessed 30 July 2018).

create a new synthesis. Such transformations would require Wall Street leaders to champion the cause. In short, the world needs capitalists with conscience. Unfortunately, the social dynamics among the elites in modern societies appear to act as restraints against the emergence of such countervailing forces. Beyond flagging off this concern, a primer for stoking such revolutions is beyond the scope of this book.[7]

However, if such campaigns or even revolutions emerge, governments should be ready with specific public policy choices that can effectively address this problem. We hope that our work is a small but vital contribution to that state of preparedness. Historically, such Overton windows on reforms have only opened up occasionally. Governments should opportunistically seize such reform moments. It is with this in mind that we have outlined our agenda for change.

Somehow, it seems an appropriate and befitting end to this book to borrow and paraphrase the concluding lines of a memorable lecture, delivered by Kenneth J. Arrow, the great economist and human being, in which he attempted to make a cautious case for socialism:[8]

> It would be a pleasure to end this [book] with a rousing affirmation one way or the other. But, as T. S. Eliot told us, that is not 'how the world will end.' Experiment is perilous, but it is not given to us to refrain from the attempt.

## Postscript: history repeats – elite capture of rule-making

Is elite capture of rule-making institutions the most disturbing trend of our times? Have the wheels of history come a full circle?

We have enough evidence today to argue that deregulation, excessive financialization and privatization, business concentration, de-unionization, and skill-biased technologies have all led to a weakening of labour's influence and a corresponding dominance of business interests in both the economy and the polity.

The result has been widening inequality and the emergence of a group of super-wealthy elites. Evidence of the dynamics that have contributed to this

---

[7] In his book *Other People's Money*, John Kay reminds himself to be optimistic by pointing to far-reaching political changes that occurred in his lifetime which he did not think were possible: closing of Britain's coalmines, privatization of its railways, gay couples and the election of a black president in the United States of America (p. 307).

[8] Kenneth J. Arrow, 'A Cautious Case for Socialism,' lecture at the third Lionel Trilling Seminar of the academic year 1977–78, on 13 April at Columbia University.

state of affairs have been piling up[9] – increasing business concentration across sectors, declining labour's share in national income,[10] decreased wages in concentrated markets,[11] booming executive compensation, soaring[12] profits,[13] growing entry barriers and anti-competitive practices, slackening anti-trust enforcement,[14] rising prices and stagnant productivity following mergers,[15] business investment declines associated with rising market power,[16] higher price mark-ups,[17] reduced competition and depressed dynamism leading to rising inequality and poor productivity growth,[18] disproportionate benefit from monetary policy, and so on.

---

[9] Noah Smith, 'The Market Power Story', Noahpinion Blog, 24 August, 2017, available at http://noahpinionblog.blogspot.com/2017/08/the-market-power-story.html (accessed on 14–15 August 2018).

[10] David Autor et al., 'Concentrating on the Fall of the Labour Share', *American Economic Review*, Papers and Proceedings 107, no. 5 (2017): 180-185, available at https://economics.mit.edu/files/12544 (accessed on 14–15 August 2018).

[11] Jose Azar, Ioana Marinescu and Marshall I Steinbaum, 'Labour Market Concentration', NBER Working Paper No. 24147, December 2017, available at http://www.nber.org/papers/w24147.pdf (accessed on 14–15 August 2018).

[12] Simcha Barkai, 'Declining Labour and Capital Shares', available at http://home.uchicago.edu/~barkai/doc/BarkaiDecliningLaborCapital.pdf (accessed on 14–15 August 2018).

[13] Nicole Bullock, 'Soaring US Profit Margins Pose Challenge for Investors', *Financial Times*, 12 August 2018, available at https://www.ft.com/content/e0973b90-9ccb-11e8-9702-5946bae86e6d (accessed on 14–15 August 2018).

[14] John Kwoka, 'Mergers, Merger Control, and Remedies: A Retrospective Analysis of US Policy', MIT Press, 19 December 2014.

[15] Bruce A. Blonigen and Justin R Pierce, 'Evidence for the Effects of Mergers on Market Power and Efficiency', Federal Reserve Board Working Paper, October 2016, available at https://www.federalreserve.gov/econresdata/feds/2016/files/2016082pap.pdf (accessed on 14–15 August 2018).

[16] German Gutierrez and Thomas Philippon, 'Investment-less Growth: An Empirical Investigation', November 2016, available at http://pages.stern.nyu.edu/~tphilipp/papers/QNIK.pdf (accessed on 14–15 August 2018).

[17] Jan De Loecker and Jan Eeckhout, 'The Rise of Market Power and the Macroeconomic Implications', 24 August 2017, available at http://www.janeeckhout.com/wp-content/uploads/RMP.pdf (accessed on 14–15 August 2018).

[18] Jason Furman and Peter Orszag, 'Slower Productivity and Higher Inequality: Are They related?', Peterson Institute for International Economics, Working Paper no. 2018-4, 21 June 2018, available at https://papers.ssrn.com/sol3/papers.cfm?abstract_id=3191984 (accessed on 14–15 August 2018).

Instead of scrambling to address the problem head-on, we are still debating the existence of this reality. Isn't all the evidence adequate to connect the dots? What more evidence do we need to call out the problem?

One could argue that even these developments, damning as they are, would have been a matter of concern but not alarm if this were all and, importantly, the safety valves of democratic politics were active and healthy. But the aforementioned dynamics have been accompanied by an increasing tendency to use the resulting economic dominance to capture the process of making the rules of the game in society, polity and economy and use them to favour the dominant group at the cost of all others. When this happens, the social contract starts breaking down. And, worryingly, we may now be staring at an advanced state of breakdown.

A rich body of recent research points definitively to capture of politics and institutions responsible for laying down the rules of the game. Business executives have unprecedented access to the highest political levels,[19] some even averaging one White House meeting a week,[20] and that access translates into decisions which unfairly favour them over others.[21] Stock market returns, and not real-world concerns, 'cause Fed policy'.[22] The Federal Open Market Committee (FOMC) is open, but it seems only for a privileged few![23]

These look like simple misdemeanours when compared with the actions of those who caused the 'Made in Wall Street' global financial crisis. Wall Street firms have since been charged with misleading clients, selling dodgy securities,

---

[19] Gretchen Morgenson and Don Van Natta Jr, 'Paulson's Calls to Goldman Tested Ethics', *New York Times*, 8 August 2009, available at https://www.nytimes.com/2009/08/09/business/09paulson.html (accessed on 14–15 August 2018).

[20] Brody Mullins, 'Google Makes Most of Close Ties to White House', *Wall Street Journal*, 24 March 2015, available at https://www.wsj.com/articles/google-makes-most-of-close-ties-to-white-house-1427242076 (accessed on 14–15 August 2018).

[21] Jeffrey Brown and Jiekun Huang, 'All the President's Friends: Political Access and Firm Value', NBER Working Paper, April 2017, available at http://www.nber.org/papers/w23356 (accessed on 14–15 August 2018).

[22] Anna Cieslak and Annette Vissing-Jorgensen, 'The Economics of the Fed Put', April 11 April 2017, available at https://www.frbsf.org/economic-research/files/Session-3-Paper-1-Vissing-Jorgensen.pdf (accessed on 14–15 August 2018).

[23] David Andrew Finer, 'What Insights Do Taxi Records Offer into Federal Reserve Leakage?' Stigler Centre for Study of the Economy and the State, Working Paper No. 18, March 2018, available at https://research.chicagobooth.edu/-/media/research/stigler/pdfs/workingpapers/18whatinsightsdotaxiridesofferintofederalreserveleakage.pdf (accessed on 14–15 August 2018).

deceiving and mis-selling to customers, rigging bids and interest rates, foreclosure abuses and mortgage misrepresentations, market manipulation, predatory sales, fraud cover-ups, and so on. In sum, the full spectrum of white collar crimes, many with outright criminal liabilities. And those at the receiving end included both retail customers, regular investors and high-net worth ones, and institutional investors, including public pension funds. Not one senior Wall Street executive has been charged with criminal liability, much less sentenced. Worse still, much the same character cast are now back to enjoying fat bonuses and lobbying to chip away at even the weak regulatory oversight on their activities put in place by the Dodd-Frank legislation.

Then there are the authoritative ringside expositions of the capture from, among others, Yanis Varoufakis,[24] William Buiter,[25] and Paul Tucker.[26] Paul Tucker has even gone to the extent of pleading for the retreat of technocracy and more space for politics, and cautioning central bankers from attending Davos![27]

These trends have become so egregious that what would have been considered scandalous in public life a few decades back is passé. When immediately after demitting office, a President of the United States[28] and a Chairman of Federal Reserve,[29] the premier executive and regulator respectively in the world's largest economy and most powerful nation, nonchalantly accept handsomely compensated speaking tours sponsored by the very same interests

---

[24] Yanis Varoufakis, 'Adults in the Room: My Battle with Europe's Establishment', *Vintage*, 2 May 2018.

[25] Willem H. Buiter, 'Central Banks – Powerful, Political, and Unaccountable?', *Journal of the British Academy* 2 (19 December 2014): 269–303, available at https://www.britac.ac.uk/sites/default/files/10%20Buiter%20Keynes%201803.pdf (accessed on 14–15 August 2018).

[26] Paul Tucker, *Unelected Power: The Quest for Legitimacy in Central Banking and the Regulatory State* (Princeton University Press, 2018).

[27] Asher Schechter, 'A Former Central Banker Tells Other Central Bankers, "Stay Away From Davos"', ProMarket Blog, 3 July 2018, available at https://promarket.org/former-central-banker-tells-central-bankers-stay-away-davos/ (accessed on 14–15 August 2018).

[28] Krissah Thompson, 'The Obamas Face the Paid Talking Circuit', *The Washington Post*, 27 April 2017, available at https://www.washingtonpost.com/lifestyle/style/the-obamas-face-the-paid-speaking-circuit--and-all-the-questions-that-come-with-it/2017/04/27/a723c280-2b65-11e7-b605-33413c691853_story.html?noredirect=on&utm_term=.2c0eaad3c838 (accessed on 14–15 August 2018).

[29] Alexandra Stevenson, 'After Fed, Bernanke Offers His Wisdom, for a Fee', *New York Times*, 20 May 2014, available at https://dealbook.nytimes.com/2014/05/20/after-fed-bernanke-offers-his-wisdom-for-a-big-fee/ (accessed on 14–15 August 2018).

who benefited the most from their policies and are arguably at the vanguard of political capture, then something is seriously wrong!

Leave aside all such research and just consider the short history of the last decade. On the one hand, the rich have benefited immensely from the ultra-low interest rates and booming stock markets, even as the middle-class and the less well-off have seen their wealth erode due to the low rates and the tanking of the housing market. Businesses and the richest individuals have been the biggest beneficiaries of tax favours of all kinds, even as public debt soars into unsustainable terrains.

On the other hand, non-elites have borne the brunt of the austerity policies that governments have pursued either on their own volition or under compulsion. Consider the direct squeeze on funding for local governments[30] and their increasing indebtedness,[31] pervasive and sharp across the US and UK; and the pruning down of welfare programmes; the creeping privatization of essential public services and their transfer to private interests with questionable intents.[32] While the richest benefit by way of even tax exemptions on their bloated (so call 'Cadillac') medical insurance policies, the poorest are left to fend for themselves by shopping for opaque insurance policies from the market.

Or consider the behaviours of the corporate titans of tech-America. They incorporate subsidiaries in off-shore tax havens, vest intellectual property rights in them, transfer almost all profits to those subsidiaries, and thereby 'avoid' paying taxes; thanks to the low interest rates they are able to borrow cheap in the US, use the money raised to finance share buy-backs, boost their own wealth and pay out massive dividends. As if all this were not enough, they claim tax exemption on the interest expenses for the debt raised, thereby avoiding paying even less of the already meagre tax dues.[33]

---

[30] Laura Hughes, 'Northamptonshire Council Agrees to "Radical" Cuts', *Financial Times*, 9 August 2018, available at https://www.ft.com/content/e81f78b2-9bd3-11e8-ab77-f854c65a4465 (accessed on 14–15 August 2018).

[31] Monica Davey and Mary Williams Walsh, 'Billions in Debt, Detroit Tumbles into Bankruptcy', *New York Times*, 18 July 2013, available at https://www.nytimes.com/2013/07/19/us/detroit-files-for-bankruptcy.html (accessed on 14–15 August 2018).

[32] Bottom Line Nation, Series of Articles in *New York Times*, 25 June to 24 December 2016, available at https://www.nytimes.com/series/private-equity-bottom-line-nation?action=click&contentCollection=DealBook&module=Collection&region=Marginalia&src=me&version=series&pgtype=article (accessed on 14–15 August 2018).

[33] Rana Foroohar, *Makers and Takers: The Rise of Finance and the Fall of American Business* (Crown Business, 2016).

In the US, in the immediate aftermath of the bursting of the sub-prime mortgage bubble, each one of the major actors – households, corporates, and financial institutions – were left with massive debt overhang. The US government and the Federal Reserve reacted with alacrity and a slew of initiatives to bail out the same financial institutions who bore the primary responsibility for inflating up the bubble. Then the extraordinary persistence with low interest rate was justified as necessary to repair corporate balance sheets and encourage investment. As regards households, somewhere in the fine print of these measures was a small programme to help those struggling with foreclosures.

While behemoth corporations were too big to fail, households had to be disciplined with foreclosures. It was as though the free-market principles of competition and moral hazard applied only to the latter and not the former.

The result is there to see. While the top 1 per cent, even the top 10 per cent, have seen their wealth rocket upwards on the back of the stock market boom, the bottom half has seen a steep fall in their wealth.[34] For the richest, it is a case of sowing the wind and letting others reap the whirlwind, all the while sitting comfortably and enjoying their lives!

In a delightful redraft of *The Communist Manifesto*, Frank Partnoy and Rupert Younger replaced the main protagonists, 'bourgeois' and 'proletarian', with 'Haves' and 'Have-Nots' respectively, and found that three-fourths of the original prose would retain relevance today.[35] They find remarkable similarity in the dynamics of class struggle between Marx's times and today's technology and finance dominated capitalism. Inequality and political capture stand out as the recurrent headline themes. Their conclusion, 'The Have-Nots have nothing to lose but their chains. They have a world to win!'[36]

Stunningly, the elites have drawn strength and credibility from the ideological and intellectual underpinning provided by the US academic establishment (barring a few honourable exceptions) and reputed institutions

---

[34] Moritz Kuhn, Moritz Schularick and Ulrike Stein, 'Income and Wealth Inequality in America 1949–2016', Federal Reserve Bank of Minneapolis Working Paper Number 9, June 2018, available at https://www.minneapolisfed.org/institute/working-papers-institute/iwp9.pdf (accessed on 14–15 August 2018).

[35] Frank Partnoy and Rupert Younger, 'What Would Karl Marx Write Today?', *Financial Times*, 9 March 2018, available at https://www.ft.com/content/603b3498-2155-11e8-a895-1ba1f72c2c11 (accessed on 14–15 August 2018).

[36] Frank Partnoy and Rupert Younger, 'Manifesto of the Activist Party, available at http://activistmanifesto.org/manifesto.html (accessed on 14–15 August 2018).

like the International Monetary Fund (IMF) in support of their actions. Free trade, liberal immigration, global citizenry, unfettered individualism, deregulation, globalization, and so on, have found ideological justification in their works. Even when some of the concerns like widening inequality have been surfaced by the likes of Thomas Piketty, these intellectual forefathers have sought to distract with obfuscation and arcane debates and superfluous digressions.[37] Needless to say, these éminences grises have, in their own differing ways, benefited from the same trends.

The flag-bearers of the Fourth Estate have played a prominent role in distilling and disseminating these ideas and the narrative. They have helped establish a Gramscian hegemony to rationalize and drive these trends. The mutually beneficial partnership which emerged has been sustained under the veneer of a noble sounding 'liberal democratic and free-market consensus.'

Even enlightened self-interest has disappeared from the playbook of the elites. Clearly, they have become so emboldened with hubris as to eschew even pretensions of propriety and fairness in their actions. Capitalism needs saving from capitalists![38] Again, history repeating itself.

It was no surprise that things started to go wrong and wheels started coming off the apparent Goldilocks economy. The global financial crisis may have been a trigger, insofar as it exposed all the cracks that had hitherto been papered over by favourable forces like rising property markets, policies that allowed gorging on debt, globalization and the rise of China, and the flush of productivity gains and opportunities that emerged from the new technologies. But, after a few moments or months of sobriety and right rhetoric, things have gone right back to where they were before 2007. Maybe worse.

This is history repeating itself big time. Across societies and polities over time, economic elites have exercised their dominance over political power and control over decision-making processes. Always, the dominance has spilled over into excesses, provoking rebellions and revolutions and sometimes assimilations that resulted in regime shifts. We are seeing our own version of this dynamic.

Hegel, though in the context of abstract ideas, described this in terms of an inexorable dialectic – thesis, anti-thesis, and synthesis. Accordingly, any

---

[37] Tyler Cowen, 'Why I Am Not Persuaded by Thomas Piketty's Argument', Marginal Revolution Blog, 21 April 2014, available at https://marginalrevolution.com/marginalrevolution/2014/04/why-i-am-not-persuaded-by-thomas-pikettys-argument.html (accessed on 14–15 August 2018).

[38] Raghuram G. Rajan and Luigi Zingales, *Saving Capitalism from the Capitalists* (Princeton University Press, 2004).

state of the world, or thesis, generates its own opposition, or anti-thesis. The contradictions are resolved through a new state of the world, or a synthesis. In some sense, humans need the 'other'; so do nations, institutions and ideologies, to sustain themselves and to hold themselves from slipping into 'excess' mode.

Adam Smith cautioned about such state capture by merchant elites and its excesses. In fact, as Paul Sagar wrote recently, 'The invisible hand was invoked not to draw attention to the problem of state intervention, but of state capture.'[39] Karl Marx adapted Hegel to the material world and made it his central thesis – 'the history of all hitherto existing society is the history of class struggles'! In more secular terms, Vilfredo Pareto and Gaetano Mosca claimed this as an immutable law, though in an acknowledgement of the dialectic, Pareto wrote about the 'circulation of elites' and described history 'as the graveyard of the elites.'[40]

C. Wright Mills wailed at the 'power elites' from political, economic and military establishments who had usurped power from elected representatives and the resultant erosion of democracy.[41] President Eisenhower was only echoing this when he warned about the dangers posed by the military-industrial complex. A host of others in recent times from James Burnham to Robert Putnam have written about the ceding of decision-making power by democratic institutions to managers and technocrats. Notice the striking similarity here with the prevailing central bank dominance over economic policymaking.

But democracies, over the past century or so, have sought to address this problem through sufficient institutional checks and balances against egregious excesses by the dominant classes. These institutions and channels of engagement and negotiations have served as safety valves. John Kenneth Galbraith described them as institutions of 'countervailing power', necessary to attenuate excesses.[42] Over the past century, faced with the onslaught from communism, these same institutional systems have helped capitalism and liberal democracy survive by giving birth to the likes of labour unions and collective

---

[39] Paul Sagar, 'The Real Adam Smith, Aeon', available at https://aeon.co/essays/we-should-look-closely-at-what-adam-smith-actually-believed (accessed on 14–15 August 2018).

[40] Hugo Drochon, 'Why Elites Always Rule', *New Statesman*, 18 January 2017, available at https://www.newstatesman.com/politics/uk/2017/01/why-elites-always-rule (accessed on 14–15 August 2018).

[41] C. Wright Mills, *The Power Elite* (Oxford University Press, 2000).

[42] John Kenneth Galbraith, *American Capitalism: The Concept of Countervailing Power* (Martino Fine Books, 2012).

bargaining, consumer organizations, welfare state, social democracies, and so on. It is not incorrect to say that capitalism co-opted elements of communism to fend off the latter.

But, that was then. Unfortunately, if we accept the aforementioned dynamics on both the economic and political realms, the space now available for such safety valves to defuse may have shrunk and even disappeared. The populist backlash across developed economies in recent times is a manifestation of this reality. It may well be the anti-thesis of our times reaching its crescendo, and creating the conditions for 'elite circulation'.

The response of the liberals has been even more disturbing. Instead of realizing the enormity of the problem facing us and the near-complete breakdown of the social contract, and advocating measures to address it, liberal intellectuals and opinion makers have acquiesced with the elites by going after the convenient straw man in Donald J. Trump (DJT). Even with all his flaws, DJT is merely a transient phenomenon, the sort of which is very likely when the social contract is tattering.

It is not DJT that is the real problem, it is the elite capture of the rules of the game and the near-complete marginalization of the voices of labour and disenfranchisement of those who struggle to make ends meet. The 'thesis' is no longer sustainable, and the 'anti-thesis' is chaotic and deeply uncertain. In the circumstances, history teaches us that all we can expect is a tumultuous period leading to a disorderly synthesis. Unless we act now to achieve a more orderly synthesis.

# Index